# THE PAN BOOK OF CHESS

Starting – for the benefit of the complete tyro – with the basic moves and rules of Chess, the author goes on to describe elementary endgame facts and the changing values and real functions of the pieces at various stages.

The next part of the book initiates the beginner into methods of exploiting the technical features such as the 'fork', the 'pin', etc.

He is now in a position to profit from the longest, most important section, in which the author demonstrates good general tactics and strategy, shows how battles are won – or lost, and examines and analyses openings and endgames.

Finally, there is a chapter on Chess problems and compositions.

Throughout, the author illustrates his lessons with examples from actual play, including many brilliant games by the masters.

# THE PAN BOOK
# OF CHESS

## GERALD ABRAHAMS

*M.A.(Oxon.), Barrister-at-Law*

A PAN ORIGINAL

REVISED EDITION, 1966

PAN BOOKS LTD : LONDON

First published 1965 by
PAN BOOKS LTD
33 Tothill Street, London S.W.1

ISBN 0 330 23073 5

*2nd Printing (revised) 1966*
*3rd Printing 1970*

*Printed in Great Britain by*
*Cox & Wyman Limited, London, Reading and Fakenham*

# CONTENTS

# The following complete games are included in this book:

# PREFACE

ONE of the greatest players of all time lectured on Common Sense in Chess. Yet many a would-be learner of Chess is deterred by the popular thought, 'Chess is strictly for geniuses': or 'You have to have a special capacity – an inborn talent', or words to that effect. But this is untrue. Certainly we do know of persons who have shown themselves at a very early age to be remarkably good at Chess. Does anything follow from this? Can we tell that those same prodigies, had they given their attention to some other topic – some language, some science – would not have displayed an extraordinary ability in one of those directions? They grow up with the advantage, in Chess, that accrues to the student of any topic who starts early enough – whose mind, that is to say, is developed enough in very early life to grasp essentials. Thus, to speak a foreign language very early is a clear preparation for mastery in that tongue; to learn early a musical technique, an engineering skill, these are great advantages. But the speed and the ease with which some people learn is no index to the difficulty or facility of the subject. Good players resolve Chess complexities so quickly that they leave a trail of wonder. Yet, done slowly, the process is completely understandable to anyone who is willing and able to concentrate within human capacity. So the listener to an advanced electronics engineer may feel that he is standing outside the gates of a closed world. But people, quite ordinary people, learn electronics, and apply it, and add to it.

Indeed, the learning of Chess is an object lesson in education – and one simple instance of education. In the general case, the child starts with words, which are responses to repeated signals, or which are associated with specific shapes and patterns of touch and sound. But to use those in ordered speech is a considerable advance. Nobody knows quite how the transition is made from limited responses to fluent communication. Yet everyone who learns a foreign language makes that transition sooner or later.

So to learn the moves of Chess, as in the first chapter, is to learn isolated words, which the active mind somehow learns to co-ordinate. Then there are phrases: short sentences: and the process continues from the very simple utterance of simple thought to the articulation of the complex.

In successive chapters one moves, as it were, from the isolated words to the meaningful sentences. The elementary statements are of the immediate and obvious – Common-sensical. Common sense goes quite a long way. As it applies itself – becoming a more uncommon sense – the transition is made from perception of isolated small points to that comprehending activity which is vision. But when vision is attained, and the discoveries of Chess vision revealed, the student who has plodded, even in a plantigrade way, should be able to realize that there is no great mystery involved, no supernatural revelation, only better concentration, and better uses of the resources available to all.

Concentration is, perhaps, the most important word in any account of how to learn Chess, or how to learn anything. Concentration is learnable, but unteachable. Just as Dr Johnson claimed to be able to provide reason, but not understanding, so the teacher of Chess can show the points to be seen, but cannot provide the effort of looking at them. Everyone must do his own concentrating. The reward of that Concentration is Awareness. No one can sell to anybody else Awareness. Looking hard at the board, through the lenses that a writer hopes to provide, the student becomes aware of possibilities (and impossibilities) among the pieces. No logical deduction, no arithmetical process, no formula, is available. The logical ordering of thoughts follows the thought, not precedes it. Ideas cannot be forced. Rather, ideas flow in, as if a window on the mind has been opened.

All the author of a Chess book can do is help to open those windows, and to clean them. The mind, however, is the reader's mind. Only he can exercise it. The best exercise is in play. This cannot be overemphasized. Actual play, with its effort, failures after effort, and its occasional successes, is absolutely essential if even the clearest of Chess books is to be of any help at all.

In that connexion, a word as to the underlying theory of the present volume. The book is written on the assumption that one cannot learn Chess by heart. Those books which provide the learner with long Opening variations do, admittedly, perform a useful function in so far as they reveal to the reader some interesting early pieces of play. To be shown these things is stimulating. But since the Chess act, at all stages, consists in the apprehension of lines of play unaided, it must be wrong to attempt to substitute the mechanical learning of variations for the task of working them out, as the mind's eye becomes aware of the possibilities.

The Author is not acquainted with any fine player who was not a good player before his learning of opening lines, or, indeed, his reading of books. It is quite a good plan to refer to a book for some opening theory after one has played a difficult opening. Then the learning is useful. But to set out to learn variations before playing them is, at best, to postpone the Chess task till later in the game. Players who do that usually fail when the effort is called for. They are not 'played in', as they would have been had they worked from the first move.

On the above reasoning, the Author of this book leaves opening theory to the end. This is not mere paradox. Chess is all Middle-Game, all play. Therefore the advice is repeated: learn your Chess by playing.

To this end the reader is advised to seek opponents slightly stronger, slightly more experienced, than himself, and grapple them to his heart until he has become better than they are. After that let him reward them with copies of a good Chess book, in which they can read similar advice. And to all readers let me say: 'Enjoy the game.' Enjoy the act of concentrating, enjoy the discoveries you make, enjoy the errors, because sometimes one learns from errors. Enjoy also the educational experience that Chess affords, as the mind moves from phantasmal daydreams to a process of directive thinking in which all the ideas are controlled. To these enjoyments, the occasional winning of a game will undoubtedly add. The desire to win is a great educator. But if there is one activity which can be enjoyed without regard to result, surely that activity is Chess. Among Chess players one finds a scientific objectivity, an ability not to judge superficially, or by results, and above all a love for the subject. Those mental riches are rewards that make Chess well worth learning, and well worth teaching.

# THE NOTATION

(This need not be read until the reader has tackled Chapter One)

CHESS is teachable in books because Chess is communicable. Once you learn that the pieces move from square to square on a standard board of 64 squares, it becomes clear that one only has to number, or letter, the squares, and any move is describable: even in such elementary symbols as $1-5$, $28-32$ etc. (which is the notation the Draughts-players use) or a—b or x—y, or (as in international telegraphy) vx—yz according to whatever codification be agreed.

It may even be the case, when one knows the rules, that one can describe a move by naming one square only, because, in that particular position, only one piece can reach that specific square: and some players, in recording their moves, make use of such economies.

In practice, Chess-players throughout the world record their moves (for non-telegraphic purposes) in detail according to one or other of two main systems: on the one hand, the *English* or *Descriptive*, Notation: on the other, the *Continental* or *Algebraic*, *Notation*. Neither is difficult. The algebraic is logically simpler; the descriptive is psychologically easier, especially for the following of a game *sans voir*.

In the Descriptive system, we work on the fact that, at the outset of a game, each player's back row (the horizontal row, 'rank', nearest to him) is completely occupied by pieces, each one having its proper square. It follows that each of the 'files' (vertical lines) can be described by reference to the piece that stands, originally, at the bottom of it. So, reading from White's left, one has Queen's Rook's file, based on the square called Queen's Rook's Square, and numbered QR1; next Queen's Knight's file, based on QKt1, then Queen's Bishop's file, Queen's file, King's file, King's Bishop's file, King's Knight's file, King's Rook's file.

From the back row upwards one numbers the squares 1–8, the back row square being 1, and the topmost square on the file being 8. So, suppose White's Bishop moves to the fourth square from the bottom (inclusive) of the fifth file (inclusive) from White's left, the move is recorded as Bishop to King's Bishop's fourth – B—KB4. Or if White's Knight moves to the third square on the third file from White's left, the move is recorded as Knight to Queen's Bishop's third – Kt—QB3.

Observe, please, that these are descriptions of moves by White pieces: and that is their description for whichever player (White or Black) is describing them. But when a Black piece is moved, the description is made (by both players) as from Black's side of the board.

Black's back row is occupied by pieces exactly similar, and exactly opposite, to White's. Black, from his left (which is White's right) describes his back row squares as KR1, KKt1, KB1, K1, Q1, QB1, QKt1, QR1. And he numbers the squares on his files, from 1–8, towards the White side. So White's QR8 is Black's QR1, and Black's QR8 is White's QR1.

Consequently if it were a Black Bishop that had settled on the square that we described as White's KB4, it would be regarded, and described, as settling on Black's King's Bishop's fifth – B—KB5. Similarly if it were a Black Knight that had gone to the square described as White's QB3, the move would be recorded, from the Black point of view, as Kt—QB6.

Thus, in the Descriptive Notation, every square on the board has two descriptions: one used in the description of White's moves, and the other for Black's moves. But, complicated as this sounds, nobody finds the double system difficult.

[NOTE: Before moving to an account of the other notation, I would mention that, in the descriptive system, economies of recording are used whenever there is no ambiguity. The Q and K of QKt, QR, QB, KKt, KB, KR, describe no differences of power: they avoid ambiguity when it can exist.

So there may be a move describable as QKt—QKt5. If either of the two Knights could reach that square on the move, this would be a proper description: but if only one can reach it (say the Queen's Knight) but the other Kt can reach the other Kt5, then one writes: QKt—Kt5 or Kt—QKt5. Now suppose we are moving a Knight to QKt5 – the only Kt that can reach that square – and there is no Knight that can reach KKt5 – then we can lessen the writing even further, and write Kt—Kt5, because it is unambiguous. Only one Knight can go to a fifth square on a Knight's file.

Similarly, if both Bishops can reach a Knight's fifth and the KB actually does so, one writes – not KB—QKt5, because the QB cannot reach QKt5: instead KB—Kt5, or B—QKt5. If the QB cannot reach a Knight's fifth, then when the KB goes to QKt5, the unambiguous description is simply B—Kt5. (To write more than is necessary has been compared to splitting an infinitive.)]

Black

1

| QR1 QKt1 QB1 Q1 | K1 KB1 KKt1 KR1 |
|---|---|
| QR8 QKt8 QB8 Q8 | K8 KKt8 KR8 |

QKt4 / QKt5 · Q4 / Q5 · KB4 / KB5

K5 / K4 · KB5 / KB4

QB6 / QB3

| QR1 QKt1 QB1 Q1 | K1 KB1 KKt1 KR1 |
|---|---|
| QR8 QKt8 QB8 Q8 | K8 KB8 KKt8 KR8 |

White

Frame of English, or Descriptive Notation

In contrast to the Descriptive Notation the Algebraic Notation is a 'one-way' system. Every move is described as from White's side of the board.

From White's left to right, the files are lettered a, b, c, d, e, f, g, h; and the squares on the files are numbered 1–8, from White's back row to Black's back row; but never the other way. So Black's King's square (K1 or K8 in the Descriptive system) is always e8 in the algebraic, whether White is moving or Black.

Black

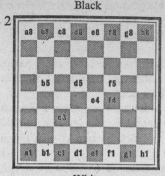

White

Frame of Continental, or Algebraic Notation

Players who use this system find it difficult at first when they are playing the Black pieces; but that difficulty is evanescent.

Strictly speaking, when one uses the algebraic, it should be sufficient to name the squares only. So a piece, moving from White's Queen's Bishop's square to White's King's Knight's fifth, does a process c1 — g5: and if that were the only piece that could reach g5, the notation g5 would appear adequate.

But the practice is not like that. On the Continental model, one writes Bc1 — g5. British players, using the Algebraic, tend to the shorter usage B — g5 – omitting the square of origin: British players, however, always name the piece. Even the humble Pawn is mentioned. So Pe2 — e4. But on the Continent, where an arrogant attitude towards infantry is traditional, the Pawn is not mentioned: so our Pawn move would be described over there as e2 — e4.

One advantage the Algebraic system holds over the descriptive. There is less danger of ambiguity. Thus it sometimes happens that (for example) White's King or Queen can capture one of two Black Pawns. One Pawn is on White's KB4; the other on White's KB5. Now if one says K × P (KB4) this may be open to the construction that, since it is a Black Pawn under notice, we are speaking of Black's KB4 (White's KB5): alternatively that, since it is a White K, the reference is to White's KB4 (and this I believe to be the correct reading). Such ambiguities are rare, but they support the 'logical' claim of the Algebraic system.

In common to both systems are certain symbols. In P—K4 and e2—e4, the — signifies 'moves to'. × signifies 'captures' (e.g. B×Kt, or Bb5×Ktc6). This × can be used in both systems: but Continental writers have long used, instead, a semicolon, or colon, to signify 'captures'; thus: c4d5: (the Russians — c4: d5) or Bc6: etc. (In each case of this usage, the captured piece is not mentioned.)

There are other markings to notice: In the British system ch. is used to signify 'check'. Some players use + to signify 'check', but this can lead to confusion, because many annotations use ⊣ to signify 'with advantage' (– being used to signify 'with disadvantage'). Continental writers use an obelus (†) to signify 'check', and a double obelus (‡) to signify 'mate'. 'Double check' is, in the continental, ††, in the British dble ch. 'Discovered check' is dis. ch. in the British. The Continental has no equivalent sign. Let is be added that the latter of these markings is not regarded as important, but it can be convenient. Other important markings are as follows:

e.p. signifies *en passant* (this and other terms will be explained later). O—O signifies 'Castles King's side', O—O—O signifies 'Castles Queen's side'. = (e.g. P=Q) describes promotion.

An exclamation mark is used by annotators in order to say: 'good move'.

A mark of interrogation (?) is used to mean 'bad, or inferior move'. Both these annotatory marks tend to be abused: so that one encounters !! to mean 'really good', and even !!! to mean 'excellent'. Parallel to this debasement of currency, we find ?? and ??? according to the feelings of the annotator.

One further system of notation is worth knowing; not for the description of moves, but for the description of positions. This is the *Forsyth Notation*.

You are looking at the board from White's side, but you are reading the board as if it were a book written in a European language, i.e. from left to right and from the farthest line down to the nearest. So you start at Black's back row, i.e. at White's top left-hand corner, and record every square – as a printer does. White pieces are initialized in capitals: Black in lower case. (This can be done in MS. diagrams, but there the preference is for ringing the Black pieces.) Vacant squares are represented by the number of sequent vacant squares on the same line. Thus we have a Black Rook at b8, Black King at g8, White Rook at c7: then 5 vacant lines: then White King at e1. This reads: 1r4kl: 2R5, 8, 8, 8, 8, 8, 4K3. More economically 1r4kl, 2R5, 4O, 4K3. Vacant lines are added together, but not usually empty squares on adjoining, partially occupied, lines. (Thus not: 1r4k 3R5.)*

Black

White

Example of Forsyth Notation
1r4k1, 2R5, 4O, 4K3

Let the reader work out for himself 5Bbk, q7, 8, p7, 8, K7, 5P2, 6Q1. There he has a study by Kubbel (White to move and win). The solution is given on p. 287. If the reader who does not solve it waits until he reaches that page, he will appreciate it more.

* One could work on files in the same way; but this is not practised.

# SOME BASIC RULES

1. In Chess the capture of the King is the end of the game.

2. But the capture of the King by accident is not allowed. To put the King *en prise* (i.e. where it can be taken) is illegal. (To prevent misunderstanding, a King must not even let itself be captured by a King, or by a piece guarding a King from check, even though the capture exposes the other King to capture. First King lost loses.)

3. A King under threat of immediate capture is said to be 'in check'. A player 'in check' has to put an immediate end to the state of check. It is customary, but not obligatory, to announce Check orally. (To announce threats to other pieces is 'not done'.)

4. It follows that the only capture of the King which terminates the game is an inevitable one. (The check is unanswerable.) Then the actual capture does not take place. We stop when it cannot be avoided! The end of the game is the situation where a King is attacked and cannot be saved from immediate capture – i.e. capture on the immediately next move. That situation is checkmate.

(In turn, people do not wait for checkmate, but resign when they think they must, by reasonable play, inevitably be mated. In order to judge this one requires study and experience of Chess processes generally.)

5. It does *not* follow that whenever the capture of the King is inevitable, the game is lost. By definition, the King is, at the moment of checkmate, in check. If the King is not in check, but its owner, having the move, can only make moves that expose it to check, the position is called STALEMATE, and paradoxically that is a draw.

6. A game is also a draw if one player has a 'perpetual check' – he can check without ceasing and without being able

to force mate. This, making the game interminable, makes it unwinnable and unlosable: i.e. a draw.

7. A draw can also be reached by agreement: also by the operation of one of two specific rules:

(a) If the identical position occurs 3 times in the game, then a valid claim to a draw can be made, instead of a move, either by the player whose impending move can cause the third occurrence, or by the player whose turn it is to move immediately the recurrence has taken place.

(b) If 50 successive moves have been played by one player (49 by the other) without any piece or Pawn having been taken, or any Pawn moved, the opponent has a valid claim to a draw.*

8. Another rule that is very important, and a very good discipline, is that to touch one of your own pieces, when it is your turn to move, creates a duty to move that piece if this can be legally done. To touch an opponent's piece when it is your turn to move creates a duty to capture it, if that can be legally done. That moves cannot be retracted goes without saying.

9. For the rest, the players move in strict rotation, White making the first move. No player may 'pass' his turn to move.

10. Capturing is always optional. The only case of compulsory capture is where the capture is the only possible way of terminating a state of check.

11. Illegal moves are not allowed to stand. They must be corrected, and all moves made between the error and the correction are void.

The above rules (or laws) are, with the moves, constitutive of the game. In addition there are regulative rules relating to match and tournament play. E.g. there are rules about time (see p. 288).

* Since some endgame positions are forced wins involving more than 50 moves, Directors of Tournaments are empowered to grant the further number required. A very complicated situation, with which the learner is not likely to be concerned.

## CHAPTER ONE

# INTRODUCING THE ELEMENTS:
# THE POWERS AND FUNCTIONS OF THE
# PIECES: SOME IMPORTANT TERMS

CHESS has been called a War-Game: and this description is, at the outset, a useful one. The learner knows that there are two ways in which a war can be won, if it is to be won at all. It can be won at the end of long campaigns during which one side gains in material strength relatively to the other, until eventually the preponderance is so massive that the stronger combatant can overwhelm the capital city and the last bastions of the defending state, and take over its government. A war can also be won, at a much earlier stage, by some devastating blow struck at the heart of the adversary; the annihilation or capture of the vital centres of administration without control of which the defender is helpless and numb, incapable of any action.

So it is in Chess. A game can be won as if after many battles and sieges; at the end, that is to say, of quite long processes of capture, processes of accumulation of force – i.e. mobile material – processes culminating in such sufficient preponderance of strength that the opponent's King – the object of the campaign – cannot be defended. A game can also be won, at a much earlier stage, if one player can so deploy his forces to the detriment of the other that he captures, or renders indefensible, the opponent's King, even while there is plenty of military potential still apparently available to the defender.

The common factor to both types of victory is the capture of the King, which is at once the target of the opposing forces, and itself a combatant: the most important combatant, but far from the strongest.*

* The notion of the fighting King is appropriate in this ancient game-product of third-century India. But if the names of the pieces were changed

If neither player succeeds in capturing his opponent's King the game is drawn: that is to say, neither player wins: and that situation is the normal result of a really well contested game. When a player comes to realize that truth in practice – i.e. when he becomes aware of the resources latent in both sets of forces – then he begins to think of the game, in a less military way, as a subtle study in the deployment of potential: even as the best generals seem to regard their wars. But that is another story.

At the outset, the learner is fighting. His field is a square board containing 64 equal squares, which are coloured alternately black and white, and symmetrically arranged to form eight adjacent ranks (horizontal lines) and, intersecting, eight adjacent files (vertical lines). The board, shown in the diagram, must be so placed that each player's first row, or rank, runs from a black left-hand corner; and along this first row he places his major pieces. Along his second row are ranged the Pawns – which have been compared to infantry, and regarded

Black

White

Chess-board with pieces. The opening scene

to fit the requirements of modern life and warfare, there would still be needed a name to distinguish some vital feature of the forces, such as the King is, in contrast with other important, physically stronger but less vital, units.

as cannon-fodder: so that he starts with a total equipment of 16 pieces (or men).*

White's pieces, reading from left to right in the Diagram, are ROOK, KNIGHT, BISHOP, QUEEN, KING, BISHOP, KNIGHT, ROOK. Black, reading from his left, has: Rook, Knight, Bishop, King, Queen, etc. The opposing Kings and Queens must face each other respectively. Each King is, at the outset, on a square of its opposite colour – i.e. White King on Black square, Black King on White square. For the rest each piece starts its career with a Pawn on the square immediately in front of it.

That is the position at the commencement of the game. From this position White moves first (in the normal game) and Black follows.† The players thereafter make one move each in strict rotation. Each player is compelled to exercise his right to move. There is no waiver. This fact is on occasion a great embarrassment.

For the purpose of studying the moves, it is advisable for the student to ignore, for the time being, the original position, and consider the powers of the pieces on the open board.

The reader will see (from a glance at the next diagram) that movement is possible along horizontal and vertical lines, and along diagonals. Most of the powers of the pieces can be described easily in these terms (Diagram 5).

Basic are the moves of Rook and Bishop. Rooks move freely along ranks or files in any direction: Bishops move freely along diagonals in any direction.

The Queen combines the powers of Rook and Bishop, and can move freely along rank or file or diagonal in any direction. The King, in the ordinary way, can move along rank or

* These words include in their denotation 'Pawns'; but very often the word 'piece' is used (with a smaller denotation) in contrast to 'Pawn', and to indicate a more valuable element. The meaning will always be clear from the context (e.g. He lost a piece for a Pawn).

† The right to move first is something of an initiative, but, in this author's opinion at least, not a sufficient initiative to bias the issue in favour of the first player.

Black

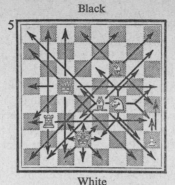

White

The moves of the pieces

file or diagonal in any direction, but only one square at a time.

The Knight has a move which is hard to describe compendiously. Some say: corner to corner of a rectangle of squares, 3 × 2, built in any direction: or 'one straight, and one diagonally away': logically the Knight exercises the minimum move to change at once its rank, its file and its diagonal.

For the rest the humble Pawn moves in single steps along its file, upwards only. Its first move can be a double one. Its captures are eccentric (diagonal). It cannot move back. When it reaches the back rank it is promoted to a piece. Descriptions will now be elaborated.

First, place the King in the middle of the board (Diagram 6)

THE KING (Roi, König, Korolj) can move one square, from the square he happens to occupy, in any direction. Thus from the point in the diagram e4, the King can move to any one of the unoccupied squares in his field: e5 or e3, or d4, or f4, or d5, or d3, or f5, or f3: a choice of eight moves. (Observe that, in Chess, pieces only move on to squares; they cannot settle on the dividing lines between squares. Also two pieces cannot share one square.) If one of the eight squares round the King were occupied by a piece of the same colour as the King, then the

Black

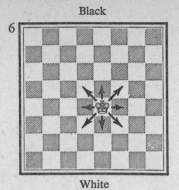

White

King's move

King could not move there. If it were occupied by an unguarded piece of the opposite colour, the King could – not must (it is normally optional) – capture that piece, i.e. remove it and occupy its place.

The King, it has already been said, has a special importance in the game. Consequently many rules surround him. We are here concerned with his normal power as an active piece. Even at this early stage, however, his prerogatives and limitations have to be appreciated.

Compendiously, the King must not move, or stay, where he can be immediately captured. A move threatening the King is called a CHECK, and this threat must be immediately countered: either by a move of the King, or by interposition of a protecting piece, or by capture of the checking piece. When there is no protection available at all, then the King is considered dead: checkmate: and the game is over – lost by the player whose King is checkmated.

Having been told so much, the learner may conclude that all positions in which the player cannot move without his King being captured are lost positions. This is, strangely, not true! If the King is *not* in check, but there is no move available which will not expose him to immediate capture, then we have, not checkmate, but Stalemate: and that is a DRAW. This is one of the most important, and thwarting, features of a game in which it is notoriously hard to win, however easy it may be to lose.

Before these terms are considered further, let other pieces be introduced.

Remove the King, and place the Queen on e4 (Diagram 7).

Black

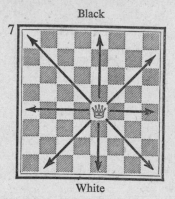

White

Queen's move

THE QUEEN (Continental – Dame: Russian – Firze [original: Vizier: cf. old English Fers]) can move in all the directions of the King's eight possible moves, but is not restricted to a move of one square. She can move in any one of eight directions, along any number of unoccupied squares, according to the desire of the player. Thus, unobstructed, the Queen has a choice of 27 possible moves, whereas the King has only eight.

The main limitations on the Queen's power are (1) the obvious one, that the Queen (and other pieces moving comparably) must keep to straight lines, including straight diagonals: e.g. a Queen moving along a White diagonal cannot end its diagonal move on a Black Square. (2) Her moves (as those of other pieces) are terminated by obstacles. Thus, place the White Queen on e4, and some other piece on b7. Now the Queen cannot move to a8. If the obstructing piece is a White one, then the White Queen cannot move farther in that direction than c6. If the obstructing piece be Black, White may (in the ordinary way it is not compulsory) capture the obstructing piece; remaining, itself, on b7 (Diagram 8).

Black

White

Queen capturing Rook
If the Rook on b7 were White, the Queen's scope would terminate at c6

This statement, be it observed, gives us a few Chess rules.

(1) With three apparent exceptions, of which two will be explained away, Chess pieces (unlike Draughts pieces) do not leap over each other.

(2) Only one piece can occupy any one square at one time.

(3) Capturing (with one exception that will be explained) consists in the move of a piece on to a square occupied, at that moment, by an opposing piece. The captured piece is removed from the board, and the capturing piece remains on the square where the capture has taken place.

The reader now has sufficient knowledge of the rules to be able to appreciate practical illustrations of MATE and STALE-MATE

Diagram 9 shows King and Queen in play against a lone King. (To avoid misunderstanding let it be observed that mate and stalemate can take place on crowded as well as empty boards: but the relatively empty board offers simpler illustrations.)

Black

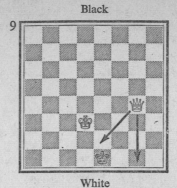

White

Mate by Q with aid of K

The White Queen can, from g4, move and deliver mate at e2 alternatively at g1. The reader will see that each of these moves gives check, and there is no escape from it.

But suppose the Queen were to move not to e2 but to f3. Now there is no check. But Black, under obligation to move, cannot do so without making his King capturable – at d1 or f1, or d2, e2, or f2 (Diagram 10).

Black

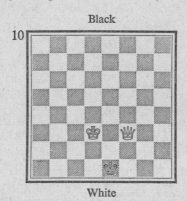

White

Black to move. Stalemate

Accordingly we have stalemate – a draw. Obviously, few players are so weak as to make the mistake that White is shown making here. But it can easily come about that, after a long closing skirmish, a player can force his opponent into stalemating. E.g. suppose the King and Queen had stood at e3 and f3, while Black still had a Queen. That Queen, going to d3, e.g. in order to capture a pawn, is captured by White, leaving a stalemate position. (It need hardly be said that stalemates occur with other pieces involved on both sides. Examples will be seen.) Meanwhile let it be noted that, partly in consequence of the stalemate rule, there is a very big margin of 'draw' in Chess. Although very slight preponderances can be exploited into victory, some quite large preponderances can fail to win.

Now, having surveyed the two pieces which can move on the diagonal as well as on the rank and file, let us substitute the pieces more limited in their powers.

*The Rook* (Tour, Turm, Ladj).

Place a Rook on e4. This piece, at one time in Chess history the strongest piece,* moves freely in any of four directions along ranks and files, but not along diagonals. So, on an empty board, it has a choice of 14 possible moves.

This is, nominally, only 6 more than the King's choice: but qualitatively its superiority is much greater, because the Rook, like the Queen, can, in two moves, go from any square on the board to any other. Because no other piece can do this, clearly both these pieces must rank high in relative values. They are called Major Pieces.

One power the Queen and Rook have in common. Each of these can, aided only by a King, deliver mate to a lone King.

Diagram 12 shows mate by a Rook. But the Rook can not only give mate: it can, in combination with a King, force mate. Thus place a Black Rook on c7, the Black King on e3, the White King on d1. A most elementary exercise in Chess is the

* Rook, Persian Rukh (the wind) had its move before the Queen, or Vizier, developed its present powers. The word Castle (for Rook) has no justification. The word Rook was corrupted into ROCCA, ROCHE, and so to fortifications.

Black

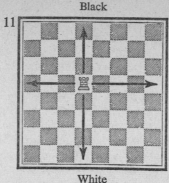

White

Rook's move

problem of now mating in two. A moment's reflection will

Black

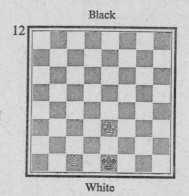

White

Mate by Rook with aid of King

show that the Rook has only to make a move on the file, to c8, c6, c5, c4 or c3. White must then move King to e1 : after which R—c1 gives mate. (Diagram 13.)

This forcing of White to move and lose is one example of what is called *zugzwang* – compulsion to move. It happens, at times, that a player's forces are so overloaded with defensive

Black

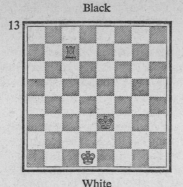

White

Black mates in 2 moves

tasks that the mere duty of moving causes the player to unguard some important point. That is *zugzwang*; and this present position is a simpler instance of it.

Let us carry the process a little farther.

Suppose the Kings were higher up the board: Black K at e6, White K at d4, Black Rook at c7. Again, by R—c8, Black would compel the White King to lose ground. If e.g. K—e4, R—c4 ch, drives it back. Or if K—d3, Black, playing K—e5, narrows its field further. Knowing this principle the reader should be able to work out a forcing process of mating with King and Rook against lone King from any points on the Board.

Let it be noted, also, that in using a Rook, there is danger of stalemate, but less than with a Queen. Thus Black King on f3, White King on h1, Black Rook on a2. Mate is forced by Kg3. But if, instead, one were to play Rg2, that would be stalemate. Such an event is usually the result of a capture.

(The Queen, by the way, is strong enough to be responsible for stalemate without the aid of its King: e.g. Q on f2: hostile King on h1.)

A thought on stalemate. It *is* illogical. It is the only *zugzwang* which is a draw. And it is a different type of draw from agreed draw – when neither sees any hope of victory; and different from that very important type of draw which is perpetual check.

In perpetual check it is clear that one player can stop the other from all positive action. The checker himself can do no better than keep checking. That is a logical draw. Stalemate is relatively illogical: but it is a source of many of the subtleties and beauties of Chess.

To revert to comparisons between the pieces, the Queen is clearly stronger than the Rook. The Rook is, equally clearly, stronger than any minor piece, though the difference between Rook and minor piece is rather less than the difference between Queen and Rook. To give a Rook for a Bishop or Knight is to 'lose the exchange' – definitely a loss, but not always a great loss. To give a Queen for a Rook is to lose the major exchange –

Black

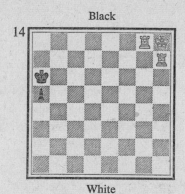

White

Mate by 2 Rooks

| | |
|---|---|
| *1.* R—Kt6 ch  K—Kt4 | *5.* R—Kt2 ch  K—B8 |
| *2.* R—R5 ch  K—B5 | *6.* R—QR2  K—Kt8 |
| *3.* R—Kt4 ch  K—Q6 | *7.* R—QKt3 and mate |
| *4.* R—R3 ch  K—K7 | next move |

If there were no Pawn at a5, the mate would be a very quick one:

*1.* R—Kt8 K moves; *2.* R—R7 mate

R—Kt8 even here also forces mate. Let the reader work it out.

usually a big loss. (To complete the account, the exchange of Bishop for Knight can be called 'loss of the minor exchange': but this is not popular terminology.)

These values are stated, of course, for normal positions with no special features. The reader will learn that, in the course of a game, the formal powers of a piece can become unimportant if it is not in a position to exercise them, and pieces of nominally smaller value prove much more effective. But, 'all things being equal' (which they sometimes are), the values are as stated.

As to the relative value of Queen and Rook, it is reasonably clear that two Rooks are very powerful and can do things that the Queen alone cannot do.

Two Rooks in collective action attacking a Pawn, defended by a King, e.g. can capture the Pawn: i.e. the capturer cannot be recaptured. A Queen could not do likewise, unsupported.

Two Rooks can force mate without the aid of a King (Diag. 14).

Black

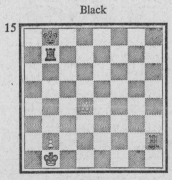

White

**Powers of Queen and of Two Rooks**
*Perpetual Check*

If Black has the move, R × P ch draws.
If White has the move he has
  (a) Perpetual check: Q—Q8, Q—R5, and Q—Q8.
  (b) Something better: There is an immediate 'fork' by Q—Q6 ch or Q—KB4 ch winning a Rook.

On the other hand, a Queen playing against two Rooks on the open board can wreak havoc if they are not mutually supporting: or can achieve that special draw which is perpetual check (Diagram 15).

Before we descend the scale in order to examine the so-called minor pieces, mention must be made of some very important, and eccentric, behaviour that can be performed by the Rook in co-operation with the King.

If the first-rank squares between the King and either Rook are vacant, then, given certain conditions, very frequently obtaining, the King and Rook can do, between them, three moves in one – the manœuvre known as CASTLING. The King moves two squares to its right or left, as the case may be, and the Rook towards which it moves leaps over it to occupy the square that the King has passed over.*

Diagram 16 shows the movement. The conditions are:

Black

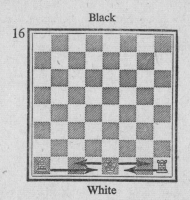

White

The process of Castling
Both instances (K side and Q side) are shown.

* Pedantically, the King should be moved first. The movement of the Rook first might be considered a complete move: whereas the long movement of the King first cannot be construed as other than the initiation of castling. Since in Chess 'to touch is to move', this is worth remembering, though few are pedantic enough to make an issue of the order in which one castles.

(1) That neither the King nor the Castling Rook shall have moved previously. (That the King has been checked is irrelevant, so long as it has not moved. This is mentioned in order to dispose of a popular error.)

(2) That the King, at the moment of Castling, shall not be in check, i.e. one cannot Castle one's way out of check.

(3) The square passed over, and the square arrived at, by the King, must not be under the threat of any hostile piece. In Diagram 16 the squares f1 and g1 must be free from attack at the appropriate moment for King's side Castling to be possible. The squares c1 and d1 must be unattacked for the purposes of Queen's side Castling. Attacks on the Rooks and threats to the square b1 are irrelevant.

(Diagram 17 shows various objections to the legality of Castling.)

Black

17

White

### Inability to Castle

*1*. Black, in Check, cannot therefore Castle. *2* If Black inserts the Kt (i.e. doesn't move the K) he may, thereafter, be free to Castle. *3*. White, when it is his turn, cannot Castle because the squares f1 and d1 are under threat by a Black piece.

If Castling is legal and done, the reader will realize that a great economy has been effected. Three moves in the time of one: the King put on to a safe square (this is by no means always the case): and the Rook brought nearer to action in the centre. The value of the Rook, diminished in the earlier part of the game by its 'out-of-placeness', is abundantly compensated by this eccentric power.

From the Rook, then, it is clear that we are going down a step to Bishop and Knight. How valuable are these relatively to each other?

To equate them is difficult. Equals, perhaps. Yet to exchange Bishop for Knight can be called losing the minor exchange. But that need not be a loss at all. That they both are formidable will be seen when we come (now) to study their movements.

*Bishop* (Fou, Laüfer, Slon).*

Black

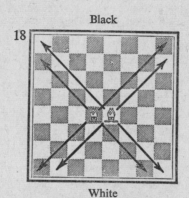

18

White

Bishop's move

Place a Bishop on e4 (Diagram 18). This is a White square. From it the Bishop moves in any of four directions, as many moves, or as few, as are desired and possible (i.e. unobstructed) along any of the White diagonals leading from e4, a total of 13 possible moves. 'Only one less than the Rook has', points out

---

* Russian Slon means elephant. This piece was called by the Arabs Alfil (elephant); corrupted into Spanish *Alfiere*: thence: *le fou* (French): *Laüfer* German). Bishop is peculiar to Anglo-Saxon: possibly relates to the association between clerics and Exchequer.

the reader. But consider the limitation. That Bishop can never control a Black square. Out of 64 squares on the board it can only visit 32. Place its companion on d4. This Bishop has a choice of 13 moves on the Black squares, and can never visit a White square. It follows that a lone Bishop with King cannot mate a lone King. Its best achievement is stalemate (e.g. Black K at e1, White K at e3, White B at e2).

But let not the power of a Bishop be underestimated. To control half the board is quite a power. Between them two Bishops can exercise formidable aggressive and defensive powers. (Put, for example, the Black King on e6 opposite two White Bishops on e4 and d4, and try to cross the board with the King.) When he considers the Knight's move, the reader may, at first sight, regard the Bishop as stronger. This, however, is to be debated.

*Knight* (Cavalier, Springer, Konj).

Black

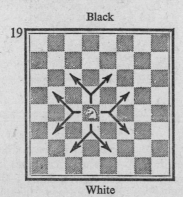

White

Knight's move

Place the Knight on e4 (Diagram 19). His move is strange. One square along the rank or file, and then one along the diagonal, away from the point of origin. Or one along the diagonal, followed by one along rank, or file, away from the point of origin: alternatively, two along the rank followed by

one along the file; or two along the file followed by one along
the rank. Directive descriptions are all useful and all slightly in-
accurate, because, in order to reach its destination the Knight
cannot be said to traverse squares; and it is not quite right to
accuse it of jumping over pieces, when it by-passes those on
immediately adjoining squares.

In order to appreciate the apparently strange power of the
Knight, fill the squares, c3, c4, c5, d3, d5, e3, e4, e5 with
pieces, and place the Knight on d4: now the Knight's moves to
e6, f5, f3, e2, c2, b3, b5, c6 are all playable (Diagram 20). He

Black

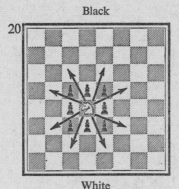

White

Knight's move

The Kt has eight possible moves, each one of which leaves the Black
Pawns undisturbed

does not leap over, rather he passes between. His apparently
illogical move has, indeed, quite a logical place in the game.
Other pieces change, with their moves, either their ranks and
diagonals or their files and diagonals, or their ranks and files;
not all three. But the Knight follows a path – incidentally the
shortest possible path – which changes in one move the piece's
rank and file and diagonal.

The power of the Knight is worth considering at length. On
first acquaintance he seems to exercise a short-range magic. He
does what a Bishop, Rook, or Queen cannot do. A Queen on e4
cannot capture a piece on f6; but a Knight on e4 can. If the

Black

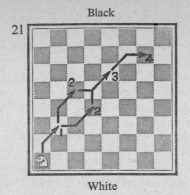

White

Knight's path a1—g7

Queen were given the Knight's power in addition to its present powers, it could deliver mate unaided! (e.g. Q on e3: hostile King on e1). As to its limitations, if you place a Knight on a1, you can see that it takes four moves to reach g7, whereas a Bishop, from a1, can reach, not only g7, but h8, in one move (Diagram 21). Yet the Knight, moving to g7, passes c2 (or b3),

Black

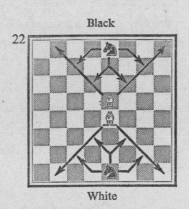

White

Knights paralysed by Bishops

and f5 (or e6) which are squares that the Bishop from a1 can never reach at all.

On the other hand, place a Bishop on e5, and a hostile Knight on e8. Now that unfortunate Knight is paralysed by the Bishop (Diagram 22). A Knight cannot so restrict a Bishop. But this possibility is abstract from the practical realities of the board. Such preponderances are the end results of complex play. Let them not bias the valuation disproportionately. Indeed the Knight has its moments. In Diagram 23 a Knight helps to 'dominate' a Bishop.

Consider, in this connexion, the following position (Diagram 24). Here a Knight works havoc among hostile Pawns. A Bishop of the wrong colour would not be able to strike at them. A Bishop of the right colour may be restricted in its movements by them.

Also a Knight is peculiarly effective against cramped or undeveloped pieces. More will be said about the Knight's 'fork' – which is not so much peculiar as spectacular. But very amusing is the smothered mate that a Knight can do. The diagram shows a piece of play called 'Philidor's legacy' – attributed to the celebrated French musician–Chess-player of the

Black

23

White

'Domination'

Black to play, loses. Wherever the B moves, the Kt, discovering check, attacks and wins it

Black

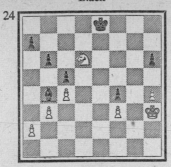

White

### Power of a Knight

If the Black King moves to Q2, White can win the KRP by Kt—B5,
followed, if the Pawn moves, by Kt—Kt7

If the King moves to the K side, then Kt—B8 docs damage to the
Q side Pawns

Black

White

### Philidor's legacy

If: *1.* .... K—Kt1        *3.* Q—Kt8 ch   R×Q
*2.* Kt—R6 double ch   K—R1        *4.* Kt—B7   Mate

eighteenth century. This is one of the popular melodies of
Chess (Diagram 25). There are many other 'smothered mates',
as the reader will learn.

Look also at this. The King wishes to cross over to its Pawn.

Black

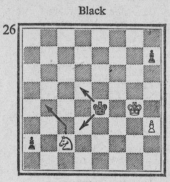

White

Knight holds King back

The reader is advised to work out for himself the result of the best
play from this position

Black

White

Knight stops Pawn

If *1.* .... P—B8 (=Q)   *2.* Kt—Kt3 ch wins the Queen

But the Knight holds it back on the other side of a curtain because of the range of checking manœuvres that will capture the pawn (Diagram 26). And so a Knight has resources to prevent the promotion of a Pawn (Diagram 27). In contrast, observe how a King thwarts a Knight. If the King is on the next square but one to the Knight's position on a diagonal, the Knight cannot achieve check in less than three moves (Diagram 28).

Black

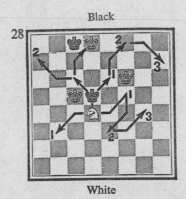

28

White

Knight's Checks

The Kings on c5 and d8 can be checked immediately. The Kings on d5 and c8 can be checked in two moves. The King on f6 can only be checked in three moves

The next diagram shows the tremendous range of Knights when they have checks, or other threats, to act as a kind of spring-board in their progress (Diagram 29).

The diagram shows the 'Domination' of a Queen by Knights and a Rook.

Of the Knight's fork, more will be said later in the chapter.

For the rest, the lone Knight with King cannot achieve mate against a lone King. The best is stalemate (Kt on f3, K on f2: adverse King on h1). Two Knights with King can give mate; but, as we shall see, cannot force mate. Two Bishops with King; or Bishop and Knight with King, can force mate. (One must

Black

White

White wins (Study by Rinck)

*1.* Kt—B3 ch   K—B4 (only move to save the King and Queen)
*2.* R—R5   Q—KB8 (only square on which to avoid forks, etc.)
*3.* R—R4   Q—B2 ch! (If this is captured, the result is stalemate)
*4.* Kt—Q7 ch   Q×Kt ch (forced)
*5.* K×Q and wins

drive the King to the corner of the Bishop's colour.) It follows that King and two Knights against King is a draw: King and 2 Bs. or B and Kt, win against lone King.*

Black

White

Power of two Bishops. This is Mate

* K and 2 Kts against K and P, can, paradoxically, be a win in some situations—fantastically difficult to exploit. (There is release from stalemate.)

Black

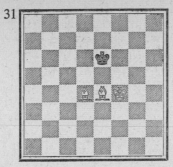

31

White

### Mate by two Bishops and King

| | | | |
|---|---|---|---|
| *1.* B—K5 | K—K2 | *7.* B—B6 ch | K—B1 |
| *2.* K—B5 | K—Q2 | *8.* B—Q6 ch | K—Kt1 |
| *3.* B—QKt7 | K—Q1 | *9.* B—K4 | K—R1 |
| *4.* K—K6 | K—K1 | *10.* K—Kt6 | K—Kt1 |
| *5.* B—B7 | K—B1 | *11.* B—Q5 ch | K—R1 |
| *6.* K—B6 | K—K1 | *12.* B—K5 | Mate |

Relatively to the Bishop the Knight has a short range: but also compensations for its short range. Suffice it, then, to say here that, unless there is very clear reason in the position for preference, it is generally assumed that a Knight is as valuable as a Bishop; so that to exchange a Bishop for a Knight constitutes no material loss: and such exchanges are frequently made in the early stages of games, even by the grandest of grand masters.

To sum up the 'minority' of minor pieces.

Minor pieces show their minority by not being able singly to force mate in conjunction with a King. King and Bishop can be placed so as to administer stalemate. So can King and Knight. But never mate.

As to the method by which King and two Bishops force mate: the task is not difficult. The two Bishops restrict the hostile King while the attacking King approaches, and they muster the opponent to the corner (Diagram 31).

The process of mate by King and Bishop and Knight is much more laborious. The technique is to force the King to a corner of the board controlled by the Bishop. The play from Diagram 32 shows the mate being achieved.

Black

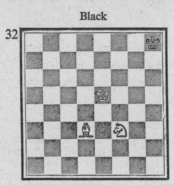

White

Mate by B and Kt with K

| | | | |
|---|---|---|---|
| 1. K—B6 | K—Kt1 | 10. B—Kt6 ch | K—Q1 |
| 2. B—K4 | K—R1 | 11. Kt—B5 | K—B1 |
| 3. Kt—Kt5 | K—Kt1 | 12. B—K4 | K—Q1 |
| 4. Kt—B7 | K—B1 | 13. Kt—K6 ch | K—B1 |
| 5. B—R7 | K—K1 | (if K—K1 B mates) | |
| 6. Kt—K5 | K—B1 | 14. K—B6 | K—Kt1 |
| (if 6. .... | K—Q1 | 15. K—Kt6 | K—B1 |
| 7. B—K4 | K—B2 | 16. B—B6 | K—Kt1 |
| 8. Kt—B4 prevents escape) | | 17. B—K7 | K—R1 |
| 7. Kt—Q7 ch | K—K1 | 18. Kt—B5 | K—Kt1 |
| 8. K—K6 | K—Q1 | 19. Kt—R6 ch | K—R1 |
| 9. K—Q6 | K—K1 | 20. B—B6 | Mate |

Observe that it is all too easy to let the defending King slip, and here the 50-move rule is relevant. A player aware of the powers of his pieces (including the King) should be able to cope with the difficulty.

Nothing would be gained by any student learning these processes by heart. Chess moves must be seen, not played as by

Black

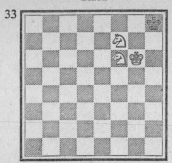

33

White

**Mate by K and 2 Kts**
*This is not forced*

1. On the previous move Black could have played to f8
2. Replace the Knight from f7 at e5. Now if it were Black to move we would have stalemate

habit. But a player who can use his pieces will soon grasp the way of forcing the King to the proper corner.

About King and two Knights there is a prevalent misunderstanding. Some say that King and two Knights cannot mate; but they *can*. Diagram 33 shows how. But what is important to grasp is that this mate cannot be forced. Examine the diagram position. The White Knight that is mating has come from e5 or d6 or d8 or g5. Now the Black King moved, on its last move, to h8. But this was not forced. It could have moved to f8.

If you construct a position from which it seems that you can force mate with K and two Knights, you will find that stalemate occurs first. (But add a Black Pawn: eg, 6K1, 4pKt2, 4Kt1K1, 4O. Here White can force mate. A rare situation.)

Last, and apparently least, we consider *the Pawn* (Pion, Bauer, Pieshka).

This, the infantry of the Chess army, is handicapped, relatively to the other pieces, by being unidirectional. The infantry can only advance. In Chess the Pawn cannot retreat. Its move is

one pace forward. Even in this it is easily thwarted. If any piece
stands in its path the Pawn cannot capture it. Yet it has a power
of capture – diagonally. The Pawn can capture any piece occu-
pying a square adjoining it on either forward diagonal.

Two changes in the course of Chess history have modified the
Pawn's power. First, the Pawn is allowed, from its base (that is
on its first move only) to move two squares forward, instead of
one, at the player's option. This option, be it understood,
cannot be reserved. A Pawn may move from b2 to b4, but *not*
from b3 to b5, or b4 to b6, etc. (Diagram 34).

Black

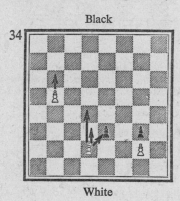

White

Pawn's move
The Pawn on g2 cannot move
The Pawn on d2 can move to d3 or d4, or can capture on e3
The Pawn on b5 can move to b6, not (in one move) to b7

From this concession a little something has been taken.

If a Pawn moves from b2 to b4, it seems, at first sight, as if a
hostile Pawn on a4 or c4 has been by-passed – because Pawn
captures are on diagonals only. But the deprived Pawn has
been granted a privilege in compensation. If a Pawn stands on
its fifth rank, and an opposing Pawn on an adjoining file makes
a move of two squares, then the by-passed Pawn can, on the
next move, and the next move only, behave as if its adversary
had only moved one square (Diagram 35).

Black

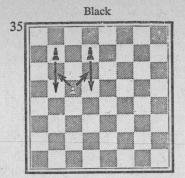

35

White

**Pawn takes *en passant***

If either Black Pawn moves one square, of course the White Pawn can capture it simply

If either Black Pawn moves two squares, the White Pawn on the next move only can capture it, exactly as if it had moved one square

This is the only case in Chess of a capture which does not place the capturer on the square vacated by the captured piece. With Castling, and promotion, it constitutes one of a very few breaches of logic in a logical set of linear moves. (The Knight's move has already been shown not to be illogical.)

Promotion is, perhaps, not irrational. When the Pawn arrives at the eighth rank, what is to become of it? To remain there dead? The answer is that one replaces it with any piece other than King or Pawn, viz. Queen, Rook, Bishop or Knight.*

That to promote to the best piece (the Queen) is not always the best move, the reader will realize without difficulty. One may wish to avoid stalemate: or one may require an immediate Knight check (Diagram 36). What requires immediately to be observed is the enhanced importance of the Pawn in the later

* Consequently a player can have on the board more than one Q, more than 2 Rooks, 2 or more Bishops of the same field, 3 or more Kts, etc.

game. We have seen that you can be left with King and Bishop, or King and Knight, or King and two Knights against a King, and have a draw – with the honours of war, for what they are

Black

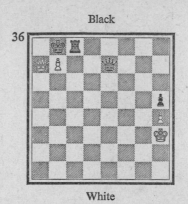

White

Under-promotion
The White Queen has captured at a7. After K×Q White captures the Rook, making a Knight, forking K and Q, and winning

worth. But if you are left with King and Pawn against King you have chances of victory. So a whole department of Chess is the technique of winning processes that may be available when there are surviving pawns on a relatively empty board. Detailed consideration of these matters must be deferred.

For the time being, let it be observed that the difficulty of winning with a Pawn and King against a King is, in practice, the most important consequence of the stalemate rule.

Before learning more about 'promotion', let the reader be introduced to a few technical terms, which illustrate the potential weaknesses of pawns.

Pawns are at their best 'Joined'. Thus put Pawns at d4 and e4. If either of these moves, the other 'guards' it; i.e. if the Pawn moving to e5 be captured, Pawn from d4 can recapture. Now if the Pawn has no companion on either side, it is said to be

'Isolated'. That is a defect because, when attacked, it will not be defensible by another Pawn – normally the most economical guard.

The fear that a Pawn is to be 'isolated' is a factor influencing players at all stages. But the fear should not be exaggerated. At least one established opening (The Tarrasch Defence to the Queen's Gambit – described later) leaves the defender with a central isolated Pawn; and this is not regarded as a fatal defect.

To revert to 'joined Pawns', they are at their best level – i.e. on the same rank. If one is one square in advance of the other, and the latter cannot draw level, because e.g. a hostile Pawn blocks the advance, the Pawns are said to be 'hanging'.* The weakness is that the support can be undermined (Diagram 37). But hanging Pawns can be strong against a lone King, which dare not move behind the forward Pawn.

Another 'disease' of Pawns is seen when Pawns are 'doubled'.

If Pawns are on e3 and e4, clearly they are doing less work and have fewer prospects than were they on separate files. Doubled Pawns are not useless: they can control squares, and in endgames, as we shall see, they gain tempo. But, by and large, a pair of doubled Pawns is of less value than a pair of un-doubled Pawns.

Also relatively unhappy is the Pawn that is 'backward'. Thus if its companion is in front, but itself cannot catch up because of some obstruction, it cannot co-operate with the promotion effort of its companion. But sometimes a backward Pawn can sacrifice itself for the benefit of its companion (Diagram 37).

The contrasting and happier state for a Pawn is to be 'Passed'.

This is the term used to describe a Pawn which has no Pawn opponent on its own file or on either adjoining file. Obviously, when it gets its chance this Pawn can run through to promotion

---

* 'Hanging' is an adjective also applied to a piece which, after a tactical *mêlée*, is left *en prise* and unguarded.

Black

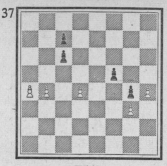

White

### Varieties of Pawn Positions

*1.* The Pawns on a4 and b4 are 'joined Pawns'. So are those on f5, g4 and on g3, h4.
*2.* The Pawns on c7 and c6 are 'doubled Pawns', also 'isolated'.
*3.* The Pawn on d4 is an 'isolated Pawn'
*4.* The pairs of Pawns f5 and g4 and g3 and h4 are described as 'hanging Pawns'. Observe that Black, with P—f4, destroys the White pair
*5.* The Pawns on a4 and h4 are 'passed Pawns'.
*6.* The Pawns on g3 and f5 are 'backward Pawns'
*7.* The Pawns on a4 and h4 are 'remote passed pawns' (see p. 111).

with less difficulty than if it had to run the gauntlet of opposing Pawns. Evidently all this is important in connexion with the promotability of Pawns.

Of mating powers, a King and two Pawns can give mate, though not forced (Diagram 38). This can influence King play when Pawns are racing for promotion. But the virtue of Pawns is that they are promotable. And the struggles that they are involved in are not struggles to inflict mate but to force their own promotion.

The basic elements of promotion play constitute a vital section of Chess, and involve some important technique.

Of Pawn triumphs and failures, a useful illustration is the following. Place the White Pawn on e4, White King on f4,

Black

38

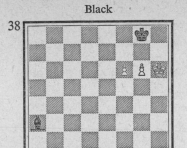

White

Mate with Pawns

After *1.* P—B7 ch if Black plays K—R1 (unforced) *2.* P—Kt7 gives
Mate. If *1.* .... K—B1. *2.* P—Kt7 ch   K×BP. *3.* K—R7 wins

Black King on e7 (Diagram 39). In this position White to play
wins: Black to play draws. How does White win?

NOT by P—e5.

Subtler, and harder for the beginner to appreciate, is Ke5.

Black

39

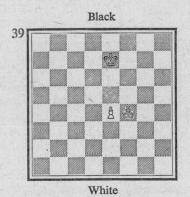

White

White to play and win
*1.* K—K5 is the first move of the winning process. (See text)

Watch what follows:

1. Ke5      Kf7
2. Kd6      Ke8
3. Ke6      Kf8
4. Kd7 (and the Pawn has a clear path)

If it were Black's move

1. .... Ke6 would lead to a draw

Thus  1. .... Ke6

2. Pe5    Ke7
3. Kf5    Kf7
4. Pe6 ch  Ke7
5. Ke5, and now be careful
5. ...... Kf8 loses
5. .... Kd8 loses

But  5. .... Ke8 draws
(6. Kf6 Kf8   7. Pe7 ch Ke8   8. Ke6 stalemate)

Alter the last position so as to give a closer order (Diagram 40).

The position has now crystallized in Black's favour. Either player to move. If White has the move he plays Kd5 and the position is not altered. Now, with White K on e5 or d5, Black, to move, can go wrong.

Black

40

White

Draw, whoever has the move. Black must play K—e8

Suppose he plays Kd8, the White plays Kd6.

Ke8 is now forced and Pe7 forces the Black King to f7, allowing White to play Kd7 winning.

Similarly if (from the diagram) *1.* .... Kf8. *2.* Kf6, etc. Therefore on the move Black must play *1.* .... Ke8! If now *2.* Kd6 Kd8. *3.* Pe7 ch Ke8. *4.* Ke6 stalemate. If, instead, *2.* Kd5 (or e5) then Ke7. *3.* Ke5 (or d5) Ke8, etc.

Contrast the next position (Diagram 41). Here White wins, whoever has the move.

If White to move

|   |   |
|---|---|
| *1.* Kf6 | Kf8 |
| *2.* Pe6 | Ke8 |
| *3.* Pe7 wins |   |

Black

41

White

White wins, whoever has the move

If Black to move

*1.* .... Kf8

*2.* Kd7 and the Pawn comes through protected by the King. Observe, then, the desirability of 'King in front of Pawn'. In deciding whether either side is likely to have a won endgame after exchanges, the value of K in front of Pawns is a great factor.

Observe, however, that slightly lower down the board the case is different (Diagram 42 companion to Diagram 39).

Black

42

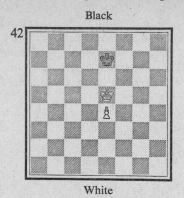

White

White to move can only draw. Black to move loses

Here White to move cannot force victory –

| | |
|---|---|
| *1.* Kf5 | Kf7 |
| *2.* Pe5 | Ke7 |
| *3.* Pe6 | Ke8! (as in Diagram 40) and this is drawn. |

But had it been Black to move White would win.

| | |
|---|---|
| *1.* .... | Kf7 (If *1*....Ke8 *2.* Ke6 etc.) |
| *2.* Kd6 | Ke8 |
| *3.* Ke6 | Kd8 |
| *4.* Kf7 or Pe5 wins | |

The reader may realize that he has witnessed a *zugzwang* of King by King. This situation is an instance of 'The Opposition'.

When two Kings are facing each other separated by one square, or an odd number of squares, on file, rank or diagonal, the King that forces the other to cede ground is said to have *The Opposition*.*

This feature of the board is particularly important when a

* Experiment with 4k3, 4o, 4P3, 4K3. A Pawn move only draws: King play is required. *1.* K—Q2, followed by K advance.

King is trying to get in among the opposing Pawns. If the opposing King has to abandon its control of the approach squares, then this inability to maintain the Opposition is usually fatal.

Sometimes a very long movement of Chess thought by a master ends in a working-out of whether or not he goes into the endgame with 'The Opposition'.

A useful rule for the reader to bear in mind is the following.

A King has the Opposition when it is separated by an odd number of squares from the opposing King, on the same rank, the same file, or the same diagonal – and *the other player has to move.*

Often the Chess-player, who normally, on a crowded board, wants to be 'on the move', finds towards the end that he wants his opponent to move. And the losing of 'tempo' becomes as

Black

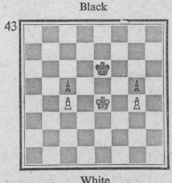

White

### Opposition and Triangulation

*1.* Black to move, loses, because White has the opposition. Whichever way the Black King moves, the White King makes ingress. *2.* But opposition is not always a winning asset, e.g. White here does not lose though Black will have opposition. But he must be careful in order to draw. Thus not *1.* K—K3 because *1.* .... K—K4 would win for Black. Good is K—Q3. If *1.* .... K—K4. *2.* K—K3. White has Triangulated. Similarly if *1.* .... K—Q3 *2.* K—Q2! or K—K2!

important as the gaining of it has been at earlier stages. In the process of tempo play, a very useful device is the King's process of triangulation, shown in Diagram 43.

Note the process *1*. K—Q3 K—Q3. *2*. K—Q2 (or K2) not K—K3. This is sometimes called Tempo play.

The term 'Tempo' is a simple one, but very important. In the diagram position (44) Black has taken a Pawn; White can recapture immediately and Black can recapture. But what is the hurry? White checks first (with R—R6) driving the hostile King away. This can be labelled a *Zwischenzug*. Then he captures. So he exploits a 'tempo' and saves a Pawn.

Black

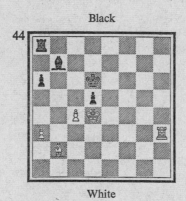

White

White uses Tempo
*1*. R—R6 ch enables him to recapture at d5 and hold the Pawn
But if *1*. P×P  B×P
*2*. R—R6 ch  B—K3

In tempo play games can be decided on very fine points – whereas others end more roughly, brutally. There is, as we have seen, a big margin of draw – players failing to win, when they have considerable material preponderance. But the subtleties of the game – the gaining of tempo, etc. – are often available to make a close finish into a winning one (Diagram 45). But tempo is not peculiar to the endgame.

Black

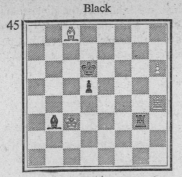

45

White

Loss of Tempo

With *1.* K—Kt2 White would obtain great advantage. Instead *1.* K—Q4 loses tempo because *1.* .... B—B7 threatens mate, and White must play either R—R3 or B—R6, enabling Black to hold the square h7

Here is an example of tempo in development, from the openings.

| | |
|---|---|
| *1.* P—Q4 | P—Q4 |
| *2.* P—QB4 | P—K3 |
| *3.* Kt—QB3 | Kt—KB3 |
| *4.* B—Kt5 | QKt—Q2 |
| *5.* P—K3 | B—K2 |
| *6.* Kt—B3 | O—O |
| *7.* B—Q3 | P×P |

Black, by delaying the capture on c4, has caused White to waste his move B—Q3. It so happens that this is no great loss, because Black has now changed the nature of the position – and that may have justified White in losing a move.

And now to some other terms that help as a guide to the tactics of the game.

First some occurrences that are calculated to fill novices with alarm. 'Discovered Check' and 'Double Check'.

Discovered check takes place when any piece or pawn moves away from a given file, rank, or diagonal, leaving a long-range piece (Queen, Rook, or Bishop) of the same colour threatening to capture the hostile King immediately (Diagram 46). This kind of check is not different logically from any move by a piece on to a square from which it gives check. A discovered

Black

46

White

Discovered Check
*1.* B—Kt6 ch forces the King to move, possibly discovering check, and wins the Queen
*2.* B—Q7 ch allows Q×R as well as P—Kt4 or a King move
*1.* B—K6 ch allows, also, K×B

check can be met by a move of the King, by an interposition, or by a capture of the checking piece. (That the King's move may capture the piece whose move has revealed the check is obvious.) A good example of discovered check is the following – which is technically important. White Q on h6, B on d3, Black King on g8, pawns on h7 and f7. The mate is achieved by *1.* B×P ch. K—R1. *2.* B—Kt6 dis. ch. K—Kt1. *3.* Q—R7 ch and mate at f7.

'Double check' is more justifiably regarded as alarming. Here (Diagram 47) the Bishop that moves away from the line of attack of the uncovered Rook (B(Q2)—Kt5 dble. ch) itself delivers a check. In this case mate follows (with R—Q8 or B—Q8, according to the King's move). (White's previous move – played by Réti against Tartakover – had been the

Black (Tartakover)

White (Réti)

(Vienna 1908)
A catastrophic double check
This is the aftermath of a fine Q sacrifice at d8. The B from Q2, not only 'discovers' the Rook's check, but administers a check. This kind of check forces the King to move. Here mate follows.

If K—B2   B—Q8 Mates
If K—K1   R—Q8 Mates

sensational Q(Q3) – Q8 ch). So a Bishop moves out of a Rook's or Queen's path, leaving check, and delivering an independent check. So a Rook can move out of a Bishop's or Queen's line: and a Knight can move out of the line of action of Queen, Rook, or Bishop, and give its own check as well. A Pawn can only achieve double check when it captures, or when it promotes itself. Obviously a King cannot give double check. Nor can a Queen, for it must come from a line on which it is already giving check. Equally obviously, a Knight cannot be the piece whose check is uncovered.

The important feature of double check is that it forces the King to move. It is impossible to intervene between the King and two pieces checking simultaneously and it is impossible to capture two checking pieces in one move.

Let the reader remember, however, that double checks, for all their terrors, may prove completely harmless.

Now some terms relating to capturing, etc. When a piece can be captured, it is said to be '*en prise*'.* Also it is said to be threatened', or 'attacked', by the piece that can take it. Generally to 'threaten' in Chess means 'to be able, unless opposed, to do a certain act'. (The threatener may not know that he can do it, but it is still a threat.)

If a piece is 'threatened' it can be 'guarded'. That means, some other piece is made available to recapture the potential capturer. Common sense often suggests the desirability of guarding economically, i.e. with the cheaper pieces. Common sense also enables a player to work out how many guards are necessary against accumulating forces. At this stage, when the reader begins to think about checks and mates, threats, guards, and defences, he is moving from a grasp of the powers of the pieces – what the rules enable them to do – to the functions of the pieces, i.e. manœuvres that the player finds for his pieces.

From the rules alone – the powers – one learns comparatively little. Psychologically Chess begins after the rules relating to the moves have been learned. Without knowing the moves, of course, no one can play; but merely to know the moves is not equivalent to even a minimal ability to play. One knows, as it were, an alphabet, without knowing the meaning of any words: or one knows isolated words without understanding or being able to construct a sentence. After the learning of isolated meanings the struggle is to put words together. Later, much later, comes fluent reading. One transition, from a knowledge of the moves to an ability to use the moves, is through the study of the processes of 'mating and slaying'. A game of Chess is won, in the last resort, by a process of mating. This process is facilitated by previous successful processes of capturing. The player to whom the game is more than a haphazard alternation of random moves wants, not only to mate, but to be able to force mate: not only to capture, but to capture by force: not only to capture much, but to capture wisely. In studying some examples of mating and capturing, he learns much about the

* This term (*never* shortened to e.p.) is often used to indicate that the thing can be captured 'for nothing'.

game, and develops a Chess attitude. He also moves from Common Sense to 'Applied Common Sense', which is different. He will be assisted in this mental development by an introduction to some examples of the functions (rather than the 'legal' powers) of the pieces, and to several instances of play, which, whether difficult or easy, are sufficiently familiar to experienced players to be called Technical. Once one has understood these possibilities, one is aware of them effortlessly. Then one has acquired some Technique. Technique, at all stages, and some tactical notions which go slightly beyond technique, are the subject-matter of the next chapter.

## CHAPTER TWO

# TECHNICAL AND TACTICAL POINTS: CHANGING VALUATIONS: THE ENDGAME

'AND mates and slays,' says Omar. Let us consider some processes of 'slaying'.

One stage in the progress of a Chess-player from absolute novice, with only a knowledge of the powers of pieces, to an initiate who can use those pieces for his purposes, is the stage at which he asks himself whether he *should* capture the piece that he can capture.*

The reader already understands the type of capture which is inadvisable because the piece can be immediately recaptured by a defending piece.

Here are examples of captures that are unwise, not because of recapture 'on the move' – but because some very short tactical operation is made possible to the opponent, causing material loss to the capturer. The first position is from a badly played opening.

|  | | |
|---|---|---|
| *1.* | P—Q4 | P—K3 |
| *2.* | P—KKt3 | P—QB4 |
| *3.* | B—Kt2 (a bad move: White should play P—Q5, or P×P or Kt—KB3) | |
| *3.* | .... .... | P×P |
| *4.* | Kt—KB3 | P—K4 |

Black's fourth move was evidently overlooked by White. Now the Black Pawn at d4 is guarded, and the Pawn at e5, which guards it, cannot be captured by the Knight because if *5.* Kt×P

---

* This is only one instance of whether he should move to the square to which he can move. But concentration on capturable pieces comes easier to the beginner.

(e5) Q—R4 ch 'forks' King and Knight, and wins the Knight (Diagram 48).

Black

48

White

Can't capture because of fork by Queen
If 5. Kt×P    Q—R4 ch
Observe that Black has moved no 'pieces': yet nevertheless he has some development. He may later return the Pawn, so as not to lose tempo, e.g. in reply to P—QB3

The expression 'fork' is a description of one of the best-known short-range aggressions.

People are apt to associate the fork with the Knight; and they think of such an event as a Knight going, via Q5 or QKt5, to QB7, checking and attacking the Queen's Rook at the same time. Also, since many find the Knight's track a little hard to follow, and since the Knight usually attacks pieces which are not able on that move to capture it, the Knight's fork is regarded with a special aversion. The Diagrams on pp. 40 and 42 *supra*, are very good examples of the Knight's subtlety.

But the power to 'fork' is not a monopoly of the Knight. Every piece can find itself attacking two pieces at the same moment, and that is a 'fork' whether done by Queen, Rook, Bishop, Knight, Pawn or King. Therefore, 'Can't capture because of fork' is a very frequent situation, and the reader can easily construct many for himself on the following lines.

Imagine a Pawn at e5 *en prise* to a Black Knight at c6. Black also has a Bishop at c5.

Now if Kt×P, White with P—Q4 forks B and Kt.

A possibility like that can make a capture impossible; and paradoxically it makes captures possible, or thinkable, as well,

Play the following opening moves:

|   |          |          |
|---|----------|----------|
| *1.* | P—K4   | P—K4     |
| *2.* | Kt—KB3 | Kt—QB3   |
| *3.* | Kt—QB3 | B—B4     |
| *4.* | Kt×P   |          |

Whether this is a good move or not is debatable (Diagram 49); but it does *not* lose a piece, because if *4.* .... Kt×Kt *5.* P—Q4 forks B and Kt, winning one of them.

Black

49

White

Capture made possible by a fork

White *can* play *4.* Kt×P because if *4.* .... Kt×Kt *5.* P—Q4 regains the piece. Black can either recapture the forking Pawn by *5.* .... B×P or *5.* .... B—Q3 *6.* P×Kt B×P etc.; or play, instead, *4.* .... B×P ch (before Kt×Kt) as a *Zwischenzug*

Neither side will gain material, if e.g. *5.* .... B×P, but the situation is full of tactical interest.

When White plays *4. Kt×P*, and the opponent realizes that Kt×Kt will lead to the recapture of a piece, Black knows at least that he has the first capturing option. Also, if he is ingenious, he thinks: 'Can I pick something up, while my opponent's piece is *en prise*? My Bishop is compromised.' (Lasker calls a piece with a destiny of loss a 'Desperado'.) With the desperado Bishop, Black can play *4. .... B×P ch.*

(This is a type of what is called *Zwischenzug* – a move 'in between' move and logical answer.) *5. K×B Kt×Kt.*

Then comes *6. P—Q4* and it is not clear whether White or Black has gained from this adventure.

Other constructions are easy. It may be that White cannot capture a Pawn with a Rook, e.g. because that move enables a Knight to fork the Rook and the Queen, and the exchange may be lost without compensation; or a Bishop may be able to step into the diagonal between Q and R. The possibilities are innumerable; and, of course, everything is subordinate to the particular position. It may pay me to lose the exchange, because, while he is capturing it, I can organize an attack on the King, etc.

Black

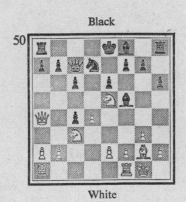

White

Fork and escape by *Zwischenzug*
White can play *12. Kt×QBP (c4)* because after *12. .... P—QKt4*
*13. Q—R5* terminates the fork and constitutes a threat

Before moving from forks, another example of *Zwischenzug* – an idea easier than the word may be.

*Zwischenzug* can emancipate a player from many tactical pressures – of which forks provide an instance. Here is quite a good example, a well-known type of opening position (Diagram 50).

White, here, may not wish to play *12*. Q×BP because of Kt×Kt, *13*. P×Kt Q×P. But he is afraid to play *12*. Kt×QBP (at c4) because of the fork 12. . . . . P—QKt4. Yet he is wrong to be put off by this. After *12*. Kt×QBP (c4) P—QKt4 *13*. Q—R5, attacking Black's Queen; and if *13*. . . . . Q×Q *14*. Kt×Q frees the Knight from attack; on the other hand, if Black guards the Queen somehow, the Knight has the tempo needed for escape.

The next example (Diagram 51) shows a 'can't capture' because of a pin. If Kt×P, R—Q1 'pins' it against the Rook, and wins it. White's best here is Kt—B3, preventing P—Q4; later he may 'blockade' (an obvious and useful notion) and so keep Black's QP 'backward'. Observe that if the Black King were at

Black

51

White

Can't capture because of 'Pin'
If Kt×P    R—Q1 pins the Knight
White's best seems to be *1*. Kt—B3 in order to prevent P—Q4.
He may later blockade with Kt—Q5 and keep Black's QP 'backward'

h8 instead of g8, White could play Kt × P, because if, then, R—Q1, Kt × P ch, forking K and R.

The word 'Pin' describes another important mode of agression.

The Queen, Rook, Bishop have this function in common. They can all PIN, i.e. they can render a lower-value piece immobile because it stands between the 'pinning' piece and one of greater value – King, Queen, Rook, etc.

Thus a Bishop pins a Knight against a Rook; or a Rook pins a Bishop against a Queen, etc. A Bishop can pin a Bishop, a Rook a Rook, a Queen a Queen; but these are less significant because the pinned piece can then capture the pinning piece, though Diagram 52 shows an amusing instance of a pin of a

Black

52

White
Unusual Pin and Double Function
(Played by Golombek)
Black has just checked. The Rook at QKt1 is pinned against the other Rook. After B—B1, Q × Q, R × Q, R × R wins the exchange. Note the 'Double function' of the R on b1, guarding the Q and the back line

Rook by a Rook where the Rook could not capture its pinner without loss. This is an unusual example of a double function imposed upon a piece. (And that, too, is an obvious and useful notion.)

Of other pieces, it is obvious that a King, a Knight, and a Pawn cannot pin.

Those pieces that can pin can also Thrust (Skewer, some call it) when the attack on the King or Queen, etc., as the case may be, causes a retreat from that line, and a piece is left capturable towards the other side of the Board. This is the complementary aspect of the 'pin' (Diagram 53).

Black

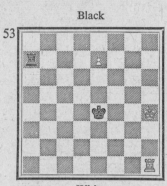

White

Can't capture because of 'Thrust' (or 'Skewer')
Black to move, loses

Black cannot capture the Pawn because of R—K1 ch by White. If he plays *1*. .... K—B5 White can check him away; alternatively can play P=Q, because the Queen can interpose itself at R5 in the event of a check. If *1*. .... R—R1 *2*. P—K8 (=Q) ch

The next diagram (54) is a trifle harder than the previous though the tactic described – 'thrust' or 'skewer' – is not particularly difficult. *25*. .... Q—K2 is played. If, then, *26*. B×Kt P, B—K1, attacking the Queen, drives the latter away, and can capture the Bishop at b5. This is a typical 'thrust' or, as some call it, 'skewer' manoeuvre.

The next (Diagram 55) is a different type of 'can't take' and is very neat. Here it looks as if Black can capture White's KtP. But this is an illusion. If *1*. .... B×P. *2*. P—R6, threatening P—R7 and 8. Black is then forced to play B—B4 to stop this, and that defence fails because White, with Kt—K6 ch, forks K and B and wins. So that KtP is 'taboo'. That fact makes White's

Black

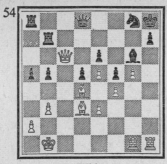

54

White

Complex involving 'Thrust' (or 'Skewer')
Black played not *25.* .... Q—Q2 which allows *26.* B × KtP; but
*25.* .... Q—K2
(Then if *26.* B × P  B—K1 (Thrust))
There followed *26.* R—QB1  B—K1
*27.* Q—Q6  K—Kt2
*28.* B × BP  P × B
*29.* Q—KB6 ch!
(Played by Samisch.)

Black

55

White

Can't capture because of Pawn promotion threat
If *1.* .... B × P
*2.* P—R6  B—B4
*3.* Kt—K6 ch wins

position very good indeed. (Incidentally, the 'promotion' threat very often prevents the capture of a backward Pawn by a K.)

Another taboo Pawn is seen in Diagram 56, where the penalty for the theft is imprisonment (P—Kt3). But place a Black piece

Black

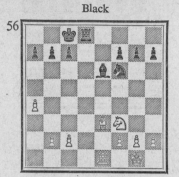

White

Can't capture because of Imprisonment

If *1.* B × P P—Kt3 followed by K—Kt2 wins the B
P—R5 is a gallant attempt at rescue which fails.

But place a Black piece on d7 and a White Bishop on e2. Then B × P is possible, because P—Kt3 would be met by B—R6 mate!

Black

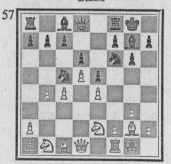

White

Can't capture because of Imprisonment

White has just attacked the Knight at c5, and this must retreat. If QKt × P, White, with P—B3, attacks it and there is no escape.

Black

White

Imprisonment of Queen

Black, with Kt—QR4, attacks the White Queen and leaves it without an escape. This is the penalty of a capture on QKt7

on d7 and a White Bishop on e2 and the theft is possible, because if P—Kt3, B—R6 mate. Cognate but in a different setting is the fate of the Knight in Diagram 57. More spectacular

Black

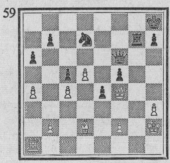

White

Can't capture because of combinative attack

| | |
|---|---|
| 27. .... Q×P? | 30. Q×Kt  Q×R |
| 28. R—QB1  Kt—K4 | 31. Q—Kt3 wins |
| 29. B—B3  Kt—B6 ch | |

(Played by A. R. B. Thomas)

is the position in Diagram 58 where a Queen is 'Imprisoned' on the open board.

The next example (Diagram 59) is rather advanced. Why cannot Black play 27. .... Q × P? There is no immediate fork, pin, thrust or improvement. Yet White's attack is in posse.

If     27. .... Q × P

    28. R—QB1, threatening B—B3 forking R and Q, and, independently, pinning R against K.

What can Black do? It seems he has a resource

    28. .... Kt—K4

    29. B—B3   Kt—B6 ch

If White's Queen takes this, the Rook is unguarded. But White does not mind losing an exchange in a good cause.

    30. Q × Kt   Q × R

    31. Q—KKt3 (and the game is over. White is threatening Q × R mate, and also threatens Q—Kt8 mate, and Black cannot stop them both. This example, at least, is more than technical. It illustrates the need for clear tactical vision.)

More advanced still is the next diagram (60) from a relatively recent game between a genius of Chess, Tal, and a competent German expert. In order to equalize, the defender captured the Knight's Pawn and the moves below the diagram show what happened. What Black lacked was the 'wisdom' that is necessary to supplement vision.

This is bringing us near to the realm of decisions that are based on general principle rather than those of which the tactical consequences can be worked out by the player using his vision. We are approaching 'strategy' and 'judgement' which will be discussed in a later chapter. Here suffice it to say that Chessplayers are notoriously chary of capturing the QKtP. 'Don't take QKtP' is an epigrammatic way of saying: don't deploy your forces away from vital centres of action. While you're going there and back, the Opponent can organize his forces in the centre and against the King, so as to render the defence difficult.

One might generalize and say: 'Don't grab.'

Black

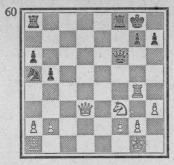

White

Very advanced example of unwise capture

After *22.* .... Q×KtP there followed: *23.* Q—Q5 ch K—R1; *24.* R—K1 QR—Q1; *25.* R—KB4 Q—Kt5; *26.* R×R ch R×R; *27.* R—K6 and White is exerting pressure on both sides of the board and wins without great difficulty

(Tal–Lehmann, 1960)

Here is an opening where a Pawn can be won, but at a cost.

| | |
|---|---|
| *1.* P—K4 | P—K4 |
| *2.* Kt—KB3 | Kt—QB3 |
| *3.* B—Kt5 | P—KB4 |

(The daring Schliemann Defence to the Ruy Lopez, an opening much discussed later.)

| | |
|---|---|
| *4.* P—Q4 | P×KP |
| *5.* Kt×P | Kt×Kt |
| *6.* P×Kt | P—QB3 |
| *7.* B—K2 | Q—R4 ch |
| *8.* B—Q2 | Q×KP |

But now scc what happens.

| | |
|---|---|
| *9.* B—R5 ch | P—Kt3 |
| *10.* B—QB3 ('thrust') | |

So Black has a difficult process of development before him, in exchange for that Pawn. That should be visible to the naked

R—D

eye, but a lot of players would avoid that capturing process by judgement or strategic instinct.

Even at the tactical level, good players still grab at Knight's Pawns without seeing pretty proximate consequences. Thus a candidate for lesser Grand Mastership, one Darga, at a Zonal Tournament towards the end of 1963, found himself with nothing to do against Pomar in the following position (61).

The opening moves were

|  |  |  |
|---|---|---|
| 1. | P—Q4 | Kt—KB3 |
| 2. | P—QB4 | P—Q3 |
| 3. | Kt—QB3 | Kt—Q2 |
| 4. | P—K4 | P—K4 |
| 5. | KKt—K2 | P—KKt3 |
| 6. | P—KKt3 | B—Kt2 |
| 7. | B—Kt2 | O—O |
| 8. | O—O | P—B3 |
| 9. | P—KR3 | (In order to keep out Black's B and to enable Pg4.) |

Black (Darga)

White (Pomar)

Misadventure
(see text)

Now Black's quite sound opening is showing its difficulty; the need for a plan. (Logical would be Kt—K1.)

But 'the devil finds work'. *9. .... Q—Kt3,* aimless unless he thinks he can 'get away with' something. Pomar obliged with *10. B—K3.* There followed *10. .... Q×KtP 11. P—R3!* See now how the Queen is imprisoned. If *Q—Kt3. 12. P×P* operates as a fork. It is the unmasking of a 'battery'.

Black had been deprived, also, of the escape hatch at *a3.* (At what stage did he overlook that? Perhaps when the midnight oil was losing candle power!) Black played, in desperation, *11. .... P×P* After *12. B×P Kt—B4 13. Kt—Q5* wins, if not the Queen, at least material. In the event the Queen was 'sacrificed' and the game quickly lost.

This position introduces a new tactical feature, which Diagram 62 illustrates simply.

Black

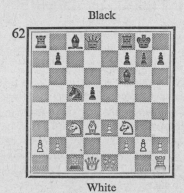

62

White

Battery

In this position White played *12. Kt×P.* The Knight is 'guarded' because if *Q×Kt 13. B × P ch* wins the Queen. Black can instead play *12. .... Kt×B ch; 13. Q×Kt B×P*

This shows a 'can't take' which is the basis of a tactical 'can take'. A 'battery', sometimes called a 'masked battery', exists when a piece can remove itself from a line of action giving check, or some terrible threat, and leaving a hostile piece exposed to capture on the line it has left.

So Pomar against Darga used batteries with the threatened

Pawn move and with the actual Knight move. Diagram 63 in contrast shows a battery which is ineffective, because of another

Black

63

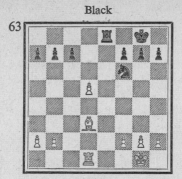

White

Battery ineffective because of back-row danger
Black can play Kt × P here, because if White replies B × P ch then, after K × B R × Kt, R—K8 is mate

important feature, the danger to the back row. Many lines of play are determined by the consideration that some piece dare not leave the back line. On that account many players make holes for their Kings at R3 or Kt3, and often unnecessarily. These examples lead us from the many instances of 'can't take' (when, at first sight, it looks as if one can) to many examples of the important obverse – the 'can't capture' that can be done – in other words, the sacrifice.

Sacrifices are not necessarily captures. One of the most spectacular sacrifices in the history of Chess was the move, by Zukertort, in play against Blackburne, of a Queen on to an empty square where it could be captured (see p. 85).

Very frequently, however, the sacrifice takes the form of capturing the apparently uncapturable.

Elementary is the following line of play.

|  |  |
|---|---|
| 1. P—K4 | P—K4 |
| 2. Kt—KB3 | P—KB3 (a bad move) |
| 3. Kt × KP |  |

White is 'sacrificing': he is apparently giving a Knight for a Pawn. But if the sacrifice be accepted, see what happens.

    *3.* .... P×Kt
    *3.* Q—R5 ch

If now *4.* .... P—KKt3

      *5.* Q×KP ch (forking King and Rook)

If instead *4.* .... K—K2

      *5.* Q×KP ch         K—B2
      *6.* B—B4 ch (and the King is exposed to a furious
            attack, and White wins)

In every game of Chess, whether in the actual play, or in the variations that are considered when moves are rejected, there occur sacrificial possibilities, just as there occur positions of 'can't capture'.

A word that the reader will encounter early is 'Gambit'.

A gambit usually takes the form of a sacrifice of a Pawn in the early stages of the game in order to enhance one's development, or one's control of the centre.

E.g. *1.* P—K4                P—K4
    *2.* P—KB4

    constitutes the King's Gambit –

   *1.* P—Q4               P—Q4
    *2.* P—QB4
    constitutes the

Queen's Gambit.

These offers are sometimes accepted, sometimes declined. In the former case, the normal expectation is that the sacrificed Pawn will be returned, or quickly recaptured. So that a gambit is a loan rather than a gift.

Of sacrifices, proper, here is the well-known 'Greek Gift'. White sacrifices his Bishop at h7, and forces a winning process if it be captured (Diagram 64).

The reader should observe that had the Black Knight been

Black

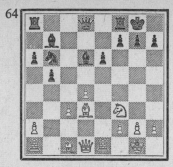

White

### Greek Gift Sacrifice

*1.* B×P ch    K×B
*2.* Kt—Kt5 ch    K—Kt3 (not K—Kt1 because of *3.* Q—R5)
*3.* Q—Kt4 threatening to unmask a battery with Kt×KPdis. ch
              If *3.* .... K—B3
                        *4.* R×P ch    P×R
                        *5.* Q×P mate

at Q2 this attack would have failed. Thus *1.* B×P ch    K×B.
*2.* Kt—Kt5    K—Kt1. *3.* Q—R5    Kt—B3.

Indeed there are a large number of cases where masters have
sacrificed at h7, and either failed to achieve anything, or been
content to drive the Black King or to keep it under pressure.

A similar observation applies to the square of f7 where
sacrifices are often made with a view to a quick attack against
the King.

In point is this old attack (played by Blackburne)

|  |  |  |
|---|---|---|
| *1.* P—K4 | P—K4 |
| *2.* Kt—KB3 | Kt—KB3 |
| *3.* B—B4 | Kt×P |
| *4.* Kt—B3 | Kt×Kt |
| *5.* QP×Kt | P—Q3 (wrong: one instance where P—KB3 is correct) |

6. Kt×P                    P×Kt (if Q—K2. 7. B×P ch
                                   followed by O—O wins)

7. B×P ch                  K×B

8. Q×Q

This badly defended Boden Kieseritsky is only one aspect of the weakness at f7 (or, in White's case, f2).

The reader should also make himself familiar with the well-known danger at a square like g5. In the position in Diagram 65, the sequence *1. .... P—KR3. 2. B—R4 P—KKt4* is

Black

65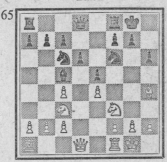

White

Breaking Barriers. Sacrifice at KKt5

If *1. ....*        P—KKt4

2. Kt×P   P×Kt

3. B×P constitutes a very strong attack.
        There could follow

3. .... Kt—QKt5 (to prevent Kt—Q5)

4. P—QR3   P—B3

5. P×Kt   B×P

6. P—B4 and Black's position is indefen-
        sible

dangerous because White plays *3. Kt×P   P×Kt. 5. B×P* and the pin on the Knight is disastrous in its effects. But once again, let it be said, this is an attack which does not succeed in every instance. Be sure that no rescue parties can be organized.

That was from the early game, showing how one breaks barriers sacrificially. From the other end of the game, so to speak, the next diagram shows a sacrificial finish (Diagram 66). A Bishop gives itself up – in order to facilitate the promotion of a Pawn. Note the very important point of order. Quite often players lose through not observing the importance of the order of the moves they are contemplating. For the rest, don't rely too much on techniques. The Greek Gift and some other sacrifices have become techniques, and are used thoughtlessly.

Black

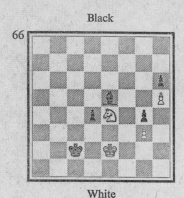

66

White

Sacrifice in end game
Point of order

| 1. . . . . | P—Q6 ch |
|------------|---------|
| 2. K—K3 | B × P wins |

But not

| 1. . . . . | B × P |
|------------|-------|
| 2. Kt × B | P—Q6 ch |
| 3. K—B2 | P—Q7 |
| 4. Kt—B1 | P=Q |
| 5. Kt—K3 ch, etc. | |

Here is a quite advanced example (Diagram 67).

This position shows the inadequacy of the 'technically' attractive. After Kt × RP. If White recaptures, and Black recaptures, Black seems to have only a perpetual check.

Can he achieve more?

Black (Shroeder)

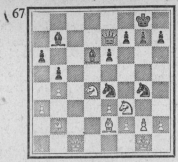

White

'Technical Sacrifice'
1. ....            Kt × RP
2. Kt × Kt         B × Kt ch
3. K × B           Q—R5 ch
4. K—Kt1           Q × P ch
5. K—R2 (not R1, because of Kt—Kt 6ch)

and it seems that there is only a draw by perpetual check. In the
actual game, White did not recapture after Kt × RP!

Try *1.* .... Kt × RP

2. Kt × Kt                 B × Kt ch
3. K × B                   Q—R5 ch
4. K—Kt1                   Q × P ch
5. K—R2 (not R1, because of *5.* .... Kt—Kt6 ch,
    followed by mate)

Now if Black moves his Kt from K5 and the Bishop inter-
venes at f3, observe that the danger to Black's back row prevents exploitation.

Let Black try, ingeniously, *5.* .... Kt—B6!

Now White cannot play B—B3, but can play *6.* Q—B1. There
could follow

6. ....            Q—Kt6 ch
7. K—Kt1           Q × KP ch
8. Q—B2            Q × Kt
9. Q × Q           Kt × B ch

10. K—B1                Kt×Q
11. B×Kt (and Black may win. But 9. B×Kt instead of
    Q×Q leaves a drawn endgame)

This position shows how easily one moves into deep waters
from the shallows.

In the actual game, by the American master Shroeder, the
opponent refused to capture the Kt when Kt×RP was played.
Was he stupid? Or had he seen that 2. .... Q—R5 was good
for Black (instead of B×Kt ch)?

This is a nice point of order.

However, these are deep waters. To revert to the shallow end,
not terribly hard is the next diagram (68) – a sacrifice of the

Black

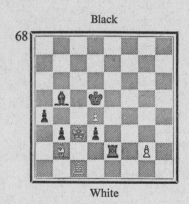

68

White

Sacrifice of the exchange in order to remove defender

| 1. | .... R×B | 5. | K—B3 | P—Kt7 |
|----|----------|----|------|-------|
| 2. | K×R    K×P | 6. | K×P | B—Q6 |
| 3. | R—B8   P—Q7 | 7. | R—K8 ch   K—B7 |
| 4. | R—Q8 ch   K—K6 | 8. | R—B8 ch   K—Kt8 |
|    |          |    | wins |  |

'exchange' – where the capture removes at once an important
defender (in the shape of the Bishop) and enables the capture of
the KP and the advance of the attacking King. Let it be added
that in the middle game a well-placed Knight or Bishop is so

strong that the exchange is often sacrificed in order to allow
this formation (Diagram 69). To revert to the examples so far

Black

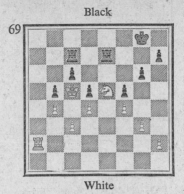

White

Knight worth a Rook
When the QBP falls, White will win

seen, none of the above sacrifices were 'long range': but the
reader, learning the language of Chess – as the pieces speak it –
has acquired from them some phrases; some short sentences;
and should by now be thinking in 'manœuvres'.

No list of manœuvres can exhaust Chess. Words like Battery,
Imprisonment, Fork, Pin, Double Function, etc., serve only to
make the student a little more conscious of the functions of the
pieces; but he has to learn to see without consulting a list of
things to look for.

One very general notion is, however, worth mentioning:
that of 'decoying'. The exploitation of 'double function' seen
in Diagram 70 is a sort of decoy. So, too, Diagram 71 shows a
well-known endgame danger. But the principle is a wide one.
All those Queen, etc., excursions after the Kt Pawns, were, in a
sense, decoys. The capturer seduced himself from the field of
battle.

On occasion there is no escape from the decoy. Diagrams 72
and 73 offer two very spectacular examples, which speak for
themselves.

Black

White

Decoy – Exploitation of Double Function
*1.* B × P ch wins the exchange and a Pawn

Black

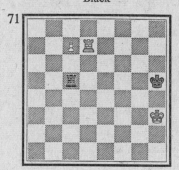

White

Decoy
*1.* R — Q5 ch wins
If the White Rook were on QKt7 *1.* R — Kt5, pinning and
decoying, would win

Black (Blackburne)

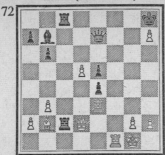

72

White (Zukertort)

Classical decoy

Black seems to be holding everything

But *28.* Q—Kt4! refutes that belief.

| If *28.* .... | Q×Q | *32.* R—Kt3 ch | K—R4 ...... |
|---|---|---|---|
| *29.* B×P ch | K×P · | *33.* R—B5 ch | K—R3 |
| *30.* R—R3 ch | K—Kt3 | *34.* B—B4 ch and mate next move | |
| *31.* R—B6 ch. | K—Kt4 | | |

In the actual game Black played *28.* .... R(*I*)—B4 met by *29.* R—B8 ch! winning quickly

Black (Torre)

73

White (Adams)

Decoy

Note the attack on the Rooks which the Queen is guarding

| *1.* Q—KKt4! | Q—Kt4 | *4.* P—QR4 | Q×RP |
|---|---|---|---|
| *2.* Q—QB4 | Q—Q2 | *5.* R—K4 | Q—Kt4 |
| *3.* Q—B7 | Q—Kt4 | *6.* Q×KtP | resigns |

Years later Black avenged himself on history by carrying out a comparable process on no less than Lasker

Those examples show, in a spectacular way, a concentration on the functions of pieces, in disregard of their apparent values.

The ordinary player is inhibited by a habit-system formed from his valuations of the pieces according to the rules (which valuation is normally valid). But the valuation must sometimes be forgotten. To achieve ability to see beyond the values is a very important stage in the evolution of a Chess-player.

Diagram 74 shows Emanuel Lasker assessing a Queen according to the needs of the position.

Now, moving from the spectacular, we find a typical Chess manœuvre, and one of the easiest to understand, in the accumulation of force against a specific point. Thus –

    *1.* P—K4               P—K4
    *2.* Kt—KB3         Kt—QB3
    *3.* B—B4              Kt—KB3
    *4.* Kt—Kt5 is a typical accumulation against a weak spot. This threat can be parried – by P—Q4; and a complex piece of play follows, which is discussed in a later chapter

Diagram 75 shows how a whole game is determined by the ability of one player to create a situation in which his aggregation of force brings a plurality of threats, not all of which can be resisted.

Here the feature to be noted is the effect of play that produces two or three threats at critical moves. At this point the learner is moving into tactical Chess. The notion of two threats enables us to return to the technical weakness of KB7.

To revert to something elementary, here is a well-known 'try', in which there are two threats, but both of them can be parried economically and the trier will have wasted his time.

    *1.* P—K4               P—K4
    *2.* B—B4              B—B4

Black (Lasker)

74

White (Euwe, 1934)

The real values

Lasker has recognized that White's *35*. Kt—K4 is not a saving resource

| | |
|---|---|
| *35*. .... Q×KP (allowing the unmasking) | *37*. R×Q    Kt×R(f6) |
| *36*. Kt—B6 ch   Q×Kt | *38*. R—QB1   Kt—K5 with a winning attack |

Black

75

White

Attacking Process

*13*. Q—Q3        P—Kt3 (forced, because B×Kt is threatened)
*14*. QR—Q1       K—Kt2
*15*. P—B5        P×P
*16*. P×P         B—K2 (if B×P   *17*. Q—B3 wins a piece)
*17*. Q—K3        Kt—Q4
*18*. B—R6 ch     K—Kt1
*19*. Q—Kt3       B—R3
*20*. B×R wins the exchange because if *20*. .... B×R   *21*. B×B followed by K×B

3. Q—R5 (White seems to be attacking the King's
      Pawn: i.e. left to its own devices, the Queen can
      take that Pawn)

3. .... Kt—QB3

(Black is obsessed with White's attack on the King's Pawn; and
overlooks another, more serious, threat, which is now carried
out.)

4. Q×BP mate

This is called the 'Scholar's Mate'* a name that could only
be justified by an unsophisticated use of the word 'Scholar'.
No experienced player would play Q—R5. Black with Q—K2
defends both threats (to KP and BP) and gains tempo, relatively to White, who, in a moment, will have to retreat his
Queen; when, e.g. Black's Kt—KB3 attacks it. There are
threats which, being seen, are refuted, but with no gain of
tempo by the defender. This is not one of them.

At this stage, it may help the reader if I repeat that, for much
of Chess, the main activities that seem to be called for are
common sense and some degree of awareness.

Thus the player who is attacked by 3. Q—R5 in the Scholar's
Mate attempt, first has to 'see' that two things are attacked, his
KP and his KBP. If he is really aware of the powers of the
pieces he will see this. Common sense then tells him to make
the move that defends both, and he must look round for a
piece that can perform those two functions in one move. He
finds the Queen. Q—K2 and Q—KB3 are both possible. But he
may think: 'I want to play my Knight later to KB3 in order to
attack White's Queen.' So he plays Q—K2. His sense is becoming more refined than ordinary 'common'. That growth is, in a
sense, the topic of this book.

* There is a shorter mate – in two: but it can only be achieved by Black.
1. P—KKt4 P—K4. 2. P—KB3 Q—R5 mate. An improbable thing, but
illustrative of the weakness of one of White's diagonals. White can do this
mate in 3 moves.

Meanwhile here is something more advanced and in the spirit of practical Chess.

| | | |
|---|---|---|
| *1.* | P—K4 | P—K4 |
| *2.* | P—Q4 | P×P |
| *3.* | Kt—KB3 | Kt—QB3 |
| *4.* | B—B4* | B—K2 |
| *5.* | P—B3 | P×P |
| *6.* | Q—Q5 | |

Here the threat of mate at KB7 can only be defended at some expense –

Thus 6. . . . . P—Q3 is useless, because of

| | | |
|---|---|---|
| *7.* | Q×P ch | K—Q2 |
| *8.* | B—K6 mate | |

Again, 6. . . . . Kt—K4 is met by Kt×Kt.

So all that is left by way of resource is

| | | |
|---|---|---|
| *6.* | . . . . | Kt—KR3 |

Then  7. B×Kt       O—O (He has no time to recapture the piece)

*8.* B—B1 (White has won a piece, and should win the game, though the process is not easy, Black has two Pawns for his piece and is now quite developed)

This last example is typical of tactical Chess in this way, that it shows the effect of a powerful threat, made possible by an opponent's desire for material gain at the expense of his development. Black had no time for *5.* . . . P×P.

Sometimes, an attack on f7 is made possible by the unwise removal of a defender. Thus in the diagram position (76) Black has just played R—K1. There followed *9.* B×P ch K×B. Perhaps Black had expected now *10.* Q—B4 ch P—Q4; *11.*

* Recently revived is P—B3 (Goring Gambit) possibly unsound. In any event *4.* . . . . P—Q6 is an available reply.

Black

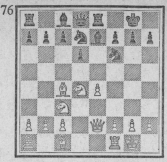

76

White

Exploitation of KBP weakness
9. B×P ch      K×B
10. Kt—K6!     K×Kt
11. Q—B4 ch
(A possible position from the Philidor, see p. 249.)

Kt×P  Kt—K4. Instead there happened *10*. Kt—K6  K×Kt (the only way of saving the Queen).

*11*. Q—B4 ch and Black is in trouble. Let it be added that, for all the familiarity of the danger, f7 remains a place of disaster. As recently as 1960 the great Reshevsky was the victim of an early sacrifice on that square. In the example given one 'possibility' was missed. A different type of mishandling occurs in the following short game from the 1962 Olympiad which shows how a quite good player can fail to anticipate the development of a fatal dilemma. (He fails to see how a double threat can develop.)

(Game played at the Varna Olympiad 1962)

| White | Black |
|---|---|
| MOHRLOCK | KRAMER |
| (West Germany) | (Holland) |
| *1*. P—K4 | P—K4 |
| *2*. Kt—KB3 | Kt—QB3 |
| *3*. B—Kt5 | |

These moves constitute the very old, and still fresh, opening known as RUY LOPEZ, or, among Continentals, as THE SPANISH OPENING. Explanations of the opening moves will be given later.

| | |
|---|---|
| 3. .... | P—QR3 |
| 4. B—R4 | P—Q3 |

The Steinitz Deferred. The Steinitz proper is

| | |
|---|---|
| 3. ... | P—Q3 |
| 5. P—Q4 | P—QKt4 |
| 6. B—Kt3 | Kt × P |
| 7. Kt × Kt | P × Kt |

Observe now that White has power to play Q × P, and apparently can do so without immediate loss. Nevertheless the move is unplayable – and constitutes the 'Noah's Ark' pitfall.

| | |
|---|---|
| If 8. Q × P | P—QB4 |

with two threats (a) to capture the Queen, (b) to push on to QB5, imprisoning the Bishop, and capturing it for less than its value.

If now 9. Q—Q5 with threat of mate at KB7 and to capture the Rook at QR8

| | |
|---|---|
| 9. .... | B—K3 |
| 10. Q—B6 ch | B—Q2 |
| 11. Q—Q5 | P—B5 |

and the Bishop falls.

Nevertheless, White has some advantage in development to compensate for the Pawn. He plays the conventional

8. P—QB3 and Black, rather than exchange, developing White's Knight, offers back the Pawn on a square less convenient to White –

| | |
|---|---|
| 8. .... | P—Q6 |

9. P—QR4 opening up lines. If Black captures, his Rook's Pawn is left isolated and weak.

Now observe further. If White is allowed to play P × P Black cannot recapture without loss, because P × P will allow R × R by White. In other words, the QRP will be 'pinned'.

So Black plays

    *9.* . . . .               B—Q2

And now the pin does not seem to matter, because the Queen guards the Rook. Nevertheless, Black is playing badly.

    *10.* P×P               P×P

He should have taken with the Bishop.

    *11.* Q—R5 winning! . . . .

Why? Because White is initiating a process that cannot be stopped. At this move Q×BP mate is threatened, and must be defended, and P—Kt3 is the only convenient way. (If B—K3. *12.* B×B (the Pawn is pinned). If *11.* . . . . Kt—R3. *12.* B×Kt. If *11.* . . . . Q—K2. *12.* R×R ch, etc.) And if he does play *11.* . . . . P—Kt3 then, with *12.* Q—Q5, White will be threatening mate again, and will now be attacking the Rook with an additional piece. If then, *12.* . . . . B—K3. *13.* not immediate capture of Rook because he does not want to lose his Bishop at Kt3, but Q—B6 ch   B—Q2.

*14.* Q×R wins a Rook.

What happened in the game was that Black played *11.* . . . . P—Q7 ch. This was captured (*12.* B×P) and Black resigned. This game was played between strong players, and illustrates the proposition that even short-range threats can be hard to see. These examples also show the importance of the King's vulnerability at early stages.

Further, this example, and the previous ones, should have equipped the reader with a notion of real values, as distinct from 'formal' values. In every position the value of any piece depends on its future dynamic prospects. A Queen is worth no more than a Pawn if the sacrifice of the Queen for the Pawn leads to mate, or is necessary in order to avoid mate.

In the first chapter the reader acquired a rough scale of the formal values of the pieces. The King: indispensable and strong at short range; the Queen: the most powerful; the Rook: a little more than half the value of the Queen, and powerful; Bishop and Knight, equally strong according to their occasions, but each significantly less powerful than the Rook. Pawns are roughly estimated as each being two-fifths of the value of a Knight or Bishop. That is a rule of thumb. But even while these assessments are being made, one realizes that they are not constant. The reader saw, in comparing Bishop with Knight, that in one set of positions, the Bishop dominates: in another set the Knight. As the game moves from opening to middle game (and, when there is anything to think about of tactical manœuvres, every part of the game is middle game) the values can change so that a sacrifice of the exchange for tempo, for mobility, may be well worth while.

Pawns are given in exchange for tempo: and entire pieces are sacrificed 'for the attack'. Even the Queen can be sacrificed, for the achievement of some fatal effect. So, according to the exigencies of position, the values are transvalued. The diagrams have shown some instances. But perhaps the greatest change, without the mediation of spectacular sacrifices, is one that supervenes as the endgame arrives. In the endgame, the middle game sacrificial disregard of values is rare. The pieces may even have recovered value. But the Pawn has grown in stature. In the ending the Pawn comes into its own, because of its promotability. In the opening and in the middle game, it was cannon-fodder, though in Chess one does not part lightly even with cannon-fodder. Certainly, at those early stages, it is rare for a Pawn to achieve victory over a Queen. But see, at the end, what a Pawn can achieve against a Queen. See what the Pawn in the next diagram (77) is doing! The learner may be surprised to be told that this position is a draw.

Notice that the Pawn is a Bishop's Pawn. Because of the stalemate that ensues when the Queen goes to c7 with the defending King at a8, or to f7 with the defending King at h8, it follows that the Queen at b6, driving the King from b8 to a8, or the Queen at g6, driving the King from g8 to h8, achieves nothing. She cannot capture the pawn, but must return to a square where she prevents promotion: e.g. c6 or f6, and the King then returns to b8 or g8 – as the case may be.

The above is the truth about Bishop's Pawns, when the

Black

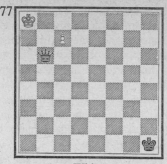

White
Pawn against Queen
Black to move. A draw

attacking King is not very near. The next diagram (78) shows a
case where the Bishop's Pawn loses. The Queen checks at c6
forcing the King to b8. Now White King to b6. The Pawn promotes to Queen. Comes Q—d6 ch, K—a8. Q—a3 ch, K—b8,
Q—a7 mate. That is the exception which tests the rule about
Bishops' Pawns; and leaves it generally valid.

Rooks' Pawns are equally privileged. What happens here is

Black

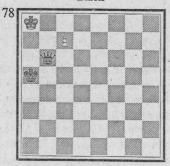

White
BP v. Q Black to move, wins

that the checking Queen drives the King on to a8 or h8: and there, unless the King be immediately released, it is stalemate. (Again a proximate White King can make a difference.)

The logic of both these draws will be appreciated when one works out the win of Queen against KtP, QP or KP (diagram 79). The Queen at d1 will zigzag, with checks and threats, till it

Black

79

White

Queen wins against Pawn

reaches e5 with check. Then, whether the White King goes to d8 or f8, Black's next move is Q d6. White must now play K—e8, and Black plays Qe6 ch. This position can always be forced by the Queen, with the aid of checks, threats, and, if necessary, pins of the Pawn (e.g. Q at e7, Pawn at d7, King c7. The defending King goes to c8, and Black plays Qc5 ch, etc.). Once the Queen has checked at e6 the King must go to d8, blocking the Pawn. This is not a stalemate set-up, because the Pawn isn't a Rook's Pawn: and the King cannot leave the Pawn to be captured, because it isn't a Bishop's Pawn. Therefore Kd8. Now, Black's King, starting from the ends of the earth, makes a move nearer. White tries Kc7. Comes Qe7, Kc8 (otherwise the Queen slips in to d8!). Q—c4 ch K—b7. Q—d6 K—c8, Qc6 ch, and again Kd8, and once again the Black King moves nearer. Eventually that King will arrive at a square like d6, and the Pawn will be capturable.

From this analysis, the reader will have learned two things –

(1) The technique of Queen against promoting Pawns.

(2) An example of the change in the strength and importance of Pawns as the game gets later and the Pawn moves higher.

Two Pawns joined on the 7th, or 6th and 7th, can equalize against a Queen provided that she cannot capture one with a check. That needs no illustration. But what the reader will, undoubtedly, be asking is: What about a Pawn against a Rook?

Obviously, its chances are better than against a Queen, because the Rook cannot zigzag down two files in the way that a Queen can. A Pawn on the 7th with King in support, and the other King away, can draw against a Rook on any of the eight files. The Rook can only check and return to the file of promotion, gaining no tempo for its King to approach.

Positions even occur in which one Pawn defeats a Rook because the Rook cannot find a convenient square.

Diagram 80 illustrates this, and introduces a quite pretty

Black

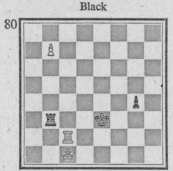

80

White
White to play and win

sacrificial complex, which should become part of the improving player's technique.

*1.* R—QKt2 is not a winning move, because *1. ...,* R×P. *2.* R×R P—Kt6 draws, e.g. *3.* R—Kt7 K—B7. *4.* K—Q1 P—Kt7. *5.* R—B7 ch K—Kt6 and promotion cannot be prevented.

Nevertheless, White has a winning line.

*1.* R—B3 ch                    R×R ch
     (the decoy already seen)

*2.* K—Kt2 (and White's promotion of the Pawn
     cannot be prevented. Remember that a slightly
     different decoy would be possible were the White
     Rook at QR2. Then R—R3 would win.)

The resultant position will be K and Q against K, R and P,
which is usually a win for the K and Q. The Queen's checks
will so dislocate the defence that the attacking King will
eventually be able to take over the task of stopping the Pawn,
while the Queen wins material.

In an introductory volume all the learning – even all the basic

Black

81

White

Fenton *v.* Potter
Black to move, cannot save the game

*1.* .... R—Kt3 ch
*2.* K—K5 (not K—B5, because of *2.* .... R—Kt8 and the Rook
     thrusts from c1, nor K—K7, because of *2.* .... R—Kt2)
*2.* ....        R—Kt4 ch
*3.* K—K4    R—Kt5 ch
*4.* K—K3    R—Kt6 ch
*5.* K—B2!    R—Kt5!
*6.* P—B8 (=R)! because if P=Q   R—B5 ch causes stalemate
*6.* .... R—QR5 in order to stop mate at QR8
*7.* K—Kt3 wins; mate and loss of Rook both threatened

E

learning – cannot find place. Let one example suffice of the
cleverness that are associated with duels between Rook and
Pawn.

Diagram 81 shows a position that occurred last century
between two English players, Fenton and Potter. It is believed
that White failed to find the right play. As a study it has been
called the SAVEDRA ENDING, after a certain clergyman who
analysed it.

Note that White must prevent *1.* A pin at b7. *2.* A thrust from
c1 when the King is on the c file. *3.* A neat danger of stalemate.

These victories of Pawn over Rook are relatively unusual.
Normal, however, is the success of the Pawn in drawing against
a Rook.

Black

82

White

White to move, draws
1. P—R4   R—Kt8 ch
2. K—B6!   (see text)

Much depends on the position of the Kings. Diagram 82 is
very instructive. The play is

1. P—R4                 R—Kt8 ch
2. K—B6 (This is very important, as will be shown)
2. ....                     R—R8
3. K—Kt5                 K—Kt7
4. P—R5                 K—B6

|       | 5. P—R6   | K—K5 |
|-------|-----------|------|
|       | 6. K—Kt6  | K—Q4 |
|       | 7. P—R7   | K—Q3 |

(If 7. .... R—Kt8 ch. 8. K—B7 forces the Rook back to a1)

|       | 8. K—Kt7  | R—Kt8 ch |

| Now   | 9. K—R8 is good, because the Rook must move away from the file in order to avoid stalemate |
| Also  | 9. K—B8 is good |
| But   | 9. K—R6 is bad, because of |
|       | 9. ....   | K—B2 |

Now White's only resource is

|       | 10. P—R8=Kt ch | K—B6 |
|-------|----------------|------|
|       | 11. K—R7       | R—Kt7 |

and White is in a bad *zugzwang* and loses the Knight at least.

This, incidentally, is the type of position in which King and Rook defeat King and Knight. In the ordinary way, with the Knight on the open board, a Knight draws against a Rook.

Now to revert to White's second move. Why was K—B6 necessary? The alternative is K—R6 (not K—R7 when R—R8 wins the Pawn).

After 2. K—R6 there follows

|       | 2. ....   | K—Kt7 |
|-------|-----------|-------|
|       | 3. P—R5   | K—B6  |
|       | 4. K—R7   | K—K5  |
|       | 5. P—R6   | K—Q4  |
|       | 6. K—R8   | K—B3  |
|       | 7. P—R7 (if K—R7 K—B2!) |  |
|       | 7. ....   | R—KR8 |
|       | 8. K—Kt8  | R—R1 mate |

This demonstrates, among other things, the remarkable speed of a King.

More will be said of this in subsequent pages.

As between Pawns and the Rook, two joined Pawns, which can occasionally draw with a Queen, can often beat a Rook. Two Pawns joined on the 6th rank can, if the Kings be

Black

83

White

White wins whoever has the move

e.g.
1. ....      R—B1
2. P—B7     R—B1
3. P—K7     R × P
4. P—K8 = Q

irrelevant, and neither Pawn can be captured on the move, inevitably defeat a Rook (Diagram 93) because, once one of them has been promoted to Queen, with the other falling, we have an ending Queen against Rook, which is a win. Queen against Rook, be it added, is a win except in occasional positions where a pin of the Queen or a thrust cannot be avoided; but it is rarely an easy win. The normal play of Queen against Rook is shown under Diagram 84. Care must be taken, when the King is against the edge of the board, to avoid the well-known stalemate.

To revert, a Pawn on the 5th, supporting a Pawn on the 6th, will just fail to cope with a Rook unless the King can help (Diagram 85).

The reader will be observing, now, that the power of the King tends to be very much enhanced in the endgame. This is because it is usually out of mating danger (there are exceptions to this principle, of course) and is relatively free to attack and defend Pawns.

An important estimate to be made in many endgames concerns the ability of the King to stop, or catch up with, a hostile advancing Pawn, or a pair of Pawns.

Black

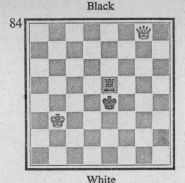

84

White

Typical win by K and Q against K and R

| | | |
|---|---|---|
| 1. K—B4 | K—B5 | If in order to avoid cramp, |
| 2. Q—Kt6 | R—K5 ch | 6. .... R—QR4 |
| 3. K—Q5 | R—K4 ch | 7. Q—K6 ch K—K4 |
| 4. K—Q4 | R—Kt4 | 8. Q—K7 ch K—Kt5 |
| 5. Q—B6 ch | K—Kt 5 | 9. Q—Q7 ch K—R4 |
| 6. K—K4 | R—KR4 | 10. K—B4 K—Kt3 |
| 7. Q—B4 ch | K—R6 | 11. Q—B6 ch. K—R4 |
| 8. K—B3 forces mate | | 12. Q—R1 ch K—Kt3 |
| | | 13. Q—QKt 1 ch |
| | | and forces a fork |

Here are some guiding principles:

(1) If a King is on a rank behind the rank where the Pawn stands, then, if the Pawn moves first the King cannot catch it. That is why 'hanging Pawns' retain a value. The King cannot take the hinder Pawn if the forward Pawn has a free run.

(2) If a King is on the same rank as a hostile Pawn or on a forward rank, it still may be unable to catch the Pawn if it is too many files away. A good idea, shown in Diagram 86, is to draw a square. One vertical side of the square consists of the square occupied by the Pawn, plus number of squares which it has to travel. (If the Pawn is on the 2nd rank, treat the 3rd rank as the base.) Complete the square by counting the proper number along the rank, and drawing imaginary lines. If the King

Black

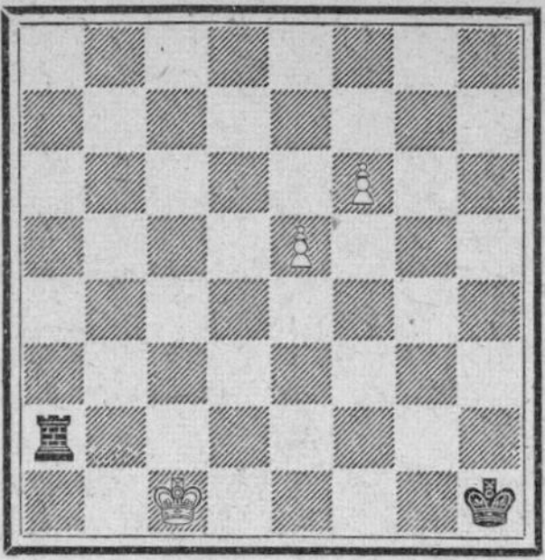

White

Black, to move, wins

e.g. *1.* .... R—KB7, then moves to KB4, captures the KP and can
return to KB4 in time to stop the BP

Note: White King is far away

Black

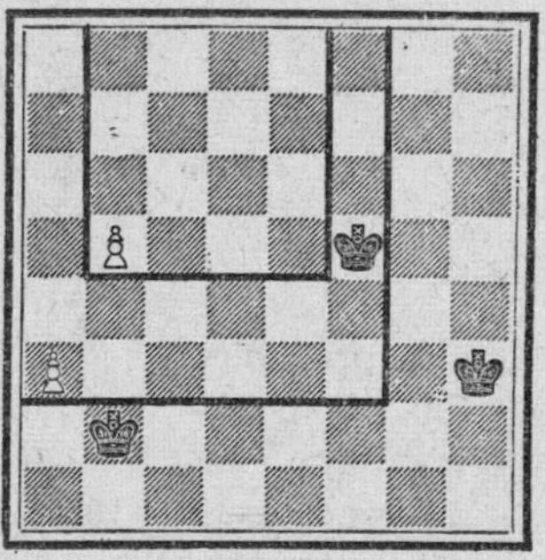

White

The Square

*1.* The King on h3 cannot catch the Pawn on a3 as it advances.

*2.* The King on f5 can only catch the Pawn on b5 if it is Black's move.

*3.* If it is White's move the King on b2 or on any 2nd-rank square,
cannot catch the Pawn on a3, or any 3rd-rank square, or on any
2nd-rank square (because of the double first move)

is outside that area when the Pawn moves, the Pawn is un-
catchable.

In thinking of this let the reader recognize that a King can look to be quite far away and still catch a Pawn. Thus K on c6 catches Pawn running down from h6. But King on b7 does not catch Pawn from h7, which can move immediately to h5.

An advanced, and brilliant, display of King's speed – not without aid – is a position played at Berlin about 1920 – and resigned by White (Diagram 87). That great master of play and endgame studies, the late Richard Réti, showed that White can

Black

87

White

White Draws (study by Réti)

1. K—Kt7  P—R5
2. K—B6  K—Kt3 (because White is threatening K—K6 which enables him to secure the promotion of his Pawn)
3. K—K5  K×P (because K—Q6 was threatened)
4. K—B4 overhauls the Black Pawn

draw. His threat to help his own Pawn home gains tempo.

Very interesting is the play of King against two Pawns.

Paradoxically two broken Pawns endanger a King as much as do two joined Pawns (Diagram 88). The subsequent diagram (89) shows the paradox strikingly.

White with King facing three joined Pawns, wins against King facing two broken Pawns. White's first move is retreat – and to one square only. He must be able to meet P—c3 with K to c2. P—d3 with K to d2 P—e3 with K to e2. His only square then is d1. 1. Kd1 and Black is in *zugzwang*. If White's Pawns

Black

White

### Kings held by Pawns

1. The holding of the White King is obvious (N.B. hanging Pawns)
2. The Black King cannot win a Pawn, because if Kc6, Pe6, and if Ke6, Pc6. He can, however, play Kc6, or e6, and in answer to Pe6 or c6, play Kc7 or e7 as the case may be, to which White cannot reply with a Pawn advance

Black

White

### Pawn Paradox
White to move, wins
1. Kd1 (see text, p. 103)

were one rank lower down, this would not be the case. The Black King could oscillate between f7, g7, h7, and White would soon be *zugzwanged*.

Diagram 90 shows a very amusing piece of Pawn play. (Against three such Pawns a triangle is a safe construction.)

Black

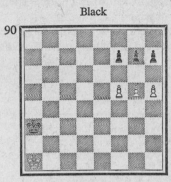

90

White

Amusing Pawn play
White wins

*1.* P—Kt6   If *1.* . . . .   RP×P
2. P—B6   P×BP
3. P—R6 and promotes itself
If *1.* . . . .   BP×P
2. P—R6   P×RP
3. P—B6 and promotes itself

If the Black Pawns had been on f6, g7, h6, they would have been impregnable

Some endgames take the form of Pawn races, with Kings removing obstacles from the paths of their protégé Pawns; other endgames are fights for access. These duels between Kings frequently depend on the 'opposition', to which the reader has already been introduced. At that point, what is taking place is a fight between two pieces, which up to this point have been relatively inactive as fighters.

In practice, one of the most frequent occurrences in well-balanced Chess – indeed the endgame framework that the

...st always bear in mind – is the reduction of the game ...King, piece and Pawn (or Pawns) against King, piece and Pawn (or Pawns). The study of this is beyond the scope of any introductory book. But the following few diagrams will show some typical technical endgame processes.

Rook and Pawn against Rook is a normal ending. One of the vital points to be observed is:

That if you can cut off the opponent's King for long enough, your Pawn, with the aid of your own King, will win.

'Cut-off' King is a well-known technical term (Diagram 91). The 'cut-off' can be from ranks (horizontal) or from files

Black

91

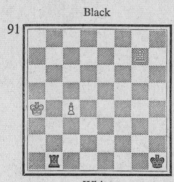

White

Cut-off King

White wins, because the Pawn's advance will be supported by the White King as soon as the Rook threatens the Pawn. The White King is only momentarily 'cut-off' – the Black King is quite out of the game. A similar effect would be obtained if the White Rook were on the second rank – the cut-off would be horizontal, instead of vertical, but equally effective. (The cut-off, to be effective, need not be so extreme as in the diagram)

(vertical). 'Cut-offs' as clear and effective as that in Diagram 91 are not easily achieved. A King can be rescued from the cut-off by the interposition of a Rook, if the exchange leaves a situation where the King can prevent the promotion of the opponent's Pawn (Diagram 92).

Black

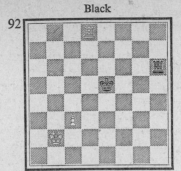

White

Ineffective Cut-off
With R—Q3, Black secures the entry of his King

Black

White

K, R and P *v.* K and R
White to play – what result?

With best defence – a draw. If P—K7 Black has a useful series of
checks

If, instead,  *1.* R—Kt1 ch   K—B1
            *2.* K—B6      R—R2!

(To pin the Pawn with R—R3 would be wrong, because then
R—QKt1 would drive the Rook back and White would have time
for R—Kt7)

            *3.* R—QKt1   R—B2 ch (can't be captured
                          because of stalemate)
            *4.* K—K5     R—B7 draws

Black

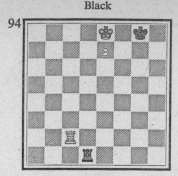

White

Lucena technique
White wins (see text)

A King which is less than two files away from an advancing
Pawn, and not too far behind, can save the game. The Rook
will check away the opposing King while the defending King
endeavours to place itself in front of the advancing Pawn.
In Diagram 93 this process is facilitated by a neat resource.
The stalemate possibility enables the Black Rook to work
its way behind the attackers and so relieve pressure on the
King.

Diagram 94 shows a win by White, where delicacy is required.
If White checks and plays his King out, Black drives it back
with checks. If White tries unsubtly to cover his King's evacua-
tion of e8 there may happen *1.* R—B7  K—Kt2. *2.* R—Q7
R—QR8. *3.* K—Q8  R—R1 ch. *4.* K—B7  K—B2 saves the
game. Correct is *1.* R—Kt2 ch  K—R2. *2.* R—Kt4  R—Q7.
(If K—R3. *3.* K—B8 wins.) *3.* K—B7  R—B7 ch. *4.* K—K6
R—K7 ch. *5.* K—Q6 R—Q7 ch. *6.* K—K5  R—K7 ch. *7.*
R—K4 wins. This is a kind of what is called 'Lucena' cover.
In analogous positions the White problem is usually to prevent
the Black King and Rook from attacking the advancing Pawn
jointly: the Black problem is to achieve the capture without the

capturing Rook being left hanging when the supporting King is checked away: alternately to manœuvre the defending King in front of the Pawn without its being mated.

The various instances of KR and P *v.* K and R do not lend themselves to easy formulae. As a matter of general technique observe that in a Rook against Pawn ending, the Rook, whether defending or attacking, prefers to be behind, rather than in front of, the advancing Pawn.

Also the proximity of Kings is all important.

Black

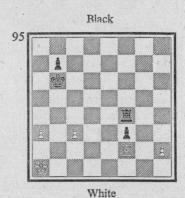

95

White

Importance of King play
White to move

Necessary is K—QKt2. But White is afraid of R—Kt5 threatening R—Kt7 and forcing a draw. He therefore plays *1.* P—R3 and now Black wins. *1.* . . . . . K—B4; *2.* K—Kt2   K—Q4; *3.* K—B2   K—K5; *4.* K—Q2   R—B3 and with checks forces his King into a dominating position. There will be threats of mate

'Make your King a fighting piece' is a Chess maxim even in the middle game. As the endgame approaches one observes, in most good games of Chess, that the Kings start moving in towards the centre very quickly.

Diagram 95 shows how a superior position can be reduced to

a loss by failure to take notice of the power of an advancing King.

Very interesting, too, is a curious exception to the centralization of Kings. In Diagram 96, what square should the King seek? Strangely, a square well away from the scene of action.

The reason arises from one of those curious pieces of resource

Black

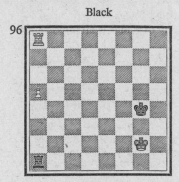

96

White

Black to move. What square?
1. . . . .      K—Kt4
2. P—R6   K—Kt3
3. P—R7   K—Kt2! This draws

But suppose the King had moved to B4, K3, Q2, then at move 4 White would play R—R8 and, in answer to R×P, R—R7 ch winning the Rook

that make the geometry of the occupied board so intriguing.

If the King occupies the 6th or lower rank, the Rook can check it. If it occupies the 3rd, 4th or 5th file from the end, then R—h8, and if R×P. 2. R—h7 ch.

Enough has now been said, it is thought, to enable the learner to realize that in the endgame the Pawn has a value as significant as that of a full piece – occasionally more.

But let him not forget that in the middle game the Pawn is a force. In the kind of game that ends before the endgame, the Pawn performs tactical functions.

Black

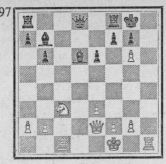

97

White

Pawn in middle game
White wins
1.  R—R8 ch   K × R
2.  Q—R5 ch and mates at h7
If the White Pawn were not available at g6, Q—R5 would not
constitute a winning attack

One example should suffice. That Pawn at g6 in Diagram 97
is the corner-stone of the mating attack.

In the building of a position the Pawn controls squares on
which hostile pieces cannot settle. This goes unnoticed by the
novice, but the good player, whenever he moves a Pawn, is
thinking of the possibility that he is permitting an opposing
piece to occupy a square from which it can operate.

Incidentally, a technical point (Diagram 98) that can occur
quite early in the game. With that opposing Pawn on a5, how
long does it take to get your Knight's Pawn to b4, supported by
a Pawn at a3? You cannot play a3 immediately because of a5 —
a4. That is how backward Pawns come into being ! So play, first,
b3 ! Then a3, then b4. And remember the pins !

Before we part from Pawns, let mention be made of one
technical strategic feature, which is of the first importance.
*Remote Passed Pawn* (or Remote Pawn, generally). In the middle
game there is a temptation not to be worried by the placing of
the Pawns, so long as equality of material is preserved. But look

Black

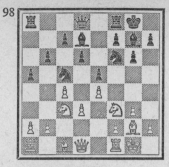

White

How to force a Pawn forward
Not *1*. P—QR3, because of *1*. . . . .　　P—R5
But *1*. P—Kt3 followed by P—R3, and B—Kt2

Black

White

Remote Passed Pawn
Whoever has the move White wins. Most favourable to Black is for
White to move first (a tempo point)
　　　　*1*. P—R5　K—Kt4
　　　　*2*. P—R6　K×P
　　　　*3*. K×P and
White then reaches the K side Pawns first

at Diagram 99. At this point the possibly accidental fact that White's is the Rook's Pawn rather than the Bishop's determines the result.

Do not overestimate this factor, however. Diagram 100 shows a situation where the general Pawn position is so much in Black's favour that the Remote Passed Pawn stands for nothing.

Black

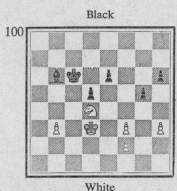

100

White

Remote passed Pawn that is useless

| 38. .... | B×Kt | | 43. K—K5 | K—B6 |
|---|---|---|---|---|
| 39. K×Kt | K—Kt4 | | 44. K×P | P—Q5 |
| 40. K—KJ | K—Kt5 | | 45. P—B4 | P—Q6 |
| 41. P—B4 | P×P | | 46. P—B5 | P—Q7 |
| 42. K×BP | K×P | | 47. P—B6 | P—Q8 (=Q) |
| | | | | wins |

Among the major pieces (in this context that means other than the Pawns) changes in value also take place. But these changes are more evident in the middle game than in the endgame.

Thus a Queen, by putting itself out of play in the middle game, can become irrelevant to the attack. In the endgame a Queen is very rarely assessable at less than full value. And so of the other pieces. Rooks in the endgame can find themselves thwarted, e.g. Rook against Bishop is usually a draw, Rook against Knight is usually a draw. In both cases there are occasions when the defending King is badly placed and the Bishop or Knight can be defeated by the Rook (101). On the other hand, the Rook never loses to Bishop or Knight.

Black

101

White

Rook defeats Bishop
*1.* K—B2
or   *1.* RQ6 wins
But transfer Black K to KR8, Black B to KKt8, White K to KKt3
Black to move, now draws (B—R7ch).

Knights and Bishops will vary relatively in the endgames according to the Pawn formations, but their strength is near enough to their full strength.

Some other pieces of information are worth recording.

(1) Rook and Bishop against Rook can be a win, but the type of position from which the win can be forced is hard to attain – can rarely be brought about by force.

(2) Rook and Knight against Rook usually fail to win.

(3) Rook and Pawn can sometimes thwart a Queen, because the Rook remains guarded. This is a particularly hard piece of Chess technique.

(4) Queen and Bishop sometimes defeat a Queen, i.e. when a mating process can be found. To sum up, in the endgame the pieces retain – even regain – their full value. If they have been 'out of play', they come back into play.

The endgame, in consequence, is as tactically dangerous and difficult as the middle game. One finds Queens struggling to organize the promotion of a Pawn while preventing the delivery of perpetual check by the opposing Queen (Diagram 102).

Black

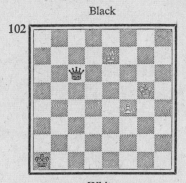

102

White

Q *v.* Q and P
Black to move. White wins

The long process is facilitated in this position by the fact that to some checks the White Queen will intervene with check or pin

So after *1.* .... Q—Kt7 ch
2. K—B6

Black's scope is limited. But there are very many positions (with this material) less favourable to the aggressor


Amusing is the device in the next position (103) in which two minor pieces combine to capture a Queen which at the moment seems unattacked.

In other words, notwithstanding changes in valuation, the problem is the same at all stages: see what the pieces can do. Also know their endgame limitations. Here are a few.

(1) Bishops may not be able to help in the liquidation of an advantage if each player has one on a different field (Diagram 104). The exceptions occur when one player has an excess on both sides of the board, and a better placed King (Diagram 104: note).

Black

White

Minor pieces capture Queen. White draws
*1*. B—B3 ch　If *1*. . . . . Q×B　*2*. Kt—Q4 ch　K moves
*3*. Kt×Q　K×Kt　*4*. K—B1 draws
If *1*. . . . . K×B　*2*. Kt—K5 ch, etc.
This idea is a feature in many elegant compositions. It is also very
useful

Black

White

Bishops of opposite colour
Typical endgame position in which Black cannot win. There are
exceptional cases: e.g. place Black Pawns here on g4, h3 and a
White on h2, and Black can win

(2) Bishop and Rook's Pawn cannot win if the defending King can occupy the corner square that is not controlled by the Bishop: e.g. White KRP, and KB: Black King on h8. The Diagram (105) shows how occasionally the King can be kept out.

Black

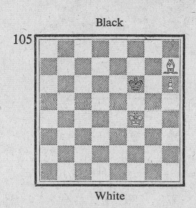

105

White

Thwarted King
A position from which the Black King cannot reach h8

(3) Knight, guarding a Pawn from in front (e.g. on e8, guarding a Pawn on d6) can prove a useless piece, if the defending King forks Kt and P and the attacking King is not in the field of play.

A Bishop guard from in front is, however, indestructible.

A Knight guarding from behind is very good, like the backward member of hanging Pawns. The King cannot capture it and then overhaul the running passed Pawn.

A Knight, be it added, can help a Rook's Pawn home where a Bishop of the wrong field fails.

(4) One point worth noticing is a Knight's defect. It cannot lose a tempo (Diagram 106). This is one of the cases where the desire to lose a move is more intense than the desire in the early game to gain one.

(5) A Rook with a Pawn *can* fail against a Bishop (107). But

Black

White

Knight cannot lose a tempo

Here Black to move loses. But White to move only draws. The Knight
moves and the King goes to f7. Now, whatever tour the Kt makes
of the board, it cannot arrive on e5 or d6, etc. without giving check.
Black will never be in *zugzwang*

Black

White

Study by del Rio

Only a draw, because the King cannot stay at g6 nor can the Bishop
be 'squeezed' so as not to be able to administer check when required

this position is exceptional. Normally that force is a winning one, and we have seen positions where the Rook, without Pawn, wins against Bishop: also exceptional. That happens when the defending King is confined to one of the four sides of the board.

This is always an important feature. So, given the right set-up, R and B can defeat R: but the 'set-up' is rare. (Diagram 108 shows the final position.)

To sum up, the pieces in the endgame do roughly what is expected of them in the light of their middle-game valuation.

The great change in value is, what the reader has already seen, the enhancement of the value of the Pawn. At the end-game stage, players can find themselves regretting their early disregard for 'cannon-fodder'.

From these facts it follows that, if a player cannot win before the endgame, he has to control his play so that the endgame will

Black

108

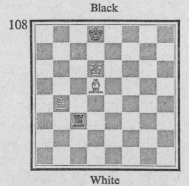

White

R and B *v.* R

In this position, arrived at by subtle manoeuvring, the process is easy

    *1.* B—B4  K—B1

    2. B—K6 ch, etc.

not be unfavourable. He must keep, at least, an endgame draw in hand.

This brings into Tactical Chess coefficients of technique and of strategy. Always consider the possible 'shape of the game', the final Pawn structure. Everything about 'isolated', 'backward', 'doubled', 'hanging', 'remote', etc., Pawns is relevant. On these features, decisions may have to be made quite early. It is in the style of some players to be obsessed with them from the beginning. And they are not wrong.

## CHAPTER THREE

# HOW BATTLES ARE WON – OR LOST
# SEEING, THINKING, JUDGING
# TACTICS AND STRATEGY
# SOME ILLUSTRATIVE GAMES

GAMES can be won, drawn, or lost, by accident. Pieces aimlessly moved produce haphazard results. Even good purposive play can be marred by blunders, involving the one who has played better on the whole in mate, or material loss (Diagram 109). Contrast this oversight with the inferior play that so often

Black

White

Error

Having gained material advantage, White relaxes and invites exchange of Queen with Q - Q3. The answer R × Kt ch, wins for Black. Yet the player of White is a person who knows all about decoys and the undermining of supports

occurs in bad positions. That is the time when good play is vital (Diagram 110). In high-class play games are less likely to be

Black

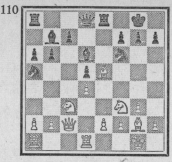

White

Error when good play vital

*14.* Q—B5

White is threatening to break up Black's King's side with B×Kt
followed by Queen exchanges and Kt–R4

*14.* .... B—QB1

*15.* Q—Kt5   P—KR3 overlooking

*16.* B×Kt winning at least a Pawn

Black, in difficulties, did not see the saving resource beginning

*14.* .... Kt—K5

lost by short-range decisions. Good players lose by excess
of effort – 'vaulting ambition o'erleaps itself' – or by impatience
in good positions – or relaxing when there is still work to be
done. (Nothing is harder than the winning of some 'won
games'.) Conduct of this type detracts from the scientific nature
of the game. But, in general, Chess differs from games of chance
in that the player who sees farther and more widely, accurately,
subtly, than his opponent, and controls his pieces within the
limits, or not too far beyond the limits, of his vision will win in
the majority of cases. Alternatively, the player who sees less
than the difficulties of the position require him to see, loses
against an opponent whose vision is adequate.

One of the tasks of Chess is the psycho-physical task of
always doing one's best. Here is an example of bad play by a
very good player against a better one: Vidmar losing to Capa-

blança at London in 1922. Let it be said, in passing, that the advantage of Chess is that everybody with a board and men and/or a knowledge of the moves, can follow master-play, and can aim at emulating Capablanca by making mental efforts in the right direction. Not many succeed, but at least one plunges early into the real depths and attempts the strong strokes of master-play, and in that way swims eventually, instead of merely paddling in a pool.

Here (Diagram 111) it requires no very strong effort to see how Vidmar goes wrong. *11. ....* P—QKt3 was badly played,

Black (Vidmar)

111

White (Capablanca)

(Played, London, 1922)

Failure of short-range vision

Here Vidmar played *11. ....* P—QKt3. A bad move because, after *12.* Kt × Kt, Black is forced to capture with the Bishop's Pawn. If *12. ....* KP × Kt, B, B—Q3 wins either KRP or QBP. Therefore *12. ....* BP × Kt (see next diagram)

because White can clear the Bishop's file for an incursion. After *12.* Kt × Kt Black cannot reply KP × Kt, because then *13.* B—Q3 forces the loss either of the KRP or the QBP. Therefore BP × P must be played. Comes *13.* B—Q3 and the KRP must be defended or moved. Then the White Queen moves to QB7, severely restricting the development of Black's pieces.

The play went as indicated, and after *13. .... P—KR3* White played *14. Q—B7* (Diagram 112). At this point Black might save himself by *14. .... Q—Q1* inaugurating a difficult

Black (Vidmar)

112

White (Capablanca)

After *12. .... BP×Kt  13. B—Q3  P—KR3*
*14. Q—B7  Q—Kt5  15. P—QR3*

Black's 14th was an error.
The only saving move was Q—Q1, after which

*15. B—Kt5  P—QR3*
*16. Q×Q  R×Q*
*17. B—B6  R—R2*

leaves Black with a defence. If, instead, white plays

*15. Q×Q  R×Q  16. R—B7, Kt—B3 or B1 or Kt1*

with a B move to follow. But Black's bid for freedom with Q—Kt5 fails

wriggle. If *15. B—Kt5  P—QR3. 16. Q×Q  R×Q. 17. B—B6 R—R2*, or *15. Q×Q  R×Q. 16. R—B7  Kt—B3 (or Kt1 or B1)* permits mobilization under pressure. But, once again, bad play when in difficulties. Vidmar preferred a dash for freedom with *14. ... Q—Kt5*, perhaps expecting White to play P—QKt3. Instead White played *15. P—QR3*, having seen (and perhaps Black had also seen it though less vividly) that *15. .... Q×KtP* loses.

Thus if *15.* ....                    Q × KtP
   *16.* R — QKt1                  Q × RP
   *17.* B — Kt5                   Q — K2

Observe that *17.* .... Kt — B3 causes the loss of the Queen by *18.* R — R1 followed by KR — Kt1. This is a typical alternative variation that has to be seen, and excluded from possibility, when the defender is making a decision.

So Black is compelled to *17.* .... Q — K2 in this line, and there would follow

   *18.* B — B6                    R — Kt1
   *19.* Kt — K5                   Q — Q1
   *20.* Q × RP                    Kt × Kt
   *21.* P × Kt (and Black has to lose his Rook or Bishop)

In this variation

   *19.* ....                     R — Q1 also fails because of
   *20.* B × Kt                    B × B
   *21.* Kt — B6 (forking, and uncapturable because of the
          pin)

So Black sees, at move 15, what White probably saw earlier, that Q × KtP is unplayable.

Therefore Vidmar played *15.* .... Q — R5 and was left with a very inferior position. There followed *16.* P — R3 (White has now time to give outlet to his King and to restrict Black's Knight).

   *16.* ....                     Kt — B3
   *17.* Kt — K5                   B — Q2
   *18.* B — B2                    Q — Kt4
   *19.* P — QR4 (observe the pressure on a piece that is
          guarding another from an awkward angle)
   *19.* ....                     Q × KtP

and now *20.* R — Kt1   Q — R7. *21.* B — Kt3 would enable White to win the Bishop at leisure.

Instead Homer nodded. White played, too quickly, Kt×B. Black now has the resource *20. . . . .* QR—B1 and if White plays Kt×Kt ch, and checks at Kt3, he still loses the Bishop at QB2.

White played

*21.* Q—Kt7 and there followed
*21.* . . . .                    Kt×Kt
*22.* B—R7 ch (unmasking a battery)
*22.* . . . .                    K×B
*23.* R×R                        R×R
*24.* Q×R and White won the exchange instead of a complete piece. It was, however, sufficient to give Capablanca victory

That example is typical of the Chess task. See: and make your moves purposive in the light of what you see.

A player may not be good enough, especially with good opposition, to find ways of obtaining advantage, or to wrest victory from advantage gained. The board has its resources, its margin of draw. But if he fails to gain the gainable, or win the winnable, the failure will be due to his own limitations; for in Chess one is playing against the limit of one's own capacity to see and to control. The player who plans correctly so as to cope with all possible variations (where the game allows it) is great indeed. But, to a degree, everyone who is really playing Chess – and not merely wood-shifting – is aiming at that ideal. To a degree one attains it in good wins, and good defences. The good player will win, moreover, without his opponent having committed any gross error, any failure to see the reasonably obvious. The slightly inferior player, who exists even at the highest levels of Chess, does not blunder, but gives his opponent chances of victory by playing with less than perfect co-ordination of forces. Then the skill that produces victory is the ability to gain what advantage can be gained, and to exploit it. The intellectual aspect of this is the clear seeing of variations – tactical lines of play – clear thinking about the ultimate shape

of the game (strategic aspects), even while the skirmishing is in
progress; and sound judgement in the innumerable positions
where a complete perspective or, as Chess-players say, a complete analysis, seems too difficult to achieve. The mind which
has the best apprehension usually makes the best decisions: i.e.
makes better, rather than worse, moves. At all levels of Chess
the apprehending and making of good moves is the way to
victory. (Good moves, not good positions, do the winning.)
Further, the reader will find, as he improves, that the only
victories which give him satisfaction are those in which his
vision gave him a control which he exploited. Good lines of
play forced a win. He will also enjoy lesser results than victory:
will enjoy draws, and even losses, if an opponent has skilfully
exploited some decision that was not a blunder, yet gave
the exploiter a chance. At that stage Chess, though not completely predictable, ceases to be a game of chance. Don't be
depressed by occasional blunders. They happen at the very highest
levels. E.g. at an Interzonal Tournament in 1961, Olafson left
a piece *en prise*. And Keres, a great player, committed the
following blunder – under fatigue. In the position 2r1r1k1,
5p1p, 6p1, 8, 3P2Q1, 2b3P1, q3BP1P, 3R1K1R, he played
(against Fischer) B—Kt5, allowing Q—Q4, forking B and
R. Don't make similar blunders by way of claim to grand-
mastery!

'But how many moves must I see ahead?' asks the novice.
The question is rather like: 'How long is a piece of string?'
You may only be called upon to see that a piece or Pawn can be
recaptured; or you may have to look down a long avenue of
moves: capture, recapture: threat, defence, further threat: etc.,
etc., and from every sequent move a long variation branch-
ing off. When that great virtuoso of Chess, Capablanca, said
that all you need to see is the next move, he omitted to
add to his epigram the thought that there very rarely exists a
'next move'. Was Capablanca's P—QR3 against Vidmar a
'next move'? Rather, the next move is an end-product of a
vision ranging far beyond the next move, in order to

ascertain that what is going to be done is a good move – i.e. the relative best.

Indeed moves tend to be seen in groups, or series, not as isolates. (That is why players often miss the nearer while seeing the farther.) Diagram 113 shows a typical endgame position in

Black (Uhlmann)

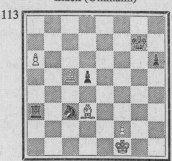

White (Golombek)

(Hastings, 1959–60)

'One Move'

*47.* P—R7 wins because after the threatened check at B7, the Pawn is forced home. If the King goes to its 3rd rank R—B6 ch followed by R—R6 wins. If K to B1, etc., R—B8 ch wins

which the move made is a small technical 'complex' in itself. The Pawn cannot be captured without loss of the Knight and its threat is otherwise unanswerable. Black cannot prevent *48.* R—B7 ch. If the King moves to the back rank, R—B8 ch ensures the promotion. If the King goes to its 3rd rank, R—B6 ch followed by R—QR6 ensure Pawn promotion.

That particular manœuvre, checking and intervening between a Pawn and a controlling, or defending, Rook, can be called 'a possibility that one has to see'. If one does not see 'the complex' one does not really see 'the move'. Incidentally, this is not the easiest of manœuvres for the learner to have always in mind. But

it is typical of 'things to be aware of'. Be expectant of the unexpected. Not the least of Chess difficulties is to be aware that
there is something to look for, something that makes the next
move less easy to select than the first glance suggests.

'Be aware.' (Or 'Beware'.)

That this precept is easier to state than to follow is evidenced
by the oversight of a very fine player indeed, David Yanofsky,
in play, at Stockholm in 1962, against the remarkable South
American, Bolbochan.

In the diagram position (114) White seems to have lost a

Black (Bolbochan)

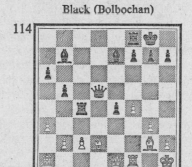

White (Yanofsky)
(Stockholm, 1962)

Surprise:
```
21. B—QB3    Q—KB4
22. R—Q1     B—KB3
23. B×B      R×P!
```

little tempo, and has problems of development to solve, while
his opponent is dynamically developed with scope for further
development. Black is threatening to capture a Pawn, and the
safe appearing defence, 21. P—B3 involves strategic disadvantages, as that the White squares in White's field are weakened,
and the scope for the Black-squared Bishop is also a trifle

restricted. Not fatal defects these, but to be avoided if possible.
Yanofsky had a good deal to analyse in respect of a possible
Pawn sacrifice by *21*. R—Q1   R×P. *22*. B—B3   Q—KB4 after
which White has no good attacking line, though there are some
*ignes fatui*.

Having to defend the Pawn, then, he elects the good-looking
developing move *21*. QB—B3 to which Black replies Q—KB4.
This move is making possible B—KB3: but White sees no
terror in this, and plays *22*. R—Q1, which, after B—KB3
B×B   Q×B   P—B3, would leave him with some control of the
only open file. Had he seen the shape of things to come, he
would probably have played *22*. Q—K2.

However, *22*. R—Q1   B—KB3 and there is a threat to leave
White with doubled Pawns at c2 and 3, under heavy attack
from Rooks. White was probably unalarmed by B—B3, because
there is no evident surprise in it. He knows that Black is not
allowing the White Rook to go to d7 and stay there, because
B—B3 will drive it away. So he plays *23*. B×B expecting
Q×B, which is to be met by *24*. P—B3. Instead, the wicked
Bolbochan ignores the Bishop, and plays *23*. .... R×P! This
cold-bloodedly wins a Pawn. If White tries to keep his Bishop
with, e.g. *24*. B—B3, there follows *24*. .... R×KB. If then
*25*. K×R (and what else is there? Q—K3 is met by Q—R6)
*25*. .... P—K6 ch. *26*. R—B3 (if K—Kt1   Q—K5) *26*. ....
Q—B7 ch. *27*. B—Q2   R—Q1 and everything falls. Naturally,
White saw this when Rook took Pawn, and did not retract
the Bishop. He played R—B2, and after exchanges (R×R,
Q×R   Q×B) he was left with a Pawn deficit for which he
had no compensation. (He might, later, have saved the
game.)

White, who is capable of seeing fine ideas, failed to see the
quite short-range sacrifice, because his mind was not on the
weaknesses of his own position. But, let it be said, this was hard
to see by master standards.

The position is further of interest because it illustrates some
technical strategic points. Notice the dynamic Pawn at e4; and
consider that this would have been less effective had it been

'blockaded' at an earlier stage by, for example, a Bishop. The advance of the Pawn not only opens a battery against the King, but gives an open line to the Black Queen. Those are the features of the position that make Black's attack possible. But logic explains: it does not enable one to see. What White missed was Black's ability not to recapture the Bishop automatically (which would also be a logical process!). White was not compelled, at move *22*, to play R—Q1. Had he played *22*. Q—K2, he would have been relatively safe from harm: and would be threatening P—KKt4 with quite an attack. (Prosaically, in a position like this many players would play *22*. Q—K2 without having seen the possibility of the quite brilliant sacrifice they are preventing.)

In every game of Chess there are stages at which one seems to have a choice of several moves, several lines of play. At others one is aware that moves are forced. If the voluntary decisions are inferior to those of the opponent, then the weaker player (or, as in the last instance, the one who is seeing less at the time) will suddenly find himself involved in a series of moves, in which each of his answers is forced. Suddenly he will find that

Black (Haida)

115

White (Marshall)
(Marienbad, 1925)
Forcing Process
After *12*. .... P—QR3  *13*. P×P  P×P. *14*. P—Q5! (see text for
the attack that follows Kt×P)

he has to terminate check, to recapture something, to retreat from attack, to avoid a fork, to abandon some line of defence that he now sees to be inadequate, while the adversary improving his position with each threat, captures some significant material, or brings about mate.

So Marshall's opponent in the position shown in Diagram 115 found himself flying through the air on his opponent's trapeze.

After *12. ....* P—QR3, made by an opponent who expected *13.* P—K5, Marshall alters the position completely with

| | |
|---|---|
| *13.* P×P | P×P |
| *14.* P—Q5 | Kt×P (If he can't do this his game is hopeless) |
| *15.* B—B4 | Q—Kt3 ch |

The check is irrelevant and White has an additional target now

| | |
|---|---|
| *16.* K—R1 | B—K3 |
| *17.* QR—Kt1 | Q—B2 |
| *18.* Kt—Kt3 | .... Marshall is acting on the principle that if you give him two Pawns you can give him three. This developing move during an attack, and doubtless seen in advance with its consequences, gives one to realize how very far and in what detail a fine combinative player can see ahead. |
| *18.* .... | Kt×KBP |

*19.* B×B ch (An attack must be able to survive exchanges)

| 19. .... | Kt × B |
| 20. Q—Q5 | QKt—Q1 |
| 21. KKt—Q4 | R—B3 |
| 22. R—K1 | Q—B1 |
| 23. Kt × Kt | Kt × Kt |

24. Kt—Q4 (White had to see, earlier, that the Black Queen cannot now play to QB4 because of Q × KtP)

24. ....          K—B2 (The last support)

| 25. R × P | Q—B4 |

26. R × B ch     .... (The breakthrough comes at an unexpected place)

| 26. .... | K × R |
| 27. Q—Kt7 ch | K—B1 |
| 28. Q × R ch | K—B2 |
| 29. Q—Kt7 ch | K—Kt3 |

30. Kt × Kt (winning a second piece and the game)

Marshall, by good development, ignoring a Pawn or two, created a situation which left many processes available to him. He saw an opportunity of a kind that few would have seen, because the direction was different from the obvious one.

Each player, therefore, must always be scanning the board to see what opportunities can develop, for himself or his opponent, from anywhere, for pieces to become co-ordinated in some threat, or series of threats. The learner, who was made aware in the last chapter of the functions of dynamic pieces, has now moved into a realm where he has to see, and suffer, co-ordination of many functions in tactical operations. From being aware of Chess phrases, he is now being aided to understand the Chess dialogue – the argument between sets of pieces.

No better introduction can be made to this than the analysis of a famous game – a game played over a century ago by one of the great geniuses of Chess, Paul Morphy. Without this game no introductory Chess book would be complete. Morphy's games are perennials of Chess, because, beneath the brilliant surface of tactics, later experts, such as Steinitz, have discerned important principles of development and strategy.

| White | Black |
|---|---|
| PAUL MORPHY | DUKE OF BRUNSWICK |
| *1.* P—K4 | P—K4 |
| 2. Kt—KB3 | P—Q3 |

Black's second move, introducing Philidor's Defence (named after a famous Musician–Chess-player of the eighteenth century), is quite sound, but needs to be more precisely followed up than would such a move as *2.* .... Kt—QB3.

> *3.* P—Q4

Already aggression. The threat (i.e. something that can be done if it is allowed) is (if *3.* .... Kt—QB3) to exchange the Pawns, and then exchange Queens, leaving Black unable to castle.

| *3.* .... | B—Kt5 |
|---|---|

This 'pin' is not a good pin. Strategically, Black is counter-attacking before he has any development, and he is unguarding a weak place on his Queen's side. Tactically he is quickly put under pressure – and loses tempo, and the minor exchange, at an early stage. Correct was *3.* .... Kt—Q2, allowing a Pawn recapture without exchange of Queens. To play *3.* .... P×P would give White control of the centre squares – a slight advantage, not a winning one.

| 4. P×P | B×Kt |
|---|---|

The element of 'force' is now being made manifest. If *4.* .... P×P White exchanges Queens and captures the King's Pawn with the unpinned Knight. Black's only alternative was *4.* .... Q—K2 with a cramped game (the Queen clogs the KB. As it happens, that cramp occurs later).

| 5. Q×B | P×P |
|---|---|
| 6. B—B4 ('developing' and, incidentally, threatening mate) | |

6. ....                          Kt—KB3

Stopping the mate, and developing a piece. An alternative was
6. .... Q—B3. Then, after 7. Q—QKt3  Kt—QB3, White can
win the QKtP, and it is doubtful whether Black can generate a
compensating counter-attack.

7. Q—QKt3 renewing the attack on the KBP,
           and attacking the QKtP (a typical double
           threat).

7. ....                          Q—K2

A good example of a forced restriction in development. The
only other move to guard the KBP is Q—Q2. After that White's
Q×QKtP would win the QR (if 8. .... Q—B3. 9. B—QKt5
wins the Q).

8. Kt—QB3, showing that Black's 7th was not inadequate.
If White were to capture the QKtP, Black, with Q—Kt5 ch,
would force exchanges, and obtain freedom at the cost of a
Pawn.

8. .... P—B3

This seems to hold everything; but Black is cramped, and has
problems of development.

9. B—KKt5

This develops White and cramps Black further. Thus it prevents P—KKt3, and threatens, *inter alia*, an exchange with
strategic consequences. If e.g. Black plays 9. .... P—KR3,
there could follow 10. B×Kt. The P must recapture. White can
then, at his leisure, bring his Kt via K2 and Kt3 to KB5 where
its effect is paralysing. (That would be an instance of the
achievement of a clear strategic advantage.) Black accordingly
makes an effort for freedom; which fails because White's
attack is already well co-ordinated, and Black's resources
unmobilized. Observe that all White's minor pieces are in play,
and the Rooks are ready for action. Black, on the other hand,
cannot begin to get castled. At this point Black seems to
have nothing better than a wriggle like Q—B2 – after which
B—K2 will still not be playable. 9. .... Kt—QR3 is also to

be considered. Then *10.* Kt—Q5 just fails: but B×QKt leaves Black with a lost endgame.

    *9.* ....               P—QKt4

Desperate, and only refuted by a neat forcing process, which the Duke had probably not anticipated.

    *10.* Kt×P             P×Kt
    *11.* B×Kt P ch      QKtQ2
    *12.* O—O—O

Observe how, when a game is well developed, the further developing moves become attacking moves.

    *12.* ....              R—Q1

Forced, in the sense that no other move guards the Knight (e.g. if *12.* .... Q—K3. *13.* B×KKt, etc.)

    *13.* R×Kt

The loss of the exchange does not matter, because another unit is being mobilized.

    *13.* ....              R×R
    *14.* R—Q1

Now there is such a pressure that there is no defence. The pinned Rook cannot be further defended by pieces less than the Queen and King.

    *14* ....              Q—K3

This is no defence, because with B×KKt, White can win the Rook. Instead Morphy finishes the game with a couple of moves calculated to demonstrate that the beautiful can be useful.

    *15.* B×R ch        Kt×B
    *16.* Q—Kt8 ch (a delightful surprise. Sacrifices on
              empty squares are harder to see than sacrifi-
              cial captures).
    *16.* ....              Kt×Q
    *17.* R—Q8 mate

Appropriately played, to the music of Rossini, in the Duke's box at the opera, this game illustrates how, given bad tactics and/or bad strategy on the part of an opponent, a good player 'forces', first a cramp, and, then, when occasion offers, an exploitation of the cramped position by co-ordination of his own 'free' pieces on their open lines. Here great accuracy is needed, lest the attempted exploitation afford a cheap release from pressure.

Not all well-won games are as clear-cut as this example. But in every game the possibilities of co-ordination to a destructive end have to be seen. There are few positions indeed in which dangers do not lurk.

Here is something quite elementary.

>  *1.* P—Q4                    P—KKt3

A defence older than the Urals, but given the modern name of Kotov-Robatsch.* Its only merit is that White may well try to exploit it more vigorously than wisely.

>  *2.* P—K4                     B—Kt2
>  *3.* B—QB4                    Kt—KB3

At this point, is not *4.* Q—B3 tempting? The threat is P—K5. So if *4.* . . . . P—Q3.

>  *5.* P—K5                     P×P
>  *6.* P×P and the Knight seems to be lost. But
>  have you noticed
>  *6.* . . . .                  B—KKt5?

If you now try a Morphy *7.* Q—QKt3, it is you, not the Duke, that is mated with *7.* . . . . Q—Q8. And if *7.* P×Kt, hoping to obtain three pieces for a Queen, *7.* . . . . B×Q stops the capture at g7, because Mate is threatened.

---

* It has been called 'The Rubbish Defence' by those who like to mispronounce. I prefer 'The Rabbit's Defence'. I am inspired to this by memory of that excellent player, the late R. C. J. Walker, who played P—KKt3 for half a century, and once said: 'I'm a rabbit: so I make a hole for myself.' May I add that I have met few players less rabbit-like in action.

So, at a very early stage, one sees, by the light of nature, a co-ordination of forces that can be disastrous.

This last example is useful in the consideration of what is meant by 'giving chances' and 'blundering'. Most players above the novice class would regard a failure to see a point like that as too gross an error to make the winner's victory meritorious. *4.* Q—B3 would be a bad error. *7.* Q—QKt3, a gross blunder. But adjectives and pejorative nouns are not very helpful.

The test is not the length of vision, but the easiness, or difficulty, to the ordinary view; and 'ordinary' is a word fairly easy to apply, though impossible to define. (There must e.g. be some allowance for class – for the strength of the players amongst whom one is playing.)

It cannot be said Yanofsky blundered in the position shown in Diagram 114. He missed something that he could have seen had his concentration been at its best. What he missed was very easy indeed to miss: indeed, hard to see. Hence its merit. On the other hand, Vidmar would undoubtedly have described his P—QKt3 as a blunder. His later move Q—Kt5 was also not good – a bad choice in a difficult position: inferior play, not so gross as a blunder. Vidmar would also have regretted that, in view of his desire to play P—QKt3, he omitted an early P—KR3, when it would have lost no tempo. Suffice it to say that Capablanca won many games against stronger resistance than Vidmar produced in the example shown.

In point is a fine winning movement by Capablanca against a redoubtable opponent, Spielmann, who was himself celebrated for clever sacrifices (Diagram 116). Before the diagram position was reached Capablanca had probably seen everything that could happen. Otherwise he would not so have restricted his Queen.

His last move was *17.* P—QR4 and Spielmann thought himself prepared for this, and played Q (from K3) – Q4. But instead of retracting the Bishop, either to B4, or via K7, so as to allow Black time for B—Kt2, Capablanca played, immediately, *18.* P×P: and now Black has nothing better than Q×B. There followed

Black (Spielmann)

White (Capablanca)
(New York, 1914)
*18.* P×P! wins (see text)

*19.* B×P (The B sacrifice was a decoy. One function
of the Queen was to guard that important
square)

| | |
|---|---|
| *19.* . . . . | R—Kt1 |

One clever feature of the play is the variation

| | |
|---|---|
| *19.* . . . . | R—R2 |
| *20.* P—Kt6! | Q×Q |
| *21.* P×R | Q×R |
| *22.* R×Q | Kt—Kt3 |
| *23.* R—Kt1 (and Black, at the moment a piece to | |

the good, is losing more than one piece)

The actual game continued:
after

| | |
|---|---|
| *19.* . . . . | R—Kt1 |
| *20.* P×P (The attack is now so good that White | |

can allow Queens to be exchanged if Black
wishes)

| | |
|---|---|
| *20.* . . . . | R—Kt4 |
| *21.* Q—B7 | Kt—Kt3 |
| *22.* P—R7 | B—R6 |

| | |
|---|---|
| *23.* KR—Kt1 | R×R ch |
| *24.* R×R | P—B4 |
| *25.* B—B3 | P—B5 |
| *26.* P×P resigns | |

The Knight must fall. If e.g. –

| | |
|---|---|
| *26.* .... | Kt—R1 |
| *27.* B×Kt | R×B |
| *28.* R—Kt8 ch, etc. | |

Here Capablanca saw a long way; but it is important to notice that his mental sweep was complete over all the variations. That 'sweep' is at least as necessary a capacity as long view. Sometimes a player approaching an endgame can, by counting Pawn moves, etc., find himself seeing more than 20 moves ahead. That can be easier than the exhausting of a set of short-range variations in a subtle opening, middle game, or endgame.

To revert to the diagram position, it is not unlikely that Spielmann, when he played Q—Q4 (or when he anticipated it), saw the possibility of P×P. He probably 'judged' that Capablanca was not getting enough value for his Bishop. Alternatively, as Black was, at that stage, slightly under pressure, he may have decided to force his opponent to a sacrifice, himself hoping for the best. The essence of the matter is that Capablanca's view was exhaustive. The position allowed a complete conspectus, and he achieved it. (Capablanca, it may be added, resembled Morphy in his flair for exploitation of anything short of the best possible 'development'.)

In practice a surprisingly large number of games are won by quite short-range failures of vision on the part of good players, because they are so much involved with long variations. The better type of win and loss is when the oversight is of a fine point arising after many moves ahead. It may well be overlooked by both players; but the one whose general control has been better is the more likely to benefit from it.

Strictly speaking that introduces elements of guesswork, and chance, into the game. Those elements are small in proportion to the vast amount of certainty that the good player apprehends. But fine players do take chances in this way. They finish an analysis, not sure of the outcome of some sub-variations: but, seeing what they do of the position that will then exist, they *judge* that there *should* be available some convincing continuation, some difficulty added to the problems of the opponent.

Thus we have it on the authority of Jonathan Penrose that when he sacrificed a Rook against Popov in the diagram position (117) he had not seen all the variations beforehand, but

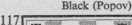

Black (Popov)

White (Penrose)
(Enschede, 1963)

A combinative attack
23. R × P! (see text)

felt sure that a draw was possible if things went wrong. Black has just played 22. .... Q(Kt5)—R5. By not retreating to K2, he suggests that he *had not seen*, rather than had misjudged, the ensuing sacrifice.

23. R × P          K × R

There is no alternative. Some offers are rebutted by their refusal: not this.

24. Q—Kt4 ch      K—R1
25. Q—R4           P—B4

(K—Kt2 would not save the Pawn, because of Q—B6 ch).

26. P × P ep.        R—B2

Against even the strongest attack there is usually available some defensive manœuvring.

| | | |
|---|---|---|
| 27. | Q × P ch | K — Kt1 |
| 28. | Q — Kt6 ch | K — B1 |
| 29. | Q — R6 ch | K — Kt1 |

Knowing that Black cannot play to K1 (because of Q — R8 ch followed by B — Kt6 ch), White gains a little time on his clock by the repetition.

| | | |
|---|---|---|
| 30. | Q — Kt5 ch | K — B1 |
| 31. | B — Kt6 | |

If White had played again *31.* Q — R6 ch then Black could claim a draw by repetition. White's checks have won tempo on the board: e.g. – the Bishop move.

| | | |
|---|---|---|
| 31. | .... | P — K4 |

Attempting to make an air-vent. No other advantage can be taken of the non-check.

The subsequent King chase was seen ahead, but there were some avenues along which the visibility was not clear.

| | | |
|---|---|---|
| 32. | Q — R6 ch | K — Kt1 |
| 33. | B × R ch | K × R |
| 34. | Q — Kt7 ch | K — K3 |
| 35. | Q — K7 ch | K — Q4 |

(If *35.* .... K — B4, *36.* Q × P ch then drives the K round the mulberry bush, and when it comes back to K3, it is checked by the Rook.)

| | | |
|---|---|---|
| 36. | Q × P ch | K — B5 |
| 37. | R — B1 ch | K — Kt6 |
| 38. | Q — B3 ch | K — R7 |
| 39. | P — QKt4 | resigns |

His King's position is farcical. This guess at a favourable finish is typical of the judgement exercised by an attacker: and similar judgement is exercised when a player, for material consideration, submits to an attack, and sees ahead of him the defensive lines of play corresponding to the choices of attack available to his opponent. He will not miss the 'cleverness': and he will take

for granted the defensibility of the position where no tactical
resource seems to be left to the other.

In practice, good players miss less in the long reaches than
they do in comparatively short range. The difference is ac-
counted for psychologically. In long variations one is aware,
expectant – even of the unexpected.

Something in the short range (not hard to see, unless one
looks with blinkered eyes), was what the great master Reuben
Fine missed, in play against Judovitch.

Black (Judovitch)

118

White (Fine)
White loses unexpectedly
9. .... Q×Kt (see text)

The opening moves were: *1.* P—Q4  P—Q4. *2.* P—QB4
P—K3. *3.* Kt—QB3  Kt—KB3. *4.* Kt—B3  P—B4 (a form of
Tarrasch Defence). *5.* B—Kt5  P×QP. *6.* Kt×P (d4) P—K4.
*7.* Kt(d4)—Kt5 (relying on a line of play that he took for
granted). *7.* .... P—QR3. *8.* Kt×P  P×Kt (b5). *9.* Kt×Kt ch.
Now, instead of making the 'obvious' recapture with the Pawn,
Judovitch recaptured with the Queen. *9.* .... Q×Kt. There
followed *10.* B×Q  B—Kt5 ch, winning the White Queen, after
which P×B, with an easy win. This is a short-range cleverness.
Fine would probably have described himself as blundering,
though others would disagree. It is of interest to observe that a
similar idea is made familiar to all who learn the Queen's
Gambit Declined.

| | |
|---|---|
| *1.* P—Q4 | P—Q4 |
| *2.* P—QB4 | P—K3 |
| *3.* Kt—QB3 | Kt—KB3 |
| *4.* B—Kt5 | QKt—Q2 |

Now why not

| | |
|---|---|
| *5.* P×P | P×P |
| *6.* Kt×P relying on the pin of the Knight? | |
| Because the pin is illusory. | |
| *6.* ...... ............ | Kt×Kt |
| *7.* B×Q | B—Kt5 ch |

capturing the Queen, and later the Bishop.

Evidently one is not always aware of what one should be aware of. Let it be added that Grandmaster Reuben Fine made very few oversights. The position cited was a rare case of his reliance on 'the book' – which all too frequently is wrong.

The position quoted is additionally valuable as an example of the consequences of 'sharp' opening play. That was a characteristic feature of wins and losses in the days when King's Gambit and Evans Gambit were combatively played. But 'sharp' play, after a period of solid play, returned to Chess in the late 1930's, and is still very frequent at the highest levels.

Now let us supplement the Morphy game with something a century nearer, between fine masters of the game. This game has different tactical features from the older game but that has nothing to do with 'period'. The play is quite 'sharp' at an early stage.

Observe, at the outset, that this win is by Black, whereas Morphy's win was with White. It must never be assumed that White holds real advantage. (An initiative is not an advantage, though it is not undesirable. More will be said about this in the chapter on Openings.)

Note also that whereas Morphy's win was the exploitation of a cramped game, this is the exploitation of a loose game, with pieces 'hanging' insecurely.

| White | Black |
|---|---|

(Played at Dallas in 1957)

| SZABO | OLAFSSON |
|---|---|
| *1.* P—Q4 | Kt—KB3 |
| *2.* P—QB4 | P—KKt3 |
| *3.* P—KKt3 | B—Kt2 |
| *4.* B—Kt2 | |

So far a King's Indian Defence on Black's part, in which, normally, White establishes a strong appearing Pawn centre, and Black plays in an effort ultimately to undermine it. But Black's next move is an attempt, inspired in the Queen's Pawn openings by Grunfeld, to weaken White's centre by occasioning its premature expansion.

| *4.* .... | P—Q4 |
|---|---|
| *5.* P×P | Kt×P |
| *6.* P—K4 | |

Perhaps (in conjunction with the last move) a bad strategic decision. Tactically it is hard for White (even with the aid of the midnight oil used on this opening) to work out all the lines of play. 'Sound' is *6.* Kt—KB3. The text is too 'committal'.

> *6.* .... Kt—Kt5 (Very quickly a forcing process)
> (Diagram 119.)

Observe that the QP, as it stands, is decisively attacked. If White defends it with e.g. Kt—KB3, or B—K3, Black plays *7.* .... B×P and on the recapture, plays *8.* .... Q×B or Kt (as the case may be). Then *9.* Q×Q is met by Kt—B7 ch. So White is committed to an advance.

The alternative course is *7.* P—QR3. To this Black could reply with *7.* .... B×P. After *8.* P×Kt B×P ch. *9.* K—K2 Q×Q ch. *10.* K×Q Kt—B3, Black will probably have three Pawns and the attack in exchange for a piece. The outcome is speculative.

G

Black (Olafsson)

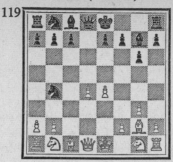

White (Szabo)
(Dallas, 1957)

Serious attack on a Pawn

The threat of 7. .... B×P is not met by K Kt—B3, because then

| 7. .... | B×P |
| 8. Kt×B | Q×B |
| 9. Q×Q | Kt—B7 ch, regains the Queen. |

7. P—Q5 (Safer, strategically, than P—QR3)
7. ...... P—QB3

Pressure on a weak point. One threat is simply to exchange Pawns and develop the QB on KB4, attacking QB7.

8. Kt—K2

Of other moves, 8. P×P Q×Q ch, and White's development is ruined. 8. P—QR3 would be met by Q—R4, after which 9. B—Q2 is ineffective, because of Kt—Q6 ch, and Q—R3. Also 8. Kt—QB3 could be met by Q—R4. Then P×QP Kt×P gives Black a superior development. The move played aims at safety for the King.

| 8. .... | P×P |
| 9. P×P | B—B4 |

(Threatening checks at QB7 and Q6. If e.g.

| 10. Kt—QR3 | Kt—Q6 ch |
| 11. K—B1 | Kt×KtP |

or (probably better) *11*. .... Q—Kt3.

White has relied on his next move as a 'saver'. But he may have had a better move).

*10*. Q—R4 ch

(To be considered was *10*. O—O. If then Kt—B7.

*11*. P—KKt4, a very interesting 'decoy'. After *11*. .... Kt×R.

*12*. P×B the Knight at White's QR1 seems to be unrescuable. However, Black is not committed. After *10*. O—O, Black can Castle, and meet P—Q6 with Kt—QB3, with a good game.

The text is too 'sharp'.)

|   | | |
|---|---|---|
| *10*. .... | | QKt—B3 |

producing a tactically rich situation. Observe that this Knight cannot be captured on the move, because of the check at White's QB2 and imminent mate.

*11*. O—O. Strangely there is no way of at once guarding the QP and securing safety for the White King. But the QP is not lost.

*11*. .... B—B7. (If Kt—B7, *12*. P—KKt4 works out well for White. If *11*. .... Kt×P. *12*. .... R—Q1 or Q—Kt5.)

*12*. Q—R3. If, instead, Q—Kt5 the Queen can be harried with either P—QR3 or BQ6. In either case Q×KtP, met by R—QKt1, loses the Queen (after P×Kt) for Rook, minor piece and Pawn (not a bad Pawn).

*12*. .... Kt×QP. A capture not without difficult consequences. At this point Black has to see quite long variations, and a big range of them.

*13*. Q—B5 (attacking two pieces)
*13*. ....                    B×Kt
*14*. B×Kt (retaining some attack)

(*14*. R×B would have allowed P—K3. White would have some attack with Kt—B3 or R—Q1. In some variations Black plays Q—Kt3 and manages to escape with his surplus Pawn.)

*14.* ....                              B—B4

*15.* B—Kt5. The recapture of the Pawn by B×Kt ch, etc.,
leaves Black Bishops in command of the board.

*15.* ....                              R—QB1

(If now *15.* .... O—O? *16.* B×Kt  P×B)

*17.* B×KP with gain of exchange.
*16.* KR—K1 creating a 'masked battery'.

Black cannot now play Kt—Q5 because of *17.* Q×P ch
Q×Q. *18.* Kt×Kt (or B×Q) with a strong attack –

*16.* ....                              O—O

*17.* Kt—B3. White could win the KP by B×Kt followed by
Q×KP; but he loses the QKtP, and a Black Rook settles on
B7. (R on the 7th is usually a big advantage as transition is
made to the endgame.) But, in avoiding this danger, he incurs
worse – perhaps he did not appreciate Black's possibilities
ahead, at move 19.

*17.* ....                              P—KR3
*18.* B—K3

(*18.* B×P would be met by Kt×B  Q×Kt  B×Kt
White is now defending a 'hanging' Bishop on his Q5. The
White Knight at QB3 can be captured, and only the Queen will
then be on guard. That Queen can be harassed, as Black now
shows.)

*18.* ....                              Kt—R4

Unmasking his battery. Where can the Queen now go in order
to keep ward on the Bishop? If Q—Kt5  P—QR3. Therefore
White tries to find a counter-attack.

*19.* Q×RP. If now Black plays B×Kt, White, with KR—Q1
(a good *Zwischenzug*) will defend the Bishop and, by threatening
to unmask his battery with B×P ch, gives himself time to
recapture at QB3. Black, however, thwarts this.

*19.* ....                              R×Kt!

*20.* KR—Q1. The alternative B—Kt6 leads to nothing but trouble after Q×B (on Q4) threatening B—R6. Merely to capture the Rook allows Q×B, and note the attack across the empty White squares around the White King. White is now lost.

| | |
|---|---|
| *20.* .... | R—Q6 |
| *21.* R×R | B×R |
| *22.* B—Kt2 | B—R3 (Very neat) |
| *23.* B—Kt6 | Q—Q3 |

*24.* Resigns, because if *24.* B×Kt   B—Q5!

That win was brought about by skirmishing, in which Black had good terrain and plenty of resource. He outplayed his opponent, but was assisted by his opponent's decisions 'to engage the enemy' and not to disengage. That kind of decision, in a slightly unbalanced game, is what Alekhine had in mind when he said that you can't win at Chess unless your opponent gives you a chance.

It cannot be said that White made any blunder after his decision was made. For the last dozen moves of the game he was endeavouring to find the resources of a disadvantageous position. When a game is developing unfavourably against a player, it is usually the case that the opponent, if strong, will be able to cope with the most ingenious of resources. This game is typical of good Chess.

At this point the reader may be anxious to understand more clearly some of the terminology I have used in connexion with the games that he has just followed: in particular, the terms TACTICS and STRATEGY.

What are Tactics? Is there a set of tactical rules? And what is Strategy? Is there a set of strategic rules? Let the reader not be disappointed if the answer fails to show him any formula, or short cut, leading to Chess success.

First as to tactics. Tactics are the essential activity of Chess. All those 'can't captures' and 'can captures' that were shown in the previous chapters are specific instances of tactical activity: typical of the points that a player should see when the pieces are in action on the board. If you have played at all, you have, with success or otherwise, played tactics. As M. Jourdain was told about prose, you have been playing tactics all the time without knowing it. Whether you have been playing strategy all the time is not quite so easy a question.

The description of tactics is quite easy. Tactics are your ordinary manoeuvres. All the specific possibilities, all the specific impossibilities, that you see when you are aware of your pieces, result in tactical decisions, tactical action: ranging from a mere capture, recapture, or short threat, to the initiation of a long forcing process.

The subsidiary question: is there a set of tactical rules? must meet a somewhat dusty answer. There are no reliable rules, because the nature of Chess is too empirical and too complex. What happens to be an important tactical feature of one position can be quite unimportant in another, not very different, position. One simple instance illustrates this. You may find yourself handicapped in a certain position because your King has no outlet from the back line, and there are mating threats to be considered. In a not very different position your back line may not be in danger, though you have to be aware of the possibilities in your analysis.

Again, one piece may find itself guarding more than one threatened square or piece. It has a double or treble function. It has been set to watch too many vineyards. Yet, in a slightly different position the task constitutes no embarrassment: any one of the recaptures gives attacking possibilities. Or it may be the case that the apparent pressure is unreal, because e.g. of pins. So one cannot lay down rules. One can, however, illustrate. The illustration of tactical operation gives a vicarious experience which does not teach rules, but which should heighten a student's awareness of the resources of the board.

Here is an example, a position from a tournament of 1962 (Diagram 120). White could probably have saved himself by 23. R (6)—R2. If that move is made Black can reply R—Kt8 ch and this Rook cannot be captured because, after 24. R×T, Q×R ch wins the R at a2 in exchange for the B at e4. But White has 24. B—B1 as a defence and 24. .... B—Q6 fails

Black (Bilek)

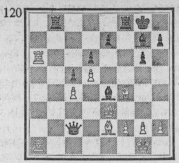

White (Schmidt)
(Olympiad of 1962)

Shortsightedness
23. R—K1?    R×B
24. Q×R     Q×B wins

after 25. R×Q  R×R. 26. Q×B. Indeed, Black probably has
nothing better than 23. .... R—Kt8 ch. 24. B—B1  R×R.
25. R×Q  B×R: and 26. P—Kt3 leaves Black with more play
than White, but no clear winning advantage. Instead, White
made the mistake 23. R—K1. Now we have 'double functions'
and 'back row danger' forcibly illustrated. Black plays 23. ....
R×B and after 24. Q×R, he plays Q×B and the Queen cannot
be captured. That fact constitutes victory. (This was easier to
see, by master standards, than what Yanofsky overlooked
against Bolbochan.)

Before we leave this position, let a word be said on the
Strategy that is latent here. Strategy is always important in
Chess, but frequently it is very difficult to isolate. In the game
between Bilek and Schmidt from which the diagram is cited
there are several strategic features. In the opening Black played
with the intention of inviting White to create a hollow centre
which, when broken, left Black's King's Bishop in strong action.
White was not lacking in compensation for this. In the later
play the coefficient of strategy was the importance for Black of

securing an open file, of which the White base was controllable by Black's Queen's Bishop. White's play was inadequate to prevent the achievement of this objective.

Objectives of this type, relating to the general frame of the game, are called strategic; because they can be planned in more general terms than the tactical lines of play. But they are very rarely thought about in abstraction from the tactics. Indeed, just as a player who knows no terminology plays tactics without knowing it, so a great many good players play strategy without knowing it. The strategic thought is involved in their vision, or in the judgement that players use when the task of vision is too difficult.

Strategy is seen fairly clearly in action when a player decides to double, or not to double, his Pawns because of the shape that the position will have, especially the ultimate endgame position. Also the decision to unbalance the game in order to attack on one side of the board is strategic as well as tactical. Not least important is general development in the opening, and later. Which files for the Rooks? which diagonals for the Bishops? These are strategic matters, though always to be thought about in the light of tactical processes.

At many stages of the game the general choice is available; what to do now that there is no coercion? Epigrammatically, it may be said: Tactics are what you do when there is something to do. Strategy is what you do when there is nothing to do. That isolation, however, is rare. Strategy is a feature, albeit unobserved, of most good tactical play. It is latent – not patent.

As for its rules, they, like the rules of tactics, are unstatable. But, generally, it can be said that to achieve at least as much scope for your pieces as your opponent has is good strategy. 'Control equal space' is a strategic maxim. Not to lose tempo when tempo matters is good strategy. Not to allow any diminution of freedom without having a plan for the regaining of it is good strategy. To keep the game well balanced unless the unbalance is clearly in your favour is also good strategy.

Many points of strategy are so familiar, and easy to grasp,

that they are embedded in the player's equipment as technique. If, for example, one of the variations of the attack leads to isolated doubled Pawns, which, sooner or later, are likely to prove indefensible, or, at least, a great endgame disadvantage, then, in avoiding that crystallization (as, e.g. in the game between Yanofsky and Bolbochan), one is behaving strategically. Again, it was a possible variation in the Morphy game that a Knight would settle and remain unassailable on KB5. That occupancy of an outpost is a very familiar idea, and a strategic feature, the use of which is an element in one's technique. Indeed, players frequently play in order to have Knights on outposts, where it occasionally turns out that they serve no useful purpose.

Thus a Knight established at QKt6, in the interstitial square between the Pawns at b7 and a6, can be very useful indeed, if the control of c8 is relevant. Always, whether in tactics or strategy, the important determinant of the value of a move, or the placing of a piece, is relevance to the total game. If it has a bearing on processes now going on, or which will take place in the foreseeable future, it is in the field of relevance, and to be considered. Irrelevant moves are bad moves: and the apprehension of what is relevant is just another way of describing Chess vision.

The effect of strategy, not the less important for being elementary, is very clearly seen in the next diagram (121) position, achieved by that great young player, Bobby Fischer. His play was so good in that game, relatively to his opponent's, and indeed by any standards, that the best his opponent could do was be left with some very clear, very simple, strategic, and/or technical disadvantages – the Queen's side Pawn minority, and, more striking, the bad Pawn position on the Queen's side. Also, in this position, White's Bishop, acting defensively as well as aggressively, is a more useful piece than Black's Knight. The reader should also be told that the doubled KBP, like the doubled QBP that occurs, at times, e.g. in the Ruy Lopez, represents a strategic risk that players sometimes take. If the

Black (Barcza)

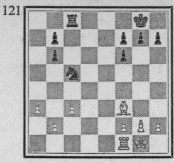

White (Fischer)

Played in an Interzonal Tournament, 1962

game comes down to an endgame, with no change in the Pawn
structure, then one player has the following advantage, that he
has four Pawns to three on one wing and because of the doubling, three against three on the other. But players incur this risk
in order to achieve quick development, and middle-game
chances.

Here are the moves with which Bobby Fischer turns advantage, inexorably, into victory.

27. R—Q1    K—B1
28. R—Q4                Note that one should not start too
                        quick an attack here for tactical
                        reasons. If 29. R—Q6  Kt—R5.

28. ....    R—B2
29. P—R3    P—B4        Restricting the squares available
                        to the Bishop.

30. R—QKt4  Kt—Q2
31. K—B1    K—K2
32. K—K2    K—Q1        Black is using his King as a
                        defensive piece. ('The King is also
                        a piece.') White, in turn, uses his
                        King as an aggressive piece.

33. R—Kt5  P—Kt3
34. K—K3  K—B1
35. K—Q4  K—Kt1
36. K—Q5

An attempt to get through which is thwarted. Fischer had evidently decided that the Rook's escape to K3 was unimportant. Nor did it turn out well.

36. ....   R—B3

Leaves one guard less on b7.

37. K—Q4  R—K3
38. P—QR4  K—B2
39. P—R5

Cannot be captured because of the attack on b7. White is 'undoubling' his opponent's pawns for reasons of attack.

39. ....   R—Q3 ch
40. B—Q5  K—B1
41. P×P  P—B3

Black has delayed recapture in such a way as to prevent exchanges. But this move lets in the Bishop.

42. K—K3  Kt×P
43. B—Kt8  K—B2

Better is 43. .... P—R3. But it leaves 44. B—R7 playable at will. Black is planning to use a little 'imprisoning' device.

44. R—B5 ch  K—Kt1

He is put to a decision before White captures the Pawn.

45. B×P  Kt—Q4 ch
46. K—B3  Kt—K2

A neat tactical device. In many positions the capture would be rendered expensive by this. But here there is an immediate mobilization of rescue party.

47. P—R4  P—Kt3
48. R—Kt5  K—Kt2
49. P—R5  K—R3

An attempt to save the KBP.

50. P—B4  P×P
51. B×P  R—Q5

See how exchanging would leave White with a power to achieve a quick King's side operation after long play against the Queen's side!

52. P—QKt3  Kt—B3
53. K—K3

Not waiting to be checked, and so drives the Rook in order to free the Knight. A nice point of order.

53. ....  R—Q1
54. B—K4  Kt—R4

Indirectly defending his KRP.

55. B—B2  P—R5
56. R—R5  R—K1 ch
57. K—Q2  R—KKt1
58. R×P  P—Kt4

R×P would be met by R—B4 winning the KBP.

59. R—B4  P×P
60. P×P  R×P
61. R×P ch  K—R2
62. K—B3  R—Kt5
63. P—B4  Kt—Kt2
64. K—Kt4 resigns

Black has no play left. White can use his QBP or KBP without interference.

The above is an important illustration of how strategic disadvantages are exploited. It is this possibility that makes them recognizable strategic disadvantages!

As to how one plays 'strategy', that is quite hard to state. Let it be repeated that, as the game proceeds there is a coefficient of strategy latent in the tactical play: occasionally patent in preparatory play, when that can be viewed in isolation.

Rules are impossible to lay down. Thus, suppose one said: 'Development is always strategically good', no player in the world, or outer space, would demur. But by what rule can one judge how much development is available to justify an attacking movement? (Nevertheless, when in doubt DEVELOP!)

It is also accepted principle that control of the centre is a good thing. If you hold the centre well, it is quite unlikely that any attack will succeed on either of your flanks. But exceptions occur. Then one says: the central control was illusory, or the development was formal rather than functional. When these sayings are translated they mean that you can very rarely move strategically, or logically, or in terms of common sense, without reference to all the specific tactical possibilities of the position. If you can make moves on first principle only, it will be when you have some very clear advantage. Even then you cannot afford 'second-best moves'.

Very interesting, in connexion with the foregoing, is a position achieved by Tarrasch (physician and Chess master) against that great English player Amos Burn. Both of these players had plenty of tactical ability, but both were famous for their strategy and logic. Indeed Tarrasch was called 'Praeceptor Germanorum' – which anybody uncharitably minded might translate as 'teacher of Teutonic pedantries'. He did, indeed, make contributions to theory. Happily his vision was brilliant enough to win more games for him than he succeeded in losing by his pedantry.

| White | Black |
|-------|-------|
| A. BURN | DR S. TARRASCH |

(Vienna 1898): Queen's Gambit Declined

| | |
|---|---|
| *1.* P—Q4   P—Q4 | |
| *2.* P—QB4   P—K3 | |
| *3.* Kt—QB3   P—QB3 | |
| *4.* P—K3 | 4. Kt—KB3 leads to a very interesting series of moves from 4. .... P×P, with which the name of the author of this book is associated. But even in 1898 they preferred to avoid it. |
| *4.* ....   B—Q3 | In ordinary Q. G. D. this would |

be the wrong square, because it is attackable from e4. But it is consistent with Black's plan here.

5. Kt—B3  P—KB4

The Stonewall. This is a defence which, well handled, gives Black plenty of play. Many of the best strategians, including the great Capablanca, have refused to adopt it, because of the difficulties that Black has in freeing his centre. Nevertheless, the opening has strategic compensations, as this game shows. Observe that White could have played 5. P—KB4.

6. B—K2

6. B—Q3 is probably better. But the text is adequate. Also playable was Q—B2 followed by P—QKt3, B—Kt2 and O—O—O, Capablanca's method.

Sporting is 6. P—KKt4. To be considered is 6. Kt—K5, but it is debatable whether 6. .... B×Kt leaves White with a strong position.

6. ....  Kt—Q2

This would not have been immediately playable after B—Q3 because, then, 7. P×P would cause the BP to recapture, leaving White with more immediate chances on the Queen's side.

7. O—O  Q—B3

Also playable is 7. .... Kt—R3 followed, at some stage, by Kt—B3. Then Black has some King's side aggression. The text, however, is good.

8. Kt—K1

Elementary Strategy and Common Sense, according to Lasker,

lay it down that one should not move the same piece twice before development is complete. That, however, is a principle which, like others, must be subordinated to the needs of the position. White has a good plan, here — to play P—KB3 followed by P—K4 with great central pressure. But the move is not good here, as it happens, for tactical reasons, which Tarrasch quickly demonstrates.

**8. .... Q—R3**

**9. P—KKt3**

Better, possibly, is 9. P—KB4; White, at move 8, was underestimating Black's reply to this 9th move.

**9. .... P—KKt4**

Obstructing the battery from the QB, and starting a Bauer–Strom against White's King's side.

**10. P—B3  Kt—K2**

**11. P—K4  P—B5**

Each is proceeding according to plan. What Tarrasch has seen is that White's next move, which looks so good 'formally', does not achieve anything. The restriction of Black's Queen's side development proves unimportant. The result indicates that White's loss of tempo by retreat of the Knight was in a bad cause.

**12. P—K5**

Better perhaps is 12. P—B5 followed by P—QKt4 with Queen's side attack, because Black's

King's side attack cannot be quick.

12. .... B—B2

13. P—KKt4

Stopping Black's Knight from reaching f5, an attacking position. Yet I regard the text as a bad move, for tactical reasons. To state the latter: White is giving a target to Black's KRP, and is enabling Black to open his KR file against the King. Evidently Burn judged that he had time and material to cope with any attack that developed from Black's limited forces.

Moves to consider are *13*. B—Q3 and *13*. P—QKt3. Also *13*. P—B5 to which P—QKt3 is not a convincing answer.

13. .... Q—Kt2

14. R—B2   P—KR4

15. R—Kt2   Kt—KKt3

Threatening Kt—R5 driving the Rook and achieving a passed Pawn.

16. KtP×P   R×P

17. B—Q3   Kt—R5

18. R—QB2   P×P!

Here is a move which, unless it is tactically successful, is strategically compromising, because it gives the square e4 to White's Knight. Thus, if *19*. B×QBP Kt—Kt3. *20*. Kt—K4 threatens, *inter alia*, to win the exchange. But Black has seen a long way.

For our purposes, I invite the reader to examine the position (Diagram 122) in the light of the question: What do you mean by development? Formally, White's development is better than Black's; but Black has all he needs, of material, space, and tempo, for fine attack.

Black (Tarrasch)

122

White (Burn)

Development?
From an apparently underdeveloped position, Tarrasch, with
18, .... P×P, commences a winning attack

| | | |
|---|---|---|
| *19.* B×QBP | Kt–KB4 | The point. Black has decoyed the Bishop in order to occupy this square. The threat is Kt×QP, and the Queen cannot recapture because of the pin from b6. |
| *20.* K–R1 | | White is suddenly faced with a terrible attack. B×KP cannot be played because Kt×QP is too destructive of the frame of White's position. |
| *20.* .... | B–Kt3! | Better than KtKt3 which allows Kt–K4 with counter-attack. |
| *21.* B×KP | | The beauty of Black's play is concealed in the inability of White to play R–Q2. If |

21. R—Q2    Kt×KP
22. P×Kt    Kt—Kt6 ch
23. K—Kt2    R×P ch
24. K×R    Q—R3 ch
25. K—Kt2    Q—R8 mate

a beautiful finish – an unheard melody.

21. ....    Kt×QP
22. B—Kt4    R—R1

Black's development looks a good deal better now!

23. R—Q2    Kt×KP!
24. B×B

If 24. R×Kt then not 24. ....
Kt×B to which R—K4 ch is a good answer but

24. ....    B×R
25. Q×B    B×B
26. P×B    R×P ch
27. K—Kt1

and not K×R, because of Kt×P ch.

In answer to 27. K—Kt1 Black cannot play Kt—B6 ch because of Kt×Kt but

27. ....    Q—R1
28. Q—K4 (to guard h1)
28. ....    O—O—O

with an easy win (and a complete development!)

24. ....    R×B
25. R×Kt    B×R
26. Q×B    R×P ch
27. K—Kt1    Q—R1
28. B×P

Desperate, in order to keep the Queen from h2.

28. ....    P×B
29. Kt—K4

Burn had intended Q×BP, but after

29. .... R—R8ch
30. K—B2 R×Kt
is unanswerable

29. ....   R—R8 ch
30. K—B2  Kt—Kt5 ch  Unmasking the battery at last.
31. Resigns.


This game illustrates many things. Not the least important is the word that springs to every Chess-player's mind when he sees Tarrasch's clever attacking sequence: 'What a combination!'.

That word Combination describes a clever attack, involving moves hard to see, and (according to Botvinnik) necessarily involving sacrifices, in the course of which attack the pieces 'combine' to force mate or the gain of material, or of some clear strategic advantage.

A good combination involves fine vision, as here, where Tarrasch not only had to see a way to create an attack, but also all the dangers, all the counterplay, all the defences, and all the subvariations, including variations of order in the moves; and see them across a changing board, with pieces disappearing and other pieces emerging into activity.

Like other useful words, the word 'Combination' is apt to be excessively used, misapplied, and strained in its application. Not every winning sacrifice can be called a combination. Such a sacrifice as the Greek gift is based on elementary tactics and only involves positional judgement. Nor, in this author's opinion, is a process the less combinative if a difficult series of moves does not happen to involve a sacrifice; though, usually, it is the element of sacrifice that constitutes the adjective 'difficult'. (An inhibition based on valuations has to be overcome in one's act of vision.)

The overused distinction in Chess is between Combinative play and Positional play. Very often combinative is used instead of the shorter 'combative'. Moreover, on the high levels of Chess, and even below, it is not possible to disentangle the

Combinative from the Positional, just as it is not possible
to disentangle the notions of Strategic play and Tactical play.
But there is a valid difference of degree. Some players of
merit are less Combinative than others. Some Combinative
players are apt to allow their positional judgement less scope.
Their play is apt to be sharper, but can be less effective in the
result.

Let it be said that no really fine player is really deficient in
combinative ability, or in positional judgement. But the great
masters of combination have produced the greatest, most
imaginative, richest Chess. Such were Morphy, Lasker,
Capablanca, Alekhine; and slightly lesser stars such as Blackburne, Zukertort, Mieses and Marshall. In our time, Fischer,
Tal and Keres have produced great combinations. So has
Botvinnik: and there are plenty of other great contemporary
names.

What is worth observing is that the positional player, with
less imagination than the fine combinative player (it is empha-
sized that the difference is only one of degree), can play quite
subtly, accurately and successfully.

Interesting, in order to illustrate this point, is a previous diagram (114). In that position, between Yanofsky and Bolbochan,
a great many players would 'judge' that Q—K2 is a better
move than R—Q1. They might like to 'overprotect' an as yet
unattacked Pawn: they might wish to control more White
squares, etc., and do this without dreaming, in their wildest
imaginings, of Bolbochan's *Zwischenzug*, made valid by a fine
combinational possibility. (This was not even in Yanofsky's
field of awareness.) So, without seeing it, they would defend
against it!

Nor must it be supposed that the combinative player is
deficient in strategy, the positional player in tactics. One
difference may well be that combinative players think more of
the time factor than of the space; and are more likely to unbalance a game or leave holes in it. There are players against
whom it is very dangerous to lose tempo; and other fine players

who are less apt to commit themselves to rapid processes of attack. Unless, of course, the end is clearly visible. That is not always the case.

Before one parts from this discussion let mention be made of the fine element of paradox that pervades the Tarrasch game. Here was one who taught that a Combination must not be thought about until an objectively discernible advantage in development had been obtained. Following Steinitz, he held that a successful combination was the logical effect of some positional superiority on the one hand, some defect on the other. Whether he could have won that game against Burn by practising that precept, or whether he really did practise it there, is an interesting speculation.

Black (Tarrasch)

White (Minckwitz)
(Leipzig, 1888)

Black plays *23*. .... P—Kt5 and secures a winning attack (see text)

In contrast to the last game, here is a position from Tarrasch's play which does show an attack emerging from an objectively discernible better development (Diagram 123).

It is clear that all Black's forces are in play, and with dynamic potential. White's pieces are 'formally' developed; but are not so dynamic. In an endgame White's Pawn structure would prove better: and, given time, he has prospects with his Rooks on the QB file. Meanwhile, he appears to have allowed his opponent too much aggression.

There followed:

| | | |
|---|---|---|
| 23. | .... | P—Kt5 |
| 24. | RP×P | BP×P |
| 25. | Kt—K5 | Q—R4! threatening P—Kt6 |
| 26. | P×P | B × Kt White has under-estimated the threat. |
| 27. | P×B | P—Kt6 |
| 28. | P×KtP | Kt×P |
| 29. | R—B3 | — forced, in order to prevent mate. |
| 29. | .... | R×R |
| 30. | P×R | R—KB1 threatening Q—R8 ch and R×P mate |
| 31. | P—B4 | Kt—K7 ch |
| 32. | K—B2 | Kt×P |
| 33. | R—Kt1 ch | K—R1 |
| 34. | B×Kt | R×B ch |
| 35. | K—K1 | Q×P ch |
| | resigns | |

That illustrates the conventional relationship, and a very important one to remember, between good development and winning attack.

Here, from, if I may say so, a lower level of Chess, yet still very good Chess, is a game that illustrates the crystallization from early tactical possibilities (or, in this case, rejection of chances), of two clear strategic policies, one was effective, and the other failed.

|          | White      | Black            |
|----------|------------|------------------|
|          | BYRNE      | THEODOROVITCH    |

(Played in U.S.A. 1962–3)

(Kotov–Robatch Defence)

| 1. | P—Q4    | P—KKt3  |
| 2. | P—QB4   | B—Kt2   |
| 3. | Kt—QB3  | P—Q3    |
| 4. | Kt—B3   | P—K4    |

After the King's side fianchetto Black is not disturbed by the prospect of an exchange of Queens on the home square. (White's QB is not well placed in the resultant game.)

| 5. | P—KKt3  | Kt—QB3  |

Inducing White to close the centre. If 6. P—K3 B—Kt5 leaves the same need.

| 6. | P—Q5    | QKt—K2  |
| 7. | B—Kt2   | KKt—B3  |

Here is where tactical considerations interfere with strategic planning. Clearly, if Black wishes to play P—KB4, for central control, he is well advised to do it before Kt—KB3. To play the Kt out first entails loss of tempo. Here Black is afraid of the variation

| 7.  | ....   | P—KB4   |
| 8.  | Kt—Kt5 | Kt—B3   |
| 9.  | Kt—K6. | But after |
| 9.  | ....   | B×Kt    |
| 10. | P×B    | P—QB3   |

the P at K6 can be ignored and Black can mobilize quite an attack. This Black, however, would not take that risk. He judged the resultant position as strategically unsatisfactory.

7. .... P—KR3 is strategically more suspect because of the resultant weakness at g6.

8. O—O    O—O

9. P—QKt4

Boldly played. Technically this should be met by 9. .... P—QR4 (before B—Kt2 makes P—QR3 playable). Black was afraid of P×P. If the R recaptures it may become a target for the KKt moving via Q2 to Kt3. As Black has counter-play with KKtQ2 aiming at QB4, and P—QKt3 he should not be afraid of the advance of White's QRP.

9. ....    Kt—K1

Black's bad tactics are making possible White's good strategy. From now on, White, judging that he can hold any King's side threat engineered by Black (who has lost tempo) organizes a formidable Queen's side demonstration.

10. B—Kt2    P—KR3

In other contexts this has been called 'country move' or 'a provincial move', disparagingly of the timidity involved. Here it is unnecessary, but it may help the KKtP forward later. Yet if he was going to play it, Black should have done so at move 7. However, it has, here, a small tactical purpose.

Black wishes to play P—K5, taking advantage of the pin of the QKt. But this would be met by Kt—Kt5 which induces

|  |  |
|---|---|
|  | P—KB4 before Black wishes to play it. |
| *11.* Q—Kt3 | Protecting or 'over-protecting' the QB and so spoiling the threat P—K5. Also the Queen is supporting, here, a Queen's side advance: and there may be an eventual battery against Black's King (e.g. were Black to play P—KB4 and meet White's side advance with P—QB3). |
|  | (Normally, Queens do not need to be moved in the opening. They are developed where they stand, but eventually they make room for Rooks.) |
| *11.* .... P—KB4 |  |
| *12.* KR—Q1 | Permitting Kt—Q4 in the event of P—K5. Also overprotecting the QP. Further, there is a maxim. 'Put your Rook on line of Queen, no matter how many pieces intervene'. White is judging, or seeing, well, in risking the KR away from the KB file. He wants the other Rook to stay on the Queen's wing. Can Black do anything against the King's side? White has enough central control to feel that this is not a danger. |
| *13.* .... P—KKt4 | If Black could quickly get his Q to KR4 and his Knights to B3 and Kt3 there would be King's side action. |
| *13.* P—B5 Kt—Kt3 | Not good. Better is Kt—KB3 followed by Q—K1. From now onwards Black is threatening |

H

nothing at all – in a very loud voice.

*14.* P—QR4  P—Kt5    On to a square that should first hold a Knight, to induce P—KR3.

*15.* Kt—Q2  P—KR4    It will take a long time for the liquidation of this Pawn and the doubling of Rooks on a well-defended KR file. Note that P—B5 will be rendered innocuous by Kt (or B)—K4.

*16.* Kt—B4  P—R5

*17.* P—R5  R—B2    Slightly defensive of the Queen's side: slightly aggressive when it slides over to KR2.

*18.* P—Kt5!    A good move proving that White's strategy has been better than Black's. There is no great immediate threat, but if Black plays

    *18.* ....  P×BP
    *19.* Kt—R4 and
    *19.* ....  P—Kt3

is impossible because of

    *20.* P—Q6. Also
    *19.* ....  Q—K2

is met by B—QR3. White is getting dominant in the centre.

*18.* ....  B—B1    Defeatism. He should fight with *18.* ....  P—K5, and Kt—K4 as a possible sequel. 'Engage the enemy' is quite a Chess maxim.

*19.* P—Kt6    Again, well played. A point that is becoming clear is the danger of a White Bishop at Q5.

*19.* ....  P×BP    *20.* P—B6 was threatened. Another threat was

|  |  |  |
|---|---|---|
| | *20.* P×BP | Q×P |
| | *21.* Kt—Kt6 | P×Kt |
| | *22.* RP×P | Q—Kt1 |
| | *23.* P—B6 but this is speculative. | |

*20.* Kt—Kt5

A very interesting demonstration of Queen's side incursion leading to full control of the board.

*20.* .... QRP×P
*21.* RP×P  R×R
*22.* R×R  P—R6

Making that Pawn irrelevant but committing the Bishop. The Queen's Pawn must be protected.

*23.* B—R1  B—Q2

If *23.* ....    P×P
    *24.* R—R8   Kt—B2
    *25.* Kt×Kt  Q×Kt
    *26.* P—Q6 is in White's favour.
If *23.* ....    P—K5
    *24.* R—R8 and
    *25.* Kt—R7 is terrible for Black.

*24.* P×P  Kt×P
*25.* Kt×Kt  Q×Kt
*26.* P—Q6

This, the easiest of White's Pawn sacrifices, is conclusive.
If *26.* ....  Q—B1
    *27.* B×KtP, etc.
If *26.* ....  Q—Q1  or  Kt1
    White has an *embarras de richesses* (including B—Q5).

*26.* ....  B×P
*27.* B—Q5

Good, leaving the B at d6 as a 'hanging piece'.

*27.* ....  Kt—R1

If *27.* ....  B—K1
    *28.* R—R8, etc.

*28.* R—Q1

Pretty and powerful. The immediate threat is Kt×B  Q×B  B×R ch, winning the Queen. Yet the text is not the best. Also playable was *28.* R—R8 ch winning a piece (after K moves) by R×Kt. If *28.* .... B—KB1. *29.* B×KP wins the Queen!

*28.* .... B—K1

Not B—KB1, because of *29.* B×KP and *30.* B×Kt.

*29.* Kt×B  Q×Kt
*30.* B×R ch

White will, or should, have seen, at move *28*, that this is a simplification leading to a reduction of his advantage. Yet a clear winning position emerges.

*30.* .... B×B
*31.* R×Q  B×Q
*32.* R—Q8 ch  K—R2
*33.* R—Q7 ch  K—Kt3
*34.* R×P  B—K3

A serious mistake. But the endgame is lost in any event.

*35.* B×P  Kt—B2
*36.* R—Kt6 resigns

Because if Kt—Q1 *37.* B—B7. And if
   *36.* .... Kt Kt4
   *37.* B—B4 has the same effect.

This game, well handled by the American Master, is of interest as an example of strategic decisions. It is quite unlikely that anyone would see all the way through Byrne's prospects. But he 'judged' that he had good chances. This 'judgement' was strengthened by an awareness of slight strategic features suggestive of Queen's side prospects. The defence was sufficiently positive to make the game valuable.

Something that the reader may have noticed in following the notes to this and previous games is that, however good the strategic position of a player is, yet he must keep on playing tactically good Chess. Few positions are so overwhelming that 'anything goes'. Frequently, on the other hand, a strategic advantage cannot be exploited without great tactical skill. Advantages do not last for ever. Indeed, they tend to diminish, as pressure on a position develops, *malgré lui*, the opponent's resources. Most good games feature, earlier or later, and quite usually at the end, some tactical stroke that turns advantage into victory. These chances are easy to miss. Play is meritorious when the winner has seen, far ahead, the final denouement, a move unexpected by the opponent, or expected too late.

In point is Diagram 124, a neat finish by the finest of contemporary Israeli players, Raaphy Persitz. During the preceding

Black

124

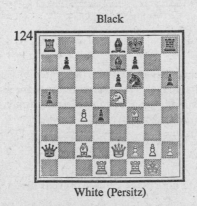

White (Persitz)

White to move and win quickly

manœuvres, Black has not seen, and White probably has seen, that now the attack does not proceed conventionally with Q—Q2, met by KtKt1. Instead, unmasking an underestimated battery, with immediate B—R7!, White wins the Queen, because, of course, if Q×Q  B×P gives mate.

Again, the opponent of the American master Schroeder must

have felt quite safe after many exchanges had left the position
in Diagram 125. Yet he resigned after a mere four or five moves

Black

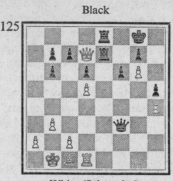

125

White (Schroeder)

White to play

further. It looks as if the 'temporarily strategic' feature, the P
at g6, has lost its virtue. Yet observe the sequence.

*1.* R—K1 pinning the Rook at e7, amusingly, so that it
cannot capture the Queen.

> *1.* .... R × R
> *2.* Q—B7 ch          K—R1
> *3.* R × R          R × R ch
> *4.* K—Kt2 and Black cannot prevent mate

He could, however, at move *1,* have played K—B1 instead of
R × R.

Then *2.* R × R          R × R
>    *3.* Q—B8 ch          R—K1
>    *4.* Q × BP          Q × QP  constitutes  a
>                   fairly  clear  winning
>                   position for White

The reader has now seen some 'brilliancies'. That word has

become a debased coin in the Chess vocabulary. One can speak of a superficial 'brilliance' contrasted with profundity. But, without semantic dogmatism, it may be said that the best use of the word 'brilliance' or 'brilliancy' is made when profundity is present below the surface of the spectacle. Indeed a long subtle analysis, with no omission of fine points, can be called a brilliant piece of work, however unspectacular. But if the word is used with restraint, to describe surprising play that should surprise a really good player, then such combinative play as Bolbochan's and Tarrasch's qualifies for the adjective.

Short brilliancies, often called 'miniatures', and usually made possible by some gross flaw in the defence, are gems of Chess because of their convincingness.

They are important to our theme, because they are so clearly tactically meritorious that one is apt to overlook the coefficient of strategy. Here is a game from a 1962 Russian Trade Union Tournament. (The Russian proletariat is now becoming as good at Chess as the Scottish miners used to be at Draughts.)

|  | White | Black |
|---|---|---|
|  | TROINOV | POPOV |
|  | (Sicilian Defence) | |
| 1. | P—K4 P—QB4 | |
| 2. | Kt—KB3 P—Q3 | |
| 3. | P—Q4 P×P | |
| 4. | Kt×P Kt—KB3 | |
| 5. | Kt—QB3 Kt—B3 | |
| 6. | B—QB4 | A move that was out of fashion until Bobby Fischer restored it to popularity. The general strategy of the Sicilian has usually been characterized by a White Bishop on f3, behind a Pawn on f4. |
| 6. | .... P—K3 | 6. Kt×P is not playable (a) because of 7. B×P ch before the recapture. From this position that process would be in White's |

favour. (b) because of 7. Kt × Kt
(e4) P—Q4 8. B—Kt5

7. O—O   B—K2
8. B—K3   O—O
9. B—Kt3

Because Kt × P, with fork to
follow, is now threatened.

9. ....   P—QR3

Normal, as a preparation for
P—QKt4, and also to keep a Kt
from b5, which might be embarrassing, say, to Q at c7.

10. P—B4   P—Q4

In many openings this move by
Black is a test of 'equality',
indicating that the initiative has
passed. Here it is ill-timed. Correct
is Q—B2. Black should not be too
afraid of White's possible P—
KKt4, etc. If that happens too
early Kt × Kt and P—K4 give
plenty of counter-action.

11. P—K5   Kt—Q2

Better is Kt—K1. Black's plan is
to develop this Kt defensively on
f8. But a better process is to aim
for g7, or to contemplate counter-
play with P—KB3, or P—KB4.

12. Q—R5

White is now threatening many
things including R—B3 and/or
P—Kt4. Black must fight back
with Kt × Kt and P—KB4. If he
wishes to move the Rook, then
first let him play P—KKt3 (with
a view to R—K1 and B—B1).

12. ....   R—K1

The move that Black makes is a
mistake. Yet this toiler cannot be
blamed for missing something
high-class.

13. Kt × QP!   P × Kt

If he does not recapture, playing,

say, B—B4, White 'gets away
with' a Pawn, e.g.

13. ....      B—B4
14. Kt×Kt    P×Kt
15. B×B      Kt×B
16. Kt—B3, etc.

Of course P—Kt3 allows Kt×B
ch. (It is always important for a
sacrificer to consider possible
refusals. They often spoil the
scheme.)

14. Q×BP ch    Making this into a Chess gem.

14. ....   K×Q    If 14. ....    K—R1
15. Kt—K6 threatens mate
and the Queen.

15. B×P ch   K—Kt3    What White had to see at move
13 (at the latest) was the sequel to

15. ....    K—B1. There could
follow
16. Kt—K6      K—Kt1
17. Kt×Q ch    K—R1
18. Kt—B7 ch   K—Kt1
19. Kt—Q6 ch   K—B1
20. Kt×R       K×Kt

and, anticlimactically, White is
left with the exchange and three
Pawns for a piece, and plenty of
play.

There are other variations. Possibly White saw them. But it may
be said that an attacker is justified in taking something for
granted. He sees ahead enough of
possibility to enable him to judge
that what he is left with will win.
In good attacks one feels that
'something will turn up'.

Now mate follows quickly.

16. P—B5 ch    K—R4
17. B—B3 ch    K—R5
18. P—Kt3 ch   K—R6
19. B—Kt2 ch   K—Kt5
20. R—B4 ch resigns      (after

          *20*. .... K—R4
          *21*. B—B3 ch  K—R3
          *22*. R—R4 mate.
   More prettily
          *21*. R—R4 ch  B×R
          *22*. B—B3 mate).

That pretty game was made possible by bad tactics and strategy on the part of the opponent. Black clogged his own game, with no sound idea for its freeing. He neither saw well, thought well, nor judged well. (The game is also an illustration of the technical weakness of f7 – already referred to.)

Frequently a defender judges, or even sees, that a very dangerous-looking attack at this, or other, point, is inadequate.

Witness the attack that Bobby Fischer survived.

| White | Black |
|---|---|
| BILEK | FISCHER |

(Played in an Interzonal Tournament 1961)

1. P—K4   P—QB4
2. Kt—KB3  P—Q3
3. P—Q4   P×P
4. Kt×P   Kt—KB3
5. Kt—QB3  P—QR3
6. B—KKt5

This is a well-known play, to prevent P—KKt3 and the Dragon Defence.

6. ....   P—K3
7. P—B4   Q—Kt3

An excursion by maps that were studied under oil-lamps at midnight.

| | |
|---|---|
| 8. Q—Q2 | with the idea of O—O—O, or R—Q1, bringing quick 'pressure' on the Queen's file. |
| 8. .... Q×P | With the following moves, a most excellent example of an attempt to steal a QKtP and 'get away with it'. |
| 9. R—QKt1  Q—R6 | |
| 10. P—K5 | Bilek saw the same map. |
| 10. .... P×P | |
| 11. P×P  KKt—Q2 | |
| 12. B—QB4 | White's King's Pawn is a 'can't take'. If *12.* .... Kt×P *13.* Kt×KP exposes Black to a destructive attack. |
| 12. ....  B—K2 | |
| 13. B×KP | The midnight oil, or tactical talent, blazes up. If *13.* ....  P×B *14.* Kt×P makes life difficult if not impossible for Black, e.g. *14.* .... B×B could be met simply by *15.* Q×B allowing Q×Kt ch (*16.* K—Q1) or by *15.* Kt—B7 ch or by *15.* Kt×P ch all producing attacks well worth a piece, even if not analysable down to finality. |
| 13. ....  O—O | An attempt to refute a sacrifice by refusal. If White now tries to disengage, Black's development may prove superior. |
| 14. O—O | Well played. The Bishop is not capturable for the moment. |

14. .... P×B

15. Kt×P forces either R×R ch or R—B2. In either case White's second Rook is in vigorous action. And there are other pieces that cannot be taken: as will appear. White's alternative

14. R—Kt3   B×B
15. Q×B   P—KR3

would have been less dangerous for Black.

14. ....   B×B
15. Q×B   P—R3

If it be asked: Why not 15. .... Q×Kt? the answer is

16. Kt—B5   [Q—B4 ch
17. K—R1]   Q×KP
18. Kt—R6 ch   K—R1
19. Kt×P ch   R×Kt
20. Q—Q8 ch   Kt—B1
21. Q×Kt ch   R×Q
22. R×R mate

15. .... P×B is more evidently disastrous after 16. Kt×P. The text, however, is very effective; and, having been seen ahead, shows that a fine attacking player such as Fischer is, for that reason, an excellent, subtle defender.

16. Q—R4

This keeps the Queen in action against d8, and it defends the Kt at d4.

16. Q—Kt3 is met by the embarrassing reply 16. .... Q—B4

16. ....   Q×Kt

Well timed. He can now beat off this dangerous attack.

| | | |
|---|---|---|
| *17.* R×KBP | | The attack, however, still seems to be going well. |

*17.* .... R×R

*18.* Q—Q8 ch   Kt—B1   Forced, because after

> *18.* .... K—R2
> *19.* B×R

seems unanswerable.

*19.* B×R ch   *19.* B×B is met by the subtle QKt Q2. *19.* Q×B leaves White, after exchanges, with material deficit. But the text looks promising.

*19.* .... K×B   The King is going into danger, but Fischer has a very clever resource.

*20.* R—B1 ch   K—Kt3

*21.* R×Kt   —   At this point White may have a drawing chance. (Not what one looks for exactly in this kind of position.)

> *22.* Q—K8 ch   K—R2
> *23.* R×Kt       Q×Kt ch
> *24.* K—B1 and Black seems to have perpetual check.

A good example of 'something turning up' during a promising attack. This usually happens if the attack is strategically not unjustified. But White wants a better 'turn-up'.

*21.* .... B—Q2   A beautiful *Zwischenzug* stopping the threatened Q—K8 ch and attacking the Kt.

*22.* Kt—B3   At this point a pretty idea just falls short of realization.

*22.*        *22.* R—   B6 ch. If
> *22.* .... P×R

23. Q—Kt8 ch  K—R4
24. Q—B7 ch  K—Kt4 (if 24.
.... K—Kt5. 26. Q—
Kt6 followed by Kt
checks).
25. Q×P ch  K—R4
26. Q—B7 ch  K—Kt4
27. Kt—B3 ch and Black must
play  Q×Kt  leaving
White with a probable
win.
But the whole move-
ment is refuted by refusal
of the sacrifice!
22. R—B6 ch  K—R2!
Then 23. R×P ch  K×R leaves
White with nothing.

22. ....  Q—K6 ch
23. K—R1

Unfortunately he cannot wriggle
clear via B1 because of B—Kt4
ch.

23. ......  Q—B8 ch
24. Kt—Kt1

An attacker out of action. But the
game is still very hard.

24. ..  Q×P
25. R—Kt8

A weak move, though a powerful
threat (Q—B6 ch).
25. Q—K7 might keep sufficient
attack for drawing purposes – at
least.

25. ....  Q—B7

Threatening B—B3 as well as
preventing Q—B6.

26. R—B8  Q×RP

A luxury he could not have
afforded had the White Queen
stood at K7 (because of 27.
R—B3).

27. R—B3  K—R2        And White lost 'on the clock'.
                       But White is lost in any event.
                       The threat is B—B3 forcing the
                       Rook to KKt3: then Q—Kt1
                       releasing the QKt and QR.

This is an excellent example of an attack justified by superior development, yet failing to achieve more than a drawing variation against the best defence. Black's position was not so clogged as was that of Black in the previous game. With an incomplete development (for the Q side pieces stayed at home) Black's position yet contained sufficient resources to hold an attack. A fine player was required in order to organize the defence, in so far as there was freedom to organize it. Another lesson from the game is that quite unbalanced games can end in draws, as all well-contested games should.

In considering the preceding games (and others to follow) the reader is well advised to consider technical features: 'hanging' pieces, outposts; open files, overloaded defences, etc., and notice to what extent they determined the outcome. He may find that those terms describe stages in a battle that was moving too fast. But when a battle is over, it can happen that what have been gained are technical — or strategic — advantages, which, for example, Bobby Fischer played for and exploited against Barcza in the position in Diagram 121 *supra*.

But there is one vague strategic principle which is, possibly, of more practical value than a lot of learning about outposts, blockades, Pawns with lust to expand (that verbal crime was committed by Nimzovitch), etc. The principle in question is the belief that miracles do not happen in Chess, or that thunder does not strike from a clear sky. Some of the sacrificial attacks already seen by the reader do illustrate this, negatively: viz. there were clear strategic indications of relative weakness or relative strength. There is pressure: or someone has gained tempo in development. Pieces are 'hanging', and the player who has the initiative is likely to win something while his opponent is endeavouring to catch up with the captures. Diagram 120 above shows a position full of warning to the defender. Diagram 124 is also ominous, though the specific thunderstroke is unexpected. But the sky is overcast. So, in the Capablanca–Spielmann position (Diagram 116) there is, to an aware player, a pervading sense of tension. But here one has to be acutely and widely aware. In Diagram 114 there is a heavy atmosphere, which might have warned the defender of danger. But the actual threat was so hard to see that White cannot be blamed for thinking that storm was not imminent.

In the light of that diagram the maxim needs elaboration. There are no miracles: but the 'natural laws' require so much detailed apprehension that strange occurrences can happen in apparently normal environments. There is no 'thunder from a clear sky', but one has to have clear vision not to miss the tiny cloud 'no bigger than a man's hand', which tells the acute observer that the atmosphere is not really serene. Nevertheless, if a player develops well relatively to his opponent's development and leaves no ordinarily apparent weaknesses, he need not spend time looking for dangers from undeveloped pieces, or immobile Pawns. Yanofsky's position in Diagram 114, would have been safer had the Pawn at e4 been blockaded by a minor piece. That is why 'technicians' blockade. But when blockading, remember that blocks can be sacrificially exploded. So look beyond the blockade along the lines which it is keeping closed, and to the pieces that can sacrifice themselves in the vicinity, in order to clear those lines.

First a diagram (126) to show the kind of position in which it is fairly obvious that sacrifices are imminent: indeed, so called-for that the moves made are hardly 'sacrificial'.

The position came at the end of a finely played game by one of the greatest English strategians, the late Atkins. Now, observe that all his pieces are functioning: and in order to make progress he must break open the defences by sacrifice.

For a heavy, but not overwhelming, atmosphere, let us cite a game by a recent great Chess star, Mikhael Tal. The whole game is worth recording. The opening is of rather special interest.

Black (Atkins)

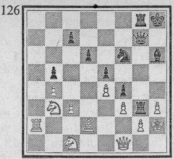

White (Wainwright)
(Played 1910)

Destruction of Blockade

| 37. .... | Kt×P | 42. K—Kt1 | B—K6 ch |
|---|---|---|---|
| 38. P×Kt | P—B6 | 43. QR—B2 | R—Kt6 |
| 39. R—KB2 | B—B5 | 44. K—R2 | B×R |
| 40. K—R1 | P×P ch | 45. R×B | R—R6 ch |
| 41. R×P | R×P ch | | forces mate |

| White | Black |
|---|---|
| UNZICKER | TAL |

(From a match between USSR and West Germany, 1960)

RUY LOPEZ

1. P—K4    P—K4
2. Kt—KB3    Kt—QB3
3. B—Kt5    P—QR3

A very usual move, because, although White, with B×Kt followed by P—Q4, can gain a King's side Pawn majority, Black has a compensating freedom of movement, greater than he obtains in the text line. So we have a strategic decision at move 4, which has become technical.

4. B—R4    Kt—B3    The Morphy Defence. 3. ....

Kt—B3 (i.e. without P—QR3) is called the Berlin defence: the difference is important in the event of Black's capturing the KP.

5. O—O   B—K2

The Tchigorin system. Black in the Lopez rarely plays the KB to QB4, because it gives White's QP a target (P—QB3 followed by P—Q4). Of other moves, Black could have played 5. .... Kt × P to which the best reply is not R—K1 (which is quite playable): but 6. P—Q4. Then the normal is

6. ..       P—QKt4
7. B—Kt3   P—Q4
8. P × P     B—K3

and there is tension against Black's centre. The defence, however, is very playable. The Tchigorin system is more popular, nowadays, because Black remains relatively uncommitted.

6. R—K1

Not only because now the KP can be more advantageously captured by Black, but this actually threatens B × Kt followed by Kt × P, winning a Pawn. 6. Q—K2 (the Worrall attack) is also playable, and leads to some Q side attack with P—QR4

6. ....   P—QKt4
7. B—Kt3—O—O

Some players prefer P—Q3 here so as to meet B—Q5 with B—Q2.

8. P—B3

Useful to preserve the B against

8. .... P—Q3

exchange by the Knight later on, and support the advance, P—Q4. 'Overprotecting' the KP and freeing the QKt and developing the QB.

Note that on move 5, Black elected to keep his KB at K2; so does not object to shutting it in.

9. P—KR3

Not a 'country move'; but 'dual purpose'.

It prevents B—Kt5 with which Black might counter-attack if White plays 9. P—Q4. Also it prepares P—KKt4, which may be played after the series P—Q4, QKt—Q2 Kt—B1, etc. The game, which began as a KP, is taking a shape analogous to the QP games in which the centre is closed.

9. .... Kt—Kt1

A move of the greatest strategic interest. The thing is not new. Breyer, a great Hungarian, played it in the 1920's. But it has not been popular. Normal, in the system is the following sequence

9. ....        Kt—QR4
10. B—B2        P—QB4
11. P—Q4        Q—B2
12. QKt—Q2      B—Q2
13. Kt—B1 and so to K3 or
        Kt3 with targets at d5
        and/or f5.

Black's position is then tenable; but the game is hard, before he achieves a King's side counter with P—KB4. In the game from which Diagram 126 is cited,

Atkins played 9. K—R1 and retired the KKt with a view to a K side thrust, which he developed patiently. Both retreats are sufficiently purposive to justify a breach of the rule against moving pieces twice in the opening.

| 10. P—Q4 | QKt—Q2 |
|---|---|

The Knight has remobilized itself. The defect is that the future of the QB is difficult. It must move to b7, and then back to c8 (if P—Q5 is played): but it does eventually come to life in most variations.

| 11. QKt—Q2 | |
|---|---|

Very high opinion favours 11. P—B4, with the threat P—B5. But it is believed that 4. .... P—B4 is adequate defence, and that 11. .... P×P is not to be excluded. The midnight oil is still burning over this. Unzicker at the time of this game had already tried 11. P—B4 in play.

| 11. .... | B—Kt2 |
|---|---|
| 12. B—B2 | |

12. P—Q5 is committal and makes Black's eventual P—KB4 reasonable.

| 12. .... | R—K1 |
|---|---|
| 13. Kt—B1 | B—KB1 |

Another retreat by way of re-organization. Note how Black is defending f5. He could not play P—KKt3 while the Rook stood at f8, or while f8 was empty because White's B—R6 would gain in tempo.

| 14. Kt—Kt3 | |
|---|---|

Perhaps Black is too well armed on the King's side now for

P—KKt4 to be promising. Kt—
K3 seems a better move, but is
rejected because after P—KKt3
and Kt—R4, f4 will be threatened.

14. ....     P—Kt3
15. P—QKt3                Takes, from the Black Queen's
                          Knight, a square that it doesn't
                          want to reach. Here White's
                          strategy is defective, because of
                          defect in tactical insight. To
                          Black's fianchetto here, the
                          proper reply seems to be B—K3,
                          followed by Q—Q2 (or Q—B1)
                          with aim at B—R6. This (better
                          in conjunction with P—KKt4)
                          can be met by K—R1 and Kt—
                          Kt1, sooner or later. But no harm
                          is done. The text (in conjunc-
                          tion with the next move) shows
                          that White has failed to see
                          some threats to the blockaded
                          centre.

15. ....     B—Kt2
16. P—Q5
16. ....     Kt—Kt3       A strange-looking move, until the
                          tactical lines are thought through.
                          The threat is P—QB3. Hence
                          White's 17th.

17. Q—K2   P—B3
18. P—B4                  Not having seen far (or clearly)
                          enough.

(See Diagram 127.)

18. ....     BP×QP
19. BP×QP                 The KP must stand so as to pre-
                          vent P—K5 and a dangerous Kt
                          move, unmasking the Bishop's

Black (Tal)

White (Unzicker)

Destruction of Blockade
White has just played *18*. P—B4
Black now wins (see text)

battery. Unzicker will undoubtedly have seen some sacrificial possibilities, but judged them inadequate. (He is relying on his 22nd and 23rd moves.) Tal saw more clearly.

19. .... KKt×QP
20. P×Kt P—K5
21. Kt×P B×R
22. B—Kt5 P—B3
23. B—K3

Unzicker may well have anticipated here.

23. .... P—B4
24. R×B P×Kt
25. Kt—Kt5 B×P
26. R—Q1 P—R3
27. B×Kt Q×B
28. R×Kt P×Kt
29. R×KKtP with quite a strong attack. If so, then

he missed a shorter vari-
ation, perhaps harder to
see, which Tal now plays.

23. ....  Kt×P!
24. R×B  Kt×B
25. Q×Kt  B×Kt
26. B×B  P—Q4

A different exploitation of the
half-pin that existed at move *23*.
White resigned at this point.

Games are lost by bad long-range decisions, and/or by bad
short-range decisions. Most are in the latter category. Even
when a player has committed himself to difficulties, he may find
good play. But the player who has done one piece of inferior
play usually does another. In point is Diagram 128, where
Fischer's opponent has already not made the most of his

Black (Bielicki)

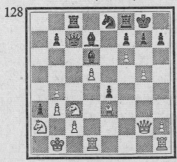

White (Fischer)
Counter and Counter-counter
(Mar del Plata, 1960)

The play went:
24. ....  B—K4?
25. Kt×P  B—B4 (threatening Q×P ch)
26. P×P  K×P
27. B—B5  Kt—Q3
28. Kt×Kt  B×Kt
29. Q—B2 with a winning K side attack

chances. But had he seen clearly he would not have played the immediate moves that he made.

In the Diagram position good moves are hard to find, but better moves are available than Black played.

24. ....  P×P is heroic but fatal: in other words, 'rash'; because of

> 25. P×P ch            K—R1
> 26. KR—Kt1            B×P
> 27. P—Q6! (and the same move refutes B—B5
>       in this variation)
> 24. ....              K—R1 is to be con-
>                         sidered

But better than the text is quite simply 24. .... B—KB4. Then 25. Kt×P is not playable because of 25. .... Q×P ch. 26. Q×Q   R×Q and if 27. K×R   B×Kt ch forking.

Admittedly, B—B4 involves difficulties:

> e.g. 24. ....            B—B4
>   25. QR—B1

If then

> 25. ....            B—Kt3
> 26. P—R4 is frightening

But there is a resource —

> 25. ....            B×P

after which may occur

> 26. B—Q4            B×Kt
> 27. B×Kt (Kt×Kt may allow P—R7 ch with
>       some counterplay)
> 27. ....            Q—Q2

and Black, still with problems to solve, has not demonstrably lost.

As the game went, Black evidently thought that after his text move, White dare not play Kt×P because of the counter-attack. But White's play, not very hard to see at that proximate stage, completely destroys the counter-chances.

Sometimes the game seizes the player by the throat, as History seized Mussolini. Then one plays desperately. Here is the Russo–Israeli Czerniak, Black against Winz, throwing away his shield (Diagram 129).

Black (Czerniak)

129

White (Winz)
(Played at Tel-Aviv, 1939)

Sudden storm
Black to move
11. .... P×P (see text)

This game had proceeded along the lines of a game Euwe–Reshevsky (Avro, 1938).

|  | | |
|---|---|---|
| | 1. P—Q4 | Kt—KB3 |
| 2. P—QB4 P—KKt3 | 3. P—B3 | P—Q4 |
| 4. P×P Kt×P | 5. P—K4 | Kt—Kt3 |
| 6. Kt—B3 B—Kt2 | 7. B—K3 | O—O |

8. P—B4 (the late F. D. Yates said that this development is always too early!) 8. .... Kt—B3. 9. P—Q5 Kt—Kt1. In the Avro game, White now played 10. Kt—B3 met by P—QB3 after which Black retained some control, and outplayed his opponent.

R—I

Here White has played *10*. P—QR4 instead of Euwe's Kt—B3, and Black has ventured *10*. .... P—K4 met by *11*. P—R5.

Now Black has apparently wasted a lot of tempo in this game. His Queen's Knight has been out and back, his King's Knight has made three moves. Will it make a fourth? On the other hand, White has used his tempo to build a position which, apart from the P at a5, is aggressive against nothing. Black feels either that he cannot waste more time, or that his development is functionally better, and sufficiently so to justify a risky aggression. It is doubtful whether either player saw the consequences very far ahead. In this type of game attackers use a judgement, and rely on the expectation, so often justified in a promising attack, that resources will be available. The game proceeded.

*11*. ....   P×P
*12*. P×Kt   P×B
*13*. R×P

> A tactical familiar feature. Capture by the Pawn would be meaningless. But the Rook capture wins a Rook. If
>
> *13*. ....   R×R
> *14*. P×R
>
> again with the strange-looking effect that the Pawn can promote without hindrance.

*13*. ....   Q—R5 ch
*14*. P—Kt3

> Not *14*. K—K2 because of
> *14*. ....      Q—B7 ch
> *15*. K—Q3   Kt—Q2
> *16*. R×R    Kt—K4 ch
> *17*. K—Q4   P—K7 mate.
> A point that Black had to see perhaps as early as move *10* (when he played P—K4).

*14*. ....   B×Kt ch

15. P×B   Q×KP

A familiar attack in a strange setting. Black is attacking with a small but surprisingly strong force. White's defence is not bad. One feels that Capablanca, had he found himself in such a position, would have won for White. (Against most players, he'd have won for Black as well!)

16. Kt—B3

Perhaps the best.
Not

    16. Q—B3   Q—B7
    17. Q×P   R×R
    18. P×R and with two checks
        Black wins that Pawn.

The variations are too many to exhaust here. Interesting is

    16. R×R⁻        Q×R
    17. R×Kt        Q×Kt
    18. Q—K2        B—Kt5
    19. R×R ch    K×R
    20. P×P          B×Q
    21. P—B8 (=Q) ch K—Kt2
    22. K×B          Q—B7 ch
    23. K—Q3        Q×B ch
    24. K×P and White seems to
        have    the    winning
        chances. But on move
        18. ....   P×P may be
        suggested.

If then

    19. P—Q6   B—Kt5
    20. R×R ch   K×R

Note now that the B cannot be taken and that if the Queen move towards the Q side

P—K7 can be played.

Also Q—Q3 leaves mate at f2.

Therefore   21. Q—KKt2   Q×Q
            22. B×Q      K—K1

and Black stands better.

In the main variation, possible for White is *19*. P—B4. If then

19. ....        B—Kt5
20. R×R ch      K×R
21. Q—KKt2      Q×Q
22. B×Q         P—KB4

is necessary in order to keep control of e2. This is a most difficult ending. Quite often an attack ends in transition to an endgame which is so difficult to estimate that the strongminded player does not proceed with the attack.

Another feature is that White cannot be left with nothing to do. Consider also the variations that spring from *17*. P×P.

Also to be considered are moves like Q—Q3 or Q—Q4, etc.

16. ....    B—Kt5
17. R×R     B×Kt
18. Q—Q3                    Not

18. R×Kt      B×Q
19. R×R ch    K×R
20. P×P       Q—B7
21. P=Q ch    K—Kt2

and White cannot prevent mate.

18. ....    Q—K4            He cannot capture the Rook because after Q exchanges P×P wins for White. Note the odd feature that a Pawn attacking a

|              |        | Kt on the back rank is attacking a piece that cannot prevent the Pawn's promotion. |
|--------------|--------|

*19.* P×P

Perhaps this is a luxury that White cannot afford.

If he plays *19.* R—Kt1 he can possibly free himself slowly from pressure and be left with the exchange to the good.

*19.* .... Q×P

P—Q6 was threatened. Also this move brings the Queen into Q side action.

*20.* R—Kt1    Q—Kt3

Threatening P—K7.

*21.* P—Kt4

As soon as he has time on his hands he makes a bad move. He is prepared to allow P—K7 relying on Q×B and, after Q×R, Q×KP.

He is afraid that *21.* B—K2 may be met by Q—Kt7 forcing Q×P and after B×B Black gets the QBP and a lot of checks.

Quite good is

   *21.* B—Kt2    P—K7
   *22.* B×B      Q×R ch
   *23.* K×P      R—K1 ch
   *24.* B—K4     P—B4
   *25.* P—Q6. But there are many complications. Black can, but may not be wise to, capture the K side pawns.

*21.* .... R—Q1!

A great turn of the wheel. Black has another piece in the attack.

*22.* R—Kt3

Because P—B4 is met by Q—Kt5 ch. forcing mate.

| | |
|---|---|
| 22. .... R×P | The Knight is irrelevant. |
| 23. R×Kt ch  K—Kt2 | |
| 24. R×B | Getting scattered material in exchange for the Queen. |
| 24. .... R×Q | |
| 25. B×R  Q—B2! | The move after! |
| 26. R—K8 | After R×KP  Q×R<br>Black has the material advantage as well as an attack. |
| 26. ....  Q×P ch | |
| 27. K—B1  Q×B ch | |
| 28. K—Kt2  Q—Q7 ch | |
| 29. K—Kt3 | Even now if White can capture that Pawn without danger the game is drawn. But the resources of the board play for Czerniak, as the stars in their courses for his Israel ancestors. |
| 29. ....  P—K7! | |
| 30. R(3)—K3  Q—K8 ch | |
| 31. K—R3  Q—B8 ch | |
| 32. K—Kt3  Q—Kt8 ch | |
| 33. K—R3  Q—B7 | The point. White is in danger of mate. If R×P  Q—B6 ch  K—R4  P—Kt4 ch wins. |
| 34. R(8)—K5 | To prevent P—KKt4. |
| 34. ....  P—QKt4 | R×P is still unplayable. |
| 35. P—Kt5  P—R4 | |
| 36. R(5)—K4 | If 36. R×P e.p. ch  K×P<br>    37. R×KP  Q—B6 ch<br>        38. K—R4  P—B3 wins.<br>But now the mate is 'off'. |
| 36. ....  P—Kt5 | |
| 37. R×KP | Fallen, but another carries on the fight. |
| 37. ....  Q—B6 ch | |
| 38. K—R4  P—Kt6 | |

*39.* R(2)—K3   Q—B7 ch
*40.* K—R3   P—Kt7
*41.* R—K8

Threatening a well-known type of what is wrongly called 'swindle'. If P=Q, R—R8 ch K×R  R—K8 ch and sacrifices itself for stalemate.

*41.* ....   Q×R ch
*42.* Resigns

The reader of the above will be interested in the next position (130) from the game Euwe–Reshevsky therein referred to. Euwe

Black (Reshevsky)

130

White (Euwe)
(Avro, 1938)

Well-timed break-up
Black to play
*22.* ....   B×Kt
*23.* R×B   P—QKt4!

allowed his opponent to spend time capturing a Pawn at f4, and developed what looked like a very promising King's side attack. But Reshevsky's greater insight had seen this to be illusory and cold-bloodedly faces King's side dangers while he breaks up White's centre.

The first nine moves are the moves of the Winz–Czerniak game (see p. 193).

There followed

|       |              |                    |
| ----- | ------------ | ------------------ |
| *10.* | Kt—B3        | P—B3               |
| *11.* | Q—Kt3        | P×P                |
| *12.* | Kt×P         | Kt×Kt              |
| *13.* | P×Kt         | Kt—Q2              |
| *14.* | B—K2         | Q—R4 ch            |
| *15.* | B—Q2         | Q—Kt3              |
| *16.* | B—B3         | B×B ch             |
| *17.* | P×B          | sacrificing the KBP |
| *17.* | ....         | Q—KB               |
| *18.* | P—B4         | Q×BP               |
| *19.* | O—O          | Q—B2               |
| *20.* | K—R1 Perhaps too slow |           |
| *20.* | ....         | Kt—B3              |
| *21.* | Q—K3         | B—Kt5              |
| *22.* | Q—R6 (see    | B×Kt               |
|       | Diagram 130) |                    |

*23.* R×B apparently developing White's threat of R—R3 and R—KB1 (with a view to R×Kt). Black seems to ignore it. The point is that after *23.* .... P—QKt4 *24.* R—KB1 is answered by Kt—Kt5 (forcing Q—R4) and P—B4, while *24.* R—R3 fails against Q—K4. That Q—K4 could have been played instead of P—QKt4, but would achieve nothing after R—K1.

There followed (to P—QKt4) *24.* P×P    Q—K4 (not Kt×P because then R—R3 followed by R—KB1 does win).

|       |       |        |
| ----- | ----- | ------ |
| *25.* | R—K1  | Kt×P   |
| *26.* | R—R3  | Q—Kt2  |

leaving White with insufficient compensation for the Pawn lost. Also we see here an illustration of the proposition that development in the centre is a safeguard against a King's side attack.

There followed

| 27. Q—Q2 | P—K3 |
| 28. R—Q3 | QR—Kt1 |
| 29. P—QR4 | · Kt—Kt3 |
| 30. Q—Kt4 | QR—B1 |

Now we begin to see the merits of 'open files'. Black did not play KR—B1 (with gain of tempo) because he may have been concerned with the nuisance value of a later Q—Q6.

| 31. P—R5  Kt—Q4 | |
| 32. Q—Kt3  R—B4 | |
| 33. B—B3  KR—Kt1 | (a very interesting decision). |
| 34. B×Kt  R(4)×P | |
| 35. Q—R2 | There is no sacrifice possible. Now Black has the advantage of doubled Rooks on an open file, and a fine diagonal for the Queen. |
| 35. .... P×B | |
| 36. R×P  Q—B6 | |
| 37. R—KB1  R—Kt7 | |
| 38. Q—R4 | 38. R—Q8 ch followed by Q×P ch comes to nothing. |
| 38. ....  R—Kt8 | |
| 39. R(5)—Q1 | Nor R(1)—Q1 because of Q—K8 ch. |
| 39. ....  R×R | |
| 40. R×R  P—QR3 | |
| 41. P—R3  R—Kt4 | |
| 42. R—R1 | From now on a precise exploitation of what, for most players, is only a small advantage. |
| 42. ....  K—Kt2 | |
| 43. Q—R2  Q—Kt7 | |
| 44. Q—R4 | He feels he has better drawing chances with Queens on. (White's Rook will be limited to one file – after exchanges.) |

| | | |
|---|---|---|
| 44. .... | R—KKt4 | Black's Rook is doing double work, but, clearly, so is White's. |
| 45. R—R2 | Q—B6 | This is a very subtle move. There are checks at e1 and g3 to be borne in mind, and Rook manœuvres threatening mate, and achieving control of the 7th rank. |
| 46. R—R1 | P—R4 | Attacking, for a 'middle-game win'. |
| 47. Q—R2 | R—KB4 | |
| 48. K—R2 | P—Kt4 | Black has play and White has none. Black's extra Pawn is guarding his King from check. |
| 49. Q—R4 | R—B5 | No longer threatening the RP because there are other interests. |
| 50. Q—R2 | P—Kt5 | |
| 51. P×P | Q—K4 | |
| 52. P—Kt3 | R—K5 | |
| 53. Q—Kt1 | R—K7 ch | |
| 54. K—R3 | P×P ch | |
| 55. K—R4 | R—R7 ch | |
| 56. K×P | Q—K7 ch resigns. | |

The mating net is interesting and clear.

The play from the diagram was a study in strategic exploitation. Black drew White's Queen's side Pawns forward, eventually liquidating whatever Queen's side advantage White held. After that there was no compensation for the Pawn. Black also exploited open files and a good diagonal, doubled Rooks, threats on both wings – the entire Chess arsenal – while having clear control of all dangers to himself from Q and Rooks.

(Reshevsky is interesting to Chess-players and others because he is one child prodigy who lost none of his 'eighth-year' powers, but increased them. Even now, in his fifties, he constitutes as strong a Chess force as can be found anywhere.)

That example was an instance of Black's defence from the

centre to the wings. A strategic benefit is gained by any player who emerges in the early middle game with greater scope in and through the centre, for his pieces.

This does not involve a powerful Pawn array – blocking the opponent's pieces. Those strong centres are often only strong in appearance. They can be eroded from the sides, as in games already seen. The centre, like development, like any concept of strength in Chess, is functional, not formal.

Diagram 131 shows the kind of case where, although Black has open lines, White's centre is better than Black's, and enables White to carry out a fine attack.

Black (Matanovic)

131

White (Naidorf)
(Mar del Plata, 1961)
The opening of lines
White to move, plays P—KB5, and later P—Q5

Black, in this game, has made the mistake of unblocking the centre for his own Bishop, not realizing that in so doing he is giving more life to White's fianchettoed Bishop, while White shows precisely how to exploit a fianchettoed Bishop, and what is meant by control of the centre.

The play up to the diagram

    NAIDORF           MATANOVIC

was

*1.* P.—Q4  Kt—KB3

2. P—QB4    P—K3
3. Kt—KB3 P—QKt3
4. P—K3

Possibly better than the frequent King's fianchetto.

4. ....    B—Kt2
4. B—Q3    B—K2

There is a strong argument for Kt—K5 here, with support from the KBP.

6. O—O    O—O
7. Kt—B3   P—Q4

It is not wrong to play this in front of the fianchettoed Bishop, but it is more justified if Black intends Kt—K5. Otherwise P—Q3 is a better move.

8. P—QKt3

Good, not only as a useful fianchetto movement, but as a defence to c4.

8. ....    QKt—Q2
9. B—Kt2   P—B4
10. Q—K2   BP×P
11. KP×P   R—QB1
12. QR—Q1  Q—B2
13. Kt—K5  P×P

Not a good decision.

14. P×P    KR—Q1
15. P—B4   Kt—B1

We now have the Diagram position, from which the play was as follows:

16. P—KB5

The Queen's Pawn is guarded by the possibility of Kt—Kt5, forking: White's move is clearing more lines of action for his pieces. It could have been stopped by earlier P—KKt3 but that would have left Black very weak on those Black squares that matter in this game.

| | |
|---|---|
| *16.* .... P—QR3 | Taking a square from White's Knight Black is short of good moves, because the position has crystallized in White's favour, through White's better use of tempo, and Black's weaker planning earlier in the game. (He could so have played as to prevent White's consolidation at e5.) |
| *17.* P×P  P×P | If Kt×P, there is a very difficult-to-analyse danger of *18.* Kt×P. If K×Kt White has Q—R5 ch among other tactical possibilities. |
| *18.* K—R1 | So as to prevent *18.* .... R×QP *19.* B×Pch  Kt×B *20.* R×R B—B4 pinning White has time for this prophylactic move. |
| *18.* .... B—R1 | *Faute de mieux,* Black can contrive pressure on g2. |
| *19.* P—Q5 | Opening the long diagonal. This Pawn is guarded by the pin that White can apply, after exchanges, at c4. |
| *19.* .... R—K1 | Quite a strong counter-threat against the weakened Knight (e.g. *20.* .... P×P followed by B—Q3). But Black has missed something, including the point of White's 18th. |
| *20.* Kt—Kt4  P×P | |
| *21.* Kt×P | Another line clearance. |
| *21.* .... Kt×Kt(d5) | Wrong capture. *21.* .... B×Kt must be played. If *22.* P×B  B—Q1 *23.* Q—B3  Q—Q3 *24.* Q—B5  B—B2 gives the defence a chance. |

| | |
|---|---|
| 22. P×Kt   B×P | |
| 23. Kt—R6 ch | What Matanovic did not see early enough. |
| 23. ....   K—R1 | Because P×Kt is answered by Q—Kt4 ch. B—Kt4. *25.* Q—Q4. |
| 24. Q—Kt4   B—Q3 | |
| 25. Kt—B7 ch resigns | Q is 'cut-off' from g7. |

The winner of the next game, David Bronstein, has been responsible for the bringing of an element of surrealism into Chess. He finds himself investigating, from the inside, difficulties into which he has inveigled himself, and discovering some factor of detonation in the game. Then there explodes a surprising combination.

This game was played at Mar del Plata in 1960.

| White | Black |
|---|---|
| WEXLER | BRONSTEIN |
| *1.* P—Q4 | Kt—KB3 |
| *2.* P—QB4 | P—B4 |
| | The Benoni Defence, calculated to make White expand his centre, leaving a hollow, as well as targets for Black Pawns. |
| *3.* P—Q5   P—K3 | *3 . . . .* P—Q3 is often played |
| *4.* Kt—QB3   P×P | |
| *5.* P×P   P—Q3 | Black's Pawn position has merits and defects: a Queen's side majority, but a 'backward Pawn'. |
| *6.* P—K4   P—KKt3 | |
| *7.* Kt—B3 | If White intends to meet P—QR4, and to develop his Kt via f3, d2, to c4, then he must play P—KR3 first. Other moves that are playable, are 7. P—QR4 |
| | 7. B—KKt5, and |
| | 7. B—B4 |

| | | |
|---|---|---|
| 7. .... | P—QR3 | |
| 8. P—QR4 | | committing himself. |
| 8. .... | B—Kt5 | One of those relatively rare occasions of a move specifically made for the purpose of exchanging B for Kt. Black loses little if any tempo here, because the recapturer, whether Q or B, will not be on its best square. |
| 9. B—K2 | | 9. P—KR3 seems more purposive, giving a square to the QB later on. |
| 9. .... | B×Kt | |
| 10. B×B | QKt—Q2 | |
| 11. O—O | B—Kt2 | |
| 12. B—B4 | | Observe that Bronstein did not play 11. .... Kt—K4 because he would not want to exchange it yet for either of White's Bishops. |
| 12. .... | Q—Kt1 | A subtle move. He does not play Q—K2, because after R—K1 the Queen can be compromised. Nor |

12. .... Q—B2 because of
13. P—K5 Kt×P
14. B×Kt P×B
15. P—Q6!

attacking the Queen and gaining tempo.

| | | |
|---|---|---|
| 13. B—K2 | | Defending the Q side and freeing the KBP. |
| 13. .... | O-O | |
| 14. B—Kt3 | R—K1 | |
| 15. Q—B2 | Q—B2 | Black, in order to develop his QR, and to work on the c file, is not afraid, or ashamed, of moving the same piece twice. |

*16.* P—B4   P—B5

A typical strategic dichotomy. White intends to do his best on the K side, Black on the Q side. Here the appearances are that Black's K side is very well defended.

*17.* K—R1

Not merely in case a check interrupts his play. The text prevents .... P—QKt4,  P×P  P×P  Kt×P  Q—B4 ch.

*17.* ....   QR—B1

*18.* P—R5

If he wishes to prevent .... Kt—B4  B×BP  QKt×KP, the text move is irrelevant. Better is QR—B1 or KR—B1. White's plan, however, seems to involve R—R4. He is making his QRP vulnerable, but estimating that Black will not be able to afford to capture it.

*18.* ....   Q—Q1

A third time! But in this type of position, tempo tends to matter less than the exact placing of pieces. However, Bronstein's timing is not bad!

*19.* KR—K1   R—B4

*20.* R—R4

Defending by counter-attack. There is, however, something to be said for letting Black consume time, as well as the QRP: e.g. After
   *20.* B—B3 (or B—B1) R×RP
   *21.* R—Q1 and P—K5
will do damage.

*20.* ....   R×RP

*21.* R×P

White is leaving Black's Rook badly placed. The alternative
    *21.* R×R  Q×R
    *22.* B×P
is met by Kt—R4! weakening White's prospects in the centre.

*21.* .... P—QKt4

*22.* R—Kt4

The need for this move shows how clearly Bronstein has seen. White cannot play
    *22.* R—B6  Kt—Kt1
    *23.* P—Kt4  Kt×R
    *24.* P×Kt  R—R6
    *25.* Q—Kt2 because
    *25.* .... R×Kt
    *26.* Q×R  Kt×KP is destructive.

Now the limitation on the scope of Black's Rook is partly offset by the narrow scope of White's Rook. However, this may increase.

*22.* .... Q—Kt3

Black's Queen manœuvres are becoming even more interesting.

*23.* B—B3

White has no idea of what is happening. Otherwise he might have kept his B on the f1 diagonal.

*23.* .... Q—B4

*24.* R—Kt3

Evidently, Wexler is convinced that if Black plays
    *24.* .... P—Kt5 then
    *25.* P—K5 gives him a good game, viz.
    *25.* .... Kt—R4
    *26.* B—B2
followed by P—K6. The outcome

is not clear. But one thing is clear, that White did not see what Black 'could' do.

24. .... Q—B5!    Proceeding with a combination worthy of a player who has tied a match for the World Championship.

25. B—K2    'All unconscious of their doom the little victims play.' But it is hard for White to find good moves here.
If 25. R—QB1 Black can play R—QB1 retaining a very tight grip.
Also 25. .... Kt—B4 is playable. After which R—R3  R×R P×R  Kt×KP. 25. B—B2 is met by 25. .... Kt×QP. If then
26. P×Kt  R×R ch
27. B×R  Q—B8 mate

25. .... Kt×KP!    Creating a totally new battery, and other complexities.

26. B×Q  Kt×B ch    This must be recaptured.
27. K—Kt1  B—Q5 ch!

27. P×Kt  R×R ch
28. K—R2  R(4)—R8
29. P—Kt4  R(R)—B8

30. Q—B2    Q—Q2 is not played because after P×B, and B×Kt, R—Q8 will give Black a square on the third rank, and allow Kt—B3

30. .... P×B
31. R—Kt7  B×Kt
32. P×B  R—R8 ch
Resigns.

That was Chess with an element of strangeness and subtlety.

One felt that the winner was using tempo unnaturally. But the fight was in a relatively stable strategic frame, in which tempo mattered less than accuracy.

Generally, good Chess looks natural. An unnatural process is likely to be a wrong one. In the position in Diagram 132, Black has allowed a very high concentration of power against

Black (Yanofsky)

132

White (Alexander)
(Hastings, 1950)

Overstrain

| | | | |
|---|---|---|---|
| *14.* B—R5 | P—Kt3 | *17.* P—R5 | P—KB5 |
| *15.* Kt×KtP | P×Kt | *18.* B×P | P×P |
| *16.* B×P | Kt×B | *19.* P×Kt wins | |

If *19.* ....    R—Kt2    *20.* Q—R3
constitutes a winning attack

his King's side, and is relying on equalization on the other wing where his attacking force is not formidable. Such an impression of unnatural development creates doubts as to the soundness of Black's position, and it proved to be very unsound.

On the other hand, the student must always be expectant of the unexpected; at least, in the short tactical range. As far as the eye can see let there be no cloud.

Study of the Illustrative games will have revealed some dangers to be avoided. Don't, for example, allow your opponent's pieces loose in your field, as Winz did in his game against

Czerniak. Control of squares is a very important strategic, technical notion.

The player of White in Diagram 133 has lost control of the Black squares in his own field and is in difficulties (not necessarily fatal). His development has not been as purposive as his opponent's. He is biting on granite.

Black

133

White

Dangers of loss of field-control

The actual game went:

| | | |
|---|---|---|
| *1.* | Q—K2 | B—Q5 ch (in a good cause) |
| *2.* | Kt×B | P×Kt |
| *3.* | Kt—Kt5 | Kt—K6 |
| *4.* | R—K1 | B—Kt5 |
| *5.* | Q—KB2 | P—K4 with a strong game |

Diagram 134 shows a subtlety of play for control of squares. In virtually forcing White to play B×Kt Black gains for himself a better control of the Black squares than his opponent can enjoy.

In the actual game Black wasted this. After *20.* B×Kt (following a Lopez) R×B was played. Now a vital consideration is the control of the QB file. Black can, must, and here does not, double Rooks. But after

| | | |
|---|---|---|
| *20.* | .... | R×B |
| *21.* | QR—B1 | R×R (not good) |
| *22.* | R×R | Kt—R4 |

Black

134

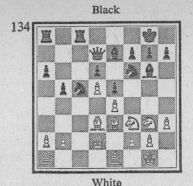

White

Control of squares

superficial tactical play has put Black at a relative disadvantage, because now Q—B3 gives White access to c6 with fine counter chances.

On the same reasoning it may be better to challenge a Rook on an open file than to proceed with one's logical development in pursuit of an attack.

Black

135

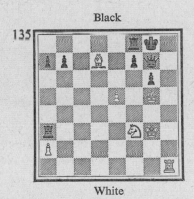

White

Concealed Battery
(see text)

Such strategic omissions lose many games. But more are lost by tactical oversights.

How easy to lose in a good position. In point is Diagram 135. If White plays Q—K7 he will probably win. If he plays, instead, P—K6, see what happens:

| | |
|---|---|
| 1. .... | R × Kt ch |
| 2. K × R | P × P dis. ch. |

A player who makes that error is doing what many do, seeing ideas in his own programme, without paying sufficient attention to initiatives that can be introduced by the opponent.

Such a player is not really seeing his own lines clearly, because he is not seeing the terrain through which they run. Try and see both sides of the board. Eventually you will see the entire board as a whole.

## CHAPTER FOUR

# SURVEY OF THE OPENINGS
# IS CHESS EXHAUSTED? IS BLACK INFERIOR?

THE text of this book, so far, has been designed to show (in graduated stages as the reader has advanced) the difficulties that present themselves to the player sitting at the chessboard, relying on his own unaided brains. The reader has seen how some of these problems have been solved: and he may have decided (as I think, rightly) that the concentration of a capable mind – with experience of concentration – will find for its owner good moves at all stages of the game. Those good moves will win against all but the equally capable mind of the strong opponent. Is there any more to Chess than that?

Do players ever win because they know a bit more of precedent, of what was done in master-games? Can a player win by reason of knowledge of long lines of opening play? or lose by ignorance of these lines? If this is not the case, why do so many players prefer to have White and choice of first move?

The last query opens up arguments which may be postponed for the moment. But as to the learning, certainly there are many processes to be learned in Chess. But one should not regard as essential learning any exhaustive treatment of opening lines.

Naturally, people are always seeking ways of making the game easier for themselves, though some persons adopt strange methods to that end. Normally, experience equips and strengthens a player. As he grows he acquires a technique. What once required thought ceases to require thought. Many of the processes seen in this book – typical ways of attack and defence, modes of development, endgame operations, etc.—become, as it were, part of one's knowledge of the rules of the game. Many possible functions of the pieces, in isolation or in co-operation, become part of one's knowledge of 'the moves'. This acquisition of technique is achieved 'naturally', through experience – which is acquired in one's own games, and in endeavours to understand the play of others. Methods can be explained, reasons given, and, to that extent, there is learning in Chess – and teaching.

But when we consider opening play, we find that here there has been a tendency for people to try and learn too much. The nervousness of the diffident player – and most players are diffident at the outset of the game – makes him want to seek assurance: 'to make assurance double sure' by making a bond with the author of a book of opening lines. In this way, the effort to learn becomes a mnemonic effort: and that effort has changed the conception of the Chess task in far too many heads.

In the field of opening play there has, naturally, been achieved a general agreement on the need for development, and on some obvious ways of development. But, going farther than this, many practising players have set out to find 'authority' for every move they make, for as long as it is possible to emulate the great. They want to learn by heart large numbers of honoured variations, going far into the middle-game. In this way they disregard the truth that somebody once 'saw' these moves unaided: and that there will come a moment when the 'learned' player will have to see a move unaided. If, at that moment, he has not 'thought through' all his previous moves, he will not be mentally geared for good Chess.

Secondly, and legitimately, there has been a good deal of midnight-oil research. 'What kind of a game do I get if, at move 13 or 14 of this line, or earlier or later, I play X instead of Y?' And one explores: and discoveries are made. I would say that few discoveries are made that are so important that every player must know them by heart. What Lipschütz saw, by his oil-lamp, Rabinovitch can improvise, by the light of nature, in the actual game. Nothing very long and convincing, and/or forcing to victory, has ever been discovered, which the judgement, and insight, of a master should not be able to find as move follows move. There is not likely to be any desperately cunning, fantastically obscure, move, which the light of nature will never find. Chess is not like that.

Nevertheless there are some opening lines which are quite hard Chess, and which, being known, save labour. In some openings, some lines have been explored a long way because problems of development of major importance present themselves early in those lines; and the variations are many. This has tempted writers – though not recently – to suggest that Chess can be exhausted, as (in some opinions) Draughts is exhausted. Capablanca, at the height of his powers, suggested that so much had been learned in Chess that novelty was on the wane. He suggested the addition of extra pieces on a larger board. But he lived to discover that Chess was richer than he had thought it to be. Today there is more research than ever, but the best that can be said of most of it is this: that if you discover a subtle way of getting some initiative (if it amounts to more than that, it is not likely to be overlooked in play) you still have a problem of how to turn it to advantage – or into 'an advantage'. There are, I think, no programmers capable of equipping an Electronic Computer with sufficient variations, and sufficient rules for the guidance of its judgement, to make it more than a mediocre 'lightning player'.

What requires to be learned in the human player is (a) General Principle in practice: (b) A few movements that can be called 'hard' – and of which the knowledge saves too great an effort too early in the game.

Typical is a line of play in the *Ruy Lopez*, which expresses the results of a good deal of experiment.

| | | |
|---|---|---|
| *1.* | P—K4 | P—K4 |
| *2.* | Kt—KB3 | Kt—QB3 |
| *3.* | B—Kt5 | P—QR3 (introducing either the Steinitz Deferred or the Morphy Defence) |

R—K

By this move Black selects from many well-tried lines, many of which are eminently playable: e.g. *3. . . . .* Kt—B3, the Berlin Defence: *3. . . . .* P—Q3 the Steinitz Defence: *3. . . . .* B—B4, the Classical Defence. None of these moves is bad, though each carries with it problems of development.

More difficult, though they do not lose, are *3. . . . .* KKt—K2 (the Alapin) and a Fianchetto (flank development) by *3. . . . .* P—KKt3. Bold, but not bad, is *3. . . . .* P—KB4 (Schliemann's Defence).

*4.* B—R4. Possible is *4.* B×Kt (Exchange variation) which can be answered by QP×Kt (the usual) or KtP×Kt, quite playable, though unpopular.

After the capture by QP (*4. . . . .* QP×B) White can play *5.* P—Q4: and, after exchanges on that square, hold a King's side Pawn majority. This is technically important. The three Queen's side Pawns, if they are placed, in an endgame, at a3, b2, c3, can hold all four of Black's Queen's side Pawns, since two of the latter are a doubled pair, while White has chances with 4–3 on the King's side. But the Exchange Variation gives Black middle-game play in which he has Bishop against Knight, and plenty of open lines.

*4. . . . .* Kt—B3 (The Morphy Defence)

Playable, *inter alia*, is *4. . . . .* P—Q3 (Steinitz Deferred), one variation of which starts with *5.* B×Kt ch, more popular than the exchange on move four, because now the recapture creates a poor pawn shape.

*5,* O—O

Nobody bothers much in the Lopez about Black's King's Pawn, but at this point White's King's Pawn is an object of attention. Indeed in this variation it can be captured.

*5. . . . .* Kt×P (The Morphy-Tarrasch)
*6.* P—Q4

This move expresses the experience of those who have found that *6.* R—K1 Kt—B4. *7.* B×Kt QP×B (or KtP×B) leads to nothing convincing in the way of attack. That was easy to see: but the merit of P—Q4 has been the subject matter of research, involving such experiments as *6. ....* P×P. *7.* R—K1 P—Q4. *8.* Kt×P B—Q3. *9.* Kt×Kt B×P ch. *10.* K—R1! Q—R5. *11.* R×Kt ch P×R. *12.* Q—Q8 ch Q×Q. *13.* Kt×Q dis. ch K×Kt. *14.* K×B (the Riga Defence). If now *14. ....* P—KB4? *15.* B—KKt5 mate, constitutes an amusing example of the power of two Bishops.

| | |
|---|---|
| *6. ....* | P—QKt4 |
| *7.* B—Kt3 | (P—Q4 achieves nothing) |
| *7. ....* | P—Q4 |
| *8.* P×P | B—K3 |

And now a tense position is developing. There is a thin red line across d5 and e4. Black's Knight is on an awkward square. (Most Chess difficulties spring from pieces on awkward squares: there is something to be said for keeping to 'natural' squares, if one knows which they are!) Also a long-sighted player of Black can see here that he may be left with a backward QBP

| | |
|---|---|
| *9.* P—B3 | To prevent the Bishop from being exchanged. |
| *9. ....* B—K2 | The square QB4 may be needed for a Knight or for the QBP. *9. ....* B—B4 can be played with a view to doubtful sacrifice of Kt on f2, followed by attack on KB file. (The Dilworth.) |
| *10.* QKt—Q2 | Chosen from a few promising moves. *10.* B—K3 may be played. To that *10. ....* Kt—QR4 followed by P—QB4 is quite a defence. Very often a Lopez is determined by Black's backward QBP (especially after exchange of Knights at d4). |
| *10. ....* O—O | |

Many have tried *10. ....* Kt–B4 followed by P—Q5 and it has never been refuted.

Black

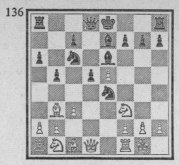

136

White

Ruy Lopez

The Morphy-Tarrasch system

10. QKt—Q2 ⎱
10. B—K3   ⎰ are usual

10. Kt—Q4 (Breslau) inviting Kt×KP
is not regarded as safe

*11.* B—B2          I quote now from a game by Broadbent, a fine English player, against van Doesburgh, a fine Dutch All-in Wrestler of the 1930's.

According to the best opinion Q—K2 is a better eleventh move than White made, the plan being R—Q1 Kt—KB1, etc. But the text is good enough.

*11.* ....                      Kt×Kt

At this point we see how an opening that has been followed to a tense position can, given a slight deviation disturbing the learned player, lead to quick attack. Black needs a good move here and finds a bad one.

(Good is *11.* .... P—KB4.)

*12.* Q×Kt. Better here then B×Kt – it saves a move for the purposes of White's attack (see move 13).

*12.* .... Kt—R4. A bad move with a good purpose: viz.

in order to have tidy Pawns in the unlikely event of an end-game: and also with a view to development of the Queen's side pieces. The immediate result is loss of time.

| | | |
|---|---|---|
| 13. Q—Q3 | P—KKt3 | A forced move now. |
| 14. Kt—Q4 | P—QB4 | It were better had the Kt stayed at c6 notwithstanding cramp, so as to exchange Knights. |
| 15. Kt×B | P×Kt | And Black has terrible weaknesses at e6 and g6. |
| 16. P—KR4! | | An exceedingly good move aiming at the g6 weakness before the Queen moves to h3. The reason why Black cannot capture is shown when he does capture. |
| 16. .... | B×P | |
| 17. Q—R3 | K—Kt2? | Black has little resource. |

If 17. .... R—K1
18. P—KKt3 drives the B back to e7.
17. .... Q—K2 deprives the B of an escape-hatch. Best seems to be R—B2.

| | |
|---|---|
| 18. P—KKt3 | B—Kt4 |
| 19. P—KB4 | B—R3 |
| 20. R—B2 | Threatening R—R2, wins. |

This example is given in order to show how a not very easy defence should not be handled. Broadbent's exploitation is sufficiently good to justify study even by those who would not have made Black's specific mistakes. One could defend a Lopez of this form without knowing this game. But 'awkward' positions do justify research and learning. Many players who feel that Black, at move 10, is compromised (this is by no means accepted doctrine) avoid the variation: and play, on move five, not 5. .... Kt×P but 5. .... B—K2, leading into the Tchigorin system. It is also possible to play 5. .... P—QKt4 followed by 6. .... P—Q3. That gives White a chance of 7.

Kt—Kt5. But Black replies with 7. .... P—Q4. 8. P×P Kt—Q5 and is attacking.

Sound is 5. .... B—K2. A consensus of opinion regards 5. .... B—B4 as dubious, though it has some merits. The point is that White's eventual P—Q4 will keep the Black Bishop out of play for quite a time.

In answer to 5. ....   B—K2 6. R—K1 is usual (Q—K2 is also playable and, in conjunction with P—QR4, constitutes the Worrall Attack which holds no terrors for the calm-minded). In answer to 6. R—K1 normal play is 6. .... P—QKt4. 7. B—Kt3 P—Q3, preparing Kt—QR4 with exchange at b3. 7. .... O—O is also playable.

Against this 7. B—Q5 B—Kt2 is complicated and not dangerous. (8. Kt×P is refuted by Kt×B.)

But the object of 7. ....   O—O is sometimes to play, after 8. P—B3, 8. ....   P—Q4, Marshall's Attack, introduced by a very clever American master, whose limitations were shown when he was annihilated in matches by Lasker and Capablanca. (Those facts are compatible with his being, nevertheless, a very fine player indeed.) In Marshall's Attack, Black sacrifices his KP

|  |  |
|---|---|
| 8. P—B3 | P—Q4 |
| 9. P×P | Kt×P |
| 10. Kt×P | Kt×Kt |
| 11. R×Kt | P—QB3 |
| 12. P—Q4 |  |

Black, with B—Q3 launches a King's side attack which White must defend very carefully, and which delays White's development. (12. .... B—Q3. 13. R—K2 Q—R5. 14.P—KKt3 Q—R6. 15. B×Kt P×B. 16. P—B3 is one possible line.) If and when it is beaten off, White emerges with a Pawn to the good.

To revert to the Tchigorin system

|  |  |
|---|---|
| 5. .... | B—K2 |
| 6. R—K1 | P—QKt4 |
| 7. B—Kt3 | P—Q3 |
| 8. P—B3 | Kt—QR4 |

|        |        |
|--------|--------|
| 9. B—B2 | P—B4 |
| 10. P—Q4 | Q—B2 |
| 11. P—KR3 (preventing B—Kt5) | |
| 11. .... | O—O |
| 12. QKt—Q2 | |

Now this position is less tense than the position we saw in the Morphy-Tarrasch system. But it is not easy. (Diagram 137.)

Black

137
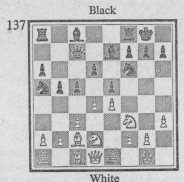

White

Ruy Lopez
Tchigorin system: typical position

White can manœuvre his Knight via KB1 and K3, to threaten Kt—B5 or (after Pawn exchanges) Kt—Q5. If Black allows the centre to loosen, by exchanging with his Pawn from e5, or by exchanging Kts at d5, White is developed against Black's King's side. Also an exchange at f5 would enable a Pawn rush against his King's side: not necessarily fatal, but very harrassing.

However, Black has plenty of play, e.g. so simple a move as K—R1 enables a process Kt—Kt1, P—Kt3 and, sooner or later P—KB4; with the kind of counter-attack that has been seen, and will be seen, in Queen's side openings, against a rigid centre. Also playable are 12. .... B—Q2 and 12. .... B—K3. 12. .... B—Kt2. 12. .... BP×P. 12. .... R—K1 (with a view to B—B1 and fianchetto) also 12. .... Kt—Q2 (to be developed on the Queen's side), or Kt—Kt1.

Russian analysts have explored *8*. P—B4 (played by Smyslov) and other deviations from the orthodox Tchigorin–Stalinist line, but no great disaster befalls Black.

The Tchigorin has been set out here in order to illustrate a line of play which could be found by a good player over the board – without learning. The Morphy–Tarrasch system, in contrast, would be hard to think through in cross-board play.

Other Lopez lines specially worth mentioning include the Steinitz Deferred –

|  |  |
|---|---|
| *1.* P—K4 | P—K4 |
| *2.* Kt—KB3 | Kt—QB3 |
| *3.* B—Kt5 | P—QR3 |
| *4.* B—R4 | P—Q3 |
| *5.* P—B3 or O—O | |

Both of these can be met by the 'freeing' *5. ....* P—KB4 (the Siesta Variation). More usual is *5. ....* B—Q2, followed by Kt—KB3, B—K2, and a quite comfortable game, so long as Black remains tactically aware of the pressure on his KP.

This pressure is best illustrated in a piece of Chess that is worth learning, and really hard to see by the light of nature. It occurs in the undeferred Steinitz Defence, where the complication of Black's P—QKt4 is not relevant.

|  |  |
|---|---|
| *1.* P—K4 | P—K4 |
| *2.* Kt—KB3 | Kt—QB3 |
| *3.* B—Kt5 | P—Q3 |
| *4.* P—Q4 | B—Q2 |

Observe that the KP is defended by a counter against White's KP (e.g. *5.* B×Kt  B×B. *6.* P×P  Kt×P, etc.).

|  |  |
|---|---|
| *5.* Kt—B3 | Kt—B3 |
| *6.* O—O | B—K2 |
| *7.* R—K1 (Diagram 138) | |

Now it's different. White is attacking the KP. Black is countering against White's KP. The defence of this is tactically complicated by the fact of White's back line being left empty of

Black (Marco)

White (Tarrasch)
(Dresden 1892)
The so-called 'Tarrasch Trap' (see text)

defence in some variations. It seems that Black can Castle. In fact, he cannot, because of the following:

| | | |
|---|---|---|
| 7. .... | .... | O—O |
| 8. B×Kt | B×B | |
| 9. P×P | P×P | |
| 10. Q×Q | QR×Q (KR×Q leads | |
| | to not dissimilar con- | |
| | sequences) | |
| 11. Kt×P | B×P | |
| 12. Kt×B | Kt×Kt | |

The White Rook is house-bound, but *13*. Kt—Q3! closing the file and pinning the Kt, gains something.

| | |
|---|---|
| *13*. .... | P—KB4 |
| *14*. P—KB3 | B—B4 ch |
| *15*. Kt×B (If *15*. KB1, B—Kt3. *16*. P×Kt | |
| P×P dis. ch., etc.) | |
| *15*. .... | Kt×Kt |

Has he escaped?

| | |
|---|---|
| *16*. B—Kt5 | R—Q4 (if *16*. .... |
| | R—Q2 *17*. B—K7) |
| *17*. B—K7 R—K1 | |
| *18*. P—QB4 wins the exchange | |

Had Black at move *10* taken with the KR, then White could, at move *15*, have played K—B1.

This, from a game Tarrasch-Marco, is called the Tarrasch Trap.

That expression justifies an excursus on the word 'Trap'.

If the word 'trap' is used to mean that one player digs a pit into which the other may fall, then it is untrue to Chess. In Chess one plays the board, not the man. One makes the best move one can see, best i.e. against all possible defences. One does not rely on the prospect of an opponent's mistake — however weak the opponent may be. If one of the variations happens to be a pit into which a simple-minded player can fall, then let it perhaps be labelled 'pitfall' but not 'trap', not so long as the latter word carries the implication of a special and cunning devising.

The one exception to this is 'desperation'. One has lost too much material, and the opponent is winning. One allows him to capture a remaining Pawn, so that thereafter one can give away one's Rooks, leaving stalemate. That was shown as a

Black

139

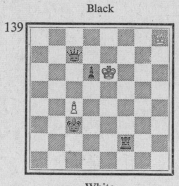

White

A trap?

After *1.* .... K × P
      *2.* Q—Q4 ch! draws

possibility at the end of the game Winz–Czerniak in the last chapter, and examples can be multiplied. Very simple is Diagram 139. White made a 'dying check'. Black greedily grabbed a Pawn – and the penalty was a draw. The word 'swindle' is also used to describe a desperate and ingenious manœuvre in order to save a game. But, for the rest, Chess is 'objective'. There should be nothing *ad hominem* in good Chess.

Thus it may have been said by the player of Black in the position in Diagram 138: 'I fell into a trap.' Without semantics one could dogmatically say to his shade: 'Your opponent set no trap. He made a good move, seeing your possible error as one variation amongst others. You chose that one. You fell into a rabbit-hole – or pitfall, but were not "trapped" by your opponent, though he found your fall helpful in his process of destroying you.' Sometimes when a player relies on a 'cleverness' and it fails, one speaks of the 'trapper trapped' but that is Chess journalism (see Diagram 140 for an example).

Black

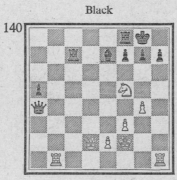

140

White

Trapper Trapped
1. .... B–Kt5
2. Q–Q4    B–B4 (the trap 'closes')
3. Q×B!   R×Q
4. Kt–K7 ch   K–R1
5. R×P ch   K×R
6. R–KR1 ch, wins

It may, of course, happen that, given a choice, one chooses the move that offers the opponent great opportunities for error, but it is rarely that one finds a 'Buredan's Ass' position, in which a decision is determined by the possible asininity of the opponent. At a middle-level there are 'trappy' players making unnecessary complications. These are not playing the best Chess. Nevertheless the word 'trap' continues to be used to describe many opening pitfalls.

The reader has already seen one pitfall in the Lopez (Noah's Ark – p. 91).

Interesting and exciting from the same opening is the RIGA defence. After *1*. P—K4 P—K4. *2*. Kt—KB3 Kt—QB3. *3*. B—Kt5 P—QR3. *4*. B—R4 Kt—B3. *5*. O—O Kt×P (Murphy–Tarrasch system). *6*. P—Q4, *P×P* (This is a bold departure from the safe P—QKt4 and P—Q4). *7*. R—K1 P—Q4 *8*. Kt×P B—Q3!? *9*. Kt×Kt B×P ch. *10*. K—R1! (If K×B, Q—R5 ch gives Black at least a perpetual check.) *10*. . . . Q—R5 threatening murder. *11*. R×Kt ch P×R (This is better than Q×R). *12*. Q—Q8 ch! Q×Q. *13*. Kt×Q dis ch K×Kt. *14*. K×B Now Black has R and 2 Pawns for 2 minor pieces. Don't play 14. . . . . P—KB4 allowing B—Kt5 mate.

The *Giuoco Piano* offers an amusing 'trap'.

| | |
|---|---|
| *1*. P—K4 | P—K4 |
| *2*. Kt—KB3 | Kt—QB3 |
| *3*. B—B4 | Kt—Q5 |

This is a move that violates opening principles. After *4*. P—QB3 Kt×Kt ch. *5*. Q×Kt White has done much more development than Black. But if White plays

*4.* Kt × P see what happens

| | |
|---|---|
| *4.* .... | Q—Kt4 |
| *5.* Kt × BP | Q × KtP |
| *6.* R—B1 | Q × KP ch |
| *7.* B—K2 | Kt—B6 mate |

an amusing 'smothered mate'.

Black played badly and White played worse.

Contrast, however, the following

| | |
|---|---|
| *1.* P—K4 | P—K4 |
| *2.* Kt—KB3 | Kt—QB3 |
| *3.* B—B4 | B—B4 |
| *4.* P—QKt4 *The Evans Gambit*, one of the great British contributions to Chess. If it is accepted by B × P there follows | |
| *5.* P—B3 | B—R4 (B4 is also playable) |
| *6.* P—Q4 | P × P |
| *7.* O—O (and White has a very free attacking game) | |

Black's position is defensible; and if he beats off the attack he may well win, but he has a difficult life. Consequently many players decline the Gambit with *4* .... B—Kt3 – the line we are considering.

Now suppose White plays, hastily, *5.* P—Kt5 and Black replies Kt—Q5, Black is laying no traps. He is playing a good move. If then, White plays *6.* Kt × P, there happens *6.* .... Q—Kt4, exactly as in the Giuoco 'trap'. This 'pitfall' is psychologically easy to fall into, because White is taking the initiative – not Black. White thinks he has won a Pawn!

Another error that is sometimes referred to as a 'trap' is the following:

| | |
|---|---|
| *1.* P—K4 | P—K4 |
| *2.* Kt—KB3 | Kt—QB3 |
| *3.* B—Kt5 | P—QR3 |
| *4.* B—R4 | Kt—B3 |
| *5.* O—O | B—K2 |
| *6.* Q—K2 | P—QKt4 |
| *7.* B—Kt3 | P—Q3 |
| *8.* P—QR4 | P—Kt5? |

*9.* Q—B4 threatening mate and the Kt. I would call P—Kt5 a simple blunder. But note that after *8.* P—QB3 B—Kt5. *9.* P—QR4 can be met by P—Kt5, because *10.* Q—B4 Kt—QR4 *11.* Q×P ch K—Q2 leaves White unable to disengage. If *12.* Kt—Kt5 good for Black (Bely–Lengyel, Hastings 1964. Was this a trap?)

Quite complex are the pitfalls in the following line:

| | |
|---|---|
| *1.* P—K4 | P—K4 |
| *2.* Kt—KB3 | Kt—QB3 |
| *3.* B—B4 | Kt—B3 |

*The Two-Knights Defence.* Not so 'safe' as *3.* .... B—B4. B—B4 makes P—Q4 more difficult for White. The text allows:

*4.* Kt—Kt5. This compels P—Q4

*5.* P×P (By his reply Black is involved in what the vulgar call 'the Fried Liver')

| | |
|---|---|
| *5.* .... | Kt×P |
| *6.* Kt×BP (Safe is P—Q4) | K×Kt |
| *7.* Q—B3 ch | K—K3 |
| *8.* Kt—B3 | QKt—K2 (or Kt—Kt5?) |
| *9.* Q—K4 | P—B3 |

White with P—Q4 maintains an excruciating pressure. Normal is, therefore, not *5.* .....: Kt×P but *5.* .... Kt—QR4

| 6 P—Q3 | P—KR3 |
|---|---|
| 7. Kt—KB3 | P—K5 |
| 8. Q—K2 | Kt×B |
| 9. P×Kt | B—K2, etc. (with a good game, though the authority of Leonhardt suggests that White stands better) |

The matter is complicated by the conduct of Bronstein who at the eighth played P×P and, after *8. .... Kt×B, 9. Q—Q4* with a strong attack. Also very interesting is

| 6. B—Kt5 ch | P—D3 |
|---|---|
| 7. P×P | P×P |
| 8. Q—B3 with an interesting attack. Black also has good chances. But 'trickier' lines here are | |
| 1. P—K4 | P—K4 |
| 2. Kt—KB3 | Kt—QB3 |
| 3. B—B4 | Kt—B3 |
| 4. P—Q4 | If now Kt×P |
| 5. R—K1 | P—Q4 |
| 6. B×P | Q×B |
| 7. Kt—B3 | Canal's attack: not terrible. |

More usual is

| 4. .... | P×P |
|---|---|
| 5. O—O | B—B4 |
| 6. P—K5 | P—Q4 |

and we are on the cake-walk of the *Max Lange*.

| 7. P×Kt | P×B |
|---|---|
| 8. R—K1 ch | B—K3 |
| 9. Kt—Kt5 | Q—Q4! |

There are pitfalls here.

If, instead of Q—Q4 Black had played Q—Q2, then

obviously, Kt × B followed by Q — R5 ch wins a piece. But what of Q — Q3?

If         9. ....                   Q — Q3
        10. P × P                   R — KKt1
        11. R × B ch                P × R
        12. Q — R5 ch               K — Q2
        13. Kt — K4                 Q — K4
        14. Kt × B ch               K — B1 (best)
        15. Q × Q (with a winning game)

However, 9. .... Q — Q4 is not too obscure to be discernible by the light of nature.

        10. Kt — B3 (an exploitation of a pin that is not
                unfamiliar in King's side openings)
        10. ....                    Q — B4

If now

        11. QKt — Kt4              O — O — O seems to hold
                                    the game for Black
                                    though after
        12. KKt × B                P × Kt
        13. P — KKt4               Q — K4

Black has anxieties, also very good counter-play.
However, consider

        11. QKt — K4              B — KB1
        12. P — KKt4              Q × P ch
        13. Q × Q                 B × Q
        14. P × P                 B × P
        15. Kt — B6 dble ch       K — B1
        16. Kt × B                P — KR4

and that Knight has no escape!
    Best seems to be 17. Kt — K3
    When the great Akiva Rubinstein first played that defence he gave his opponent a surprise. This is the kind of variation that *can* be seen in play, but calls for magnificent vision. That

variation, accordingly, can be classed with those that justify a certain amount of Chess learning. On the other hand, if a player can avoid a complication without loss of pace, or place, or, if you prefer it, 'face', he can dispense with a lot of learning and render it, for the time being, academic. For the rest, can one call Black's play 'trappy'? The recapture of the Knight is hard to see: but if *11. ....* B—B1 is a good move, because of that resource, *11. ....* B—B1 does not set a trap. The reason why B—B1 is doubtful is because of the difficulties that arise from *12.* Kt×BP – a not quite 'established', but very intriguing line of play.

The important learning in Chess is mostly to be found among the King's Pawn Attacks. So-called 'learning' abounds in many variations of both KP and QP, which adds nothing to equipment. Do you require to be told that after

| | |
|---|---|
| *1.* P—Q4 | P—Q4 |
| *2.* P—QB4 | P—K4 (*Albin's Counter-Gambit*) |
| *3.* P×KP | P—Q5 |
| *4.* P—K3 is a bad move because after | |
| *4. ....* | B—Kt5 ch |
| *5.* B—Q2 | P×P is playable? |

A good deal of learning can be rendered unnecessary by players playing 'within the visibility': and a good deal actually is within easy visibility.

If you can see short-tactical threats; if you are conscious of not having lost tempo; if your moves don't seem strained or artificial, then you are justified, in the ordinary way, in thinking that your game is good, and that no thunder is latent in the blue. As the game integrates your problems may increase, but that will be at a stage beyond the help of learning.

What is very important, however, is a conception of the shape of game that develops from any specific opening. To that end a survey may be helpful.

Let it be said that there are several ways of classifying openings. One can divide them into King's Pawn and Queen's Pawn and Irregular (which usually become QP). Another division is between Close Games and Open Games. Close are those in which the development is behind fixed Pawns; Open those in which the pieces are moving more freely. It is hard to say into which of these the Morphy–Tarrasch form of the Lopez fits. The reader may well have observed that the Tchigorin Lopez – a King's side opening – is a close game of the type that develops from many QP openings.

Another possible distinction is between 'fast and slow' openings. Some of the King's Gambits Accepted, the Evans Accepted, etc., are fast, though a good player may slow them down; and from some Queen's Pawn games a fast pace can also develop (e.g. game Szabo–Olafsson). The modern practice is to avoid variations in which attacks burn themselves out too early.

Another distinction is between the ways in which the centre is controlled. There are closed centres and fluid centres, hollow ones, solid ones: as in any box of chocolates. Perhaps one of the reasons for the movement away from the ordinary KP, by which is meant *1.* P—K4  P—K4, consists in the reluctance of many players to face immediately direct attacks on e5 made by White's QP. The tactical coefficient of the game then becomes heightened; and there is a tendency among the many to delay important skirmishing until some strategic lines are set.

We are, therefore, justified in retaining as one head of classification the openings that commence with *1.* P—K4 P—K4, the latter being still thought by many to be Black's best reply. In this class, we shall find fast and slow games; games round a fixed centre, and games in which there is a struggle for central control (very often marked by Black's ability to play P—Q4).

Another class will be King's Pawn openings to which the reply is not P—K4. There are four main openings, all very popular, under this head, namely, the French Defence (*1.* P—K4  P—K3), the Sicilian (*1.* P—K4  P—QB4), the Caro–Kahn (*1.* P—K4  P—QB3), and the Centre Counter (*1.* P—K4 P—Q4).

A fifth is Alekhine's Defence (*1.* P—K4  Kt—KB3) which

Alekhine may or may not have invented, but which he certainly did not use in any important match or tournament. That opening is typical of what used to be called the 'ultra-modern' in Chess. (The word 'ultra' adds nothing except journalistic bravura to a logical development in Chess theory, of which Nimzovitch, Tartakover and Alekhine were the pioneer exponents.) Ultra-modern is a label given, conventionally, to a number of defences and developments in the Queen's Pawn openings.

The Queen's Pawn openings start, normally, with P—Q4. But a Queen's Pawn can develop from an opening move such as *1.* Kt—KB3 – which can lead into the Réti–Zukertort system, or *1.* P—QB4 (the English), or even a fianchetto P—KKt3 or P—QKt3, or the Orang-Utan P—QKt4 – a tolerably good opening, dedicated, by Tartakover, to an ape with which he held converse once, and which evidently inspired something better, in Chess, than his London cognate has inspired in painting (though the latter makes more money).

In the Queen's Pawn a useful distinction is between openings which commence with a closed centre, and those in which the centre is closed later, or never closed at all.

However, scientific classifications (if useful at all) are matters beyond the scope of an introductory book. Suffice it here to survey briefly a number of openings that the reader should know in principle.

*The King's Pawn* (*Mutual*)

After *1.* P—K4, P—K4, White's purpose is to develop and/or attack the centre – by way of securing better development, or board-control. Very useful, though less popular in this century than in the last, is

*The King's Gambit*

    *1.* P—K4          P—K4

    *2.* P—KB4

The idea is to increase the pressure on e5 that will come from Kt—KB3, and to gain tempo in so doing. Because it was felt that White was 'trying to get away with something' the acceptance of the King's Gambit (unlike the Queen's Gambit against the more easily defensible Pawn at d5) was normal.

The Pawn could be taken, and an effort made to keep it, in the teeth of White's attack.

Typical is the 'sporting' Allgaier

| | | |
|---|---|---|
| 1. | P—K4 | P—K4 |
| 2. | P—KB4 | P×P |
| 3. | Kt—KB3 | P—KKt4 |
| 4. | P—KR4 | P—KKt5 |
| 5. | Kt—Kt5 | P—KR3 |
| 6. | Kt×P | K×Kt |

White has sacrificed a Knight and must do great damage if the sacrifice is to be justified. However, not rashly.

7. B—B4 ch can be played, which is met by 7. .... P—Q4. Then 8. B×P ch  K—K1. 9. P—Q4. But many play the Allgaier–Thorold 7. P—Q4. In both cases, the strategy aims at control of the centre and attack along the KB file. The variations are inexhaustible. In the best opinion the Allgaier should lose. In practice, it very often wins because the tactical strain is very high.* If at move five, White wishes to preserve his Knight, he can play Kt—K5 (The Kieseritzki) a line in which a Pawn can be regained; sometimes a Pawn won. This is quite a controllable game – and possibly the strategically best form of the King's Gambit Accepted. A line that has been played is:

| | | |
|---|---|---|
| 5. | Kt—K5 | P—Q3 |
| 6. | Kt×KtP | P—KR4 |
| 7. | Kt—B2 | Kt—KB3 |
| 8. | P—Q4 | B—R3 |
| 9. | Kt—B3 | Kt—Kt5 |
| 10. | Q—B3 | Kt—K6 |
| 11. | B×Kt | P×B |
| 12. | KKt—Q1 | B—Kt5 |
| 13. | Q—Kt3 | Q—B3 |
| 14. | P—K5 | |

* In the nineteenth century one of the Chess automata, Mephisto, used to play the Allgaier and win. The machine contained the diminutive but great Isador Gunsberg.

And this is 'anybody's game'. Needless to say, there was plenty of scope for deviation, and there is still a big range of choice.

More risky and aggressive is to sacrifice the Knight *in situ*. This is the Muzio.

After  *1.* P—K4                        P—K4
    *2.* P—KB4                       P×P
    *3.* Kt—KB3                      P—KKt4

the Bishop is developed.

    *4.* B—B4 and if Black attacks with
    *4.* ....                         P—Kt5 then, boldly,
    *5.* O—O

('Castle early' is not always good doctrine, but here O—O is an attacking move.)

Against this, many play

    *5.* ....                         P—Q4
    *6.* B×P                          P×Kt
    *7.* Q×P (and evidently White will, for a long time,
        have a dangerous attack)

Interesting is the following:

    *5.* ....                         P×Kt
    *6.* B×P ch — The Double Muzio
    *6.* ....                         K×B
    *7.* Q×P                          Q—B3
    *8.* P—K5                         Q×P
    *9.* P—Q4

It has been said that if White were giving odds of the Queen's Knight, he would now, in this line, have a winning position! In any case it is doubtful whether Black dare play

    *9.* ....                         Q×P ch to which
    *10.* B—K3 is an embarrassing reply.

Another form of the Gambit consists in the play of Bishop

before Knight. (The normal Chess process is Knights first because they need more developing.)

| | | |
|---|---|---|
| *1.* | P—K4 | P—K4 |
| *2.* | P—KB4 | P×P |
| *3.* | B—B4 | |

This invites Black to check at h4. This being done, however, White's development, without a Castling process, is quite vigorous. Here is a famous game:

| | | |
|---|---|---|
| *1.* | P—K4 P—K4 | |
| *2.* | P—KB4 P×P | |
| *3.* | B—B4 Q—R5 ch | |
| *4.* | K—B1 P—QKt4 | An old-fashioned decoy with tactical merits. |
| *5.* | B×KtP Kt—KB3 | |
| *6.* | Kt—KB3 Q—R3 | |
| *7.* | P—Q3 Kt—R4 | Over-ambitious at an early stage. Did he miss White's reply? |
| *8.* | Kt—R4 | If one player can move a Knight twice, why not the other? |
| *8.* | .... Q—Kt4 | |
| *9.* | Kt—B5 P—QB3 | |
| *10.* | P—KKt4 Kt—B3 | Better is P×B followed by P—KKt3. |
| *11.* | R—Kt1 | Sacrificing in order to embarrass Black's Queen. |
| *11.* | .... P×B | |
| *12.* | P—KR4 Q—Kt3 | |
| *13.* | P—R5 Q—Kt4 | |
| *14.* | Q—B3 | White has seen that this forces an awkward retreat and that there are processes available thereafter. |
| *14.* | .... Kt—Kt1 | |
| *15.* | B×P Q—B3 | White is now very well developed though uncastled. |
| *16.* | Kt—B3 B—B4 | |

| | |
|---|---|
| *17.* Kt—Q5 | At this point, with Black beginning to redevelop, White starts one of the world's great combinations. |

*17.* .... Q×P
*18.* B—Q6!  Q×R ch

| | |
|---|---|
| *19.* K—K2  B×R | Q×R is not playable, because of Kt×P ch with mate at c7. |
| *20.* P—K5  Kt—QR3 | To guard c7. |

*21.* Kt×KtP ch  K—Q1
*22.* Q—B6 ch  Kt×Q
*23.* B—K7  mate

That was played between Anderssen (White), a world champion of the 1850's and later, and Kieseritzki, the inventor of the Gambit already described.

This kind of happening, attack against imbalance, causes many players to adopt simpler or safer methods for Black.

Thus against

| | |
|---|---|
| *1.* P—K4 | P—K4 |
| *2.* P—KB4 | P×P |
| *3.* Kt—KB3  .... | P—Q4 is played, |

throwing back the Pawn for freedom.

Also possible is the more complicated *Falkbeer Counter Gambit*

| | |
|---|---|
| *1.* P—K4 | P—K4 |
| *2.* P—KB4 | P—Q4 |

Normally continued:

| | |
|---|---|
| *3.* P×QP | P—K5 |

Black King's Pawn is not worse placed than White's KBP: but it gets quickly attacked. Following is the orthodox sequence (which does not risk *4.* B—Kt5 ch.  P—B3 et seq.)

4. P—Q3    Kt—B3
5. P×P    Kt×P
6. Kt—KB3    B—QB4
7. Q—K2    B—B4    (There is a 'pitfall' here. If
7. .... B—B7 ch. 8. K—Q1
Q×Pch. 9. KKt—Q2! P—KB4
10. Kt—B3 and White is attacking. 7. .... B—B4 (the text) in
turn creates a danger for White.
If 8. P—KKt4 O—O! 9. P×B
R—K1 gives Black an attack.)

8. Kt—B3    Q—K2
9. B—K3    And exchanges leave an equal
game. Simpler is the ordinary
declining of the Gambit.

1. P—K4    P—K4
2. P—KB4    B—B4
3. Kt—KB3    P—Q3    (Better than 3. .... Kt—QB3
4. Kt×P.) Black loses no tempo,
and White has to solve the problem of Castling.
4. Kt—B3    With an expectation of Kt—QR4.

But 4. P—B3 can lead to an exciting game. On the whole, the
Declined Gambit seems favourable to Black.

Another way of bringing about a King's Gambit is through
the *Vienna*.

1. P—K4    P—K4
2. Kt—QB3    Kt—KB3
3. P—KB4

In this line, there will be no acceptance, but a counter

3. ....    P—Q4
Then 4. P×KP    Kt×P
5. Kt—B3    B—QKt5

to mention one normal line; hard play for both.

Alternatively, White has

> 5. Q—B3 (with interesting lines that can be
> thought out without the help of learning)

On the second move, Black can play Kt—QB3 (instead of KB3).

Then *3*. P—KB4 is a rather good King's Gambit, because Black's second move turns out less useful than White's. Black can decline, and offer, a gambit.

| | |
|---|---|
| *3.* .... | B—B4 |
| *4.* P×P | P—Q3 |

and there are other reasonable moves to be found. Interesting is

| | |
|---|---|
| *1.* P—K4 | P—K4 |
| *2.* Kt—QB3 | Kt—QB3 |
| *3.* B—B4 | B—B4 |
| *4.* Q—Kt4 | |

At this point the author has found that K—B1 leads to a game in which Black is the better developed.

We are now moving away from King's Gambit. This opening is relatively rare in modern masterplay: first, because so few King's Pawn (Mutual) openings are played: secondly, because White, even in King's Pawn mutual, has a big range of sound openings, fast ones, as well as the slower type in which the attack does not burn itself out so quickly. In general, it may be said that the later an attack starts the less likely it is to reach quickly the point of no return. That is one of the reasons why many players with a taste for attack prefer the Queen's Pawn openings.

On the King's side, among the longer, slower, developments with aggressive intentions, the reader has already seen the Lopez. In the lines he has seen the characteristic development includes P—QB3 and P—Q4 for White. But White can conduct the Lopez at slower tempo by playing P—Q3 instead of P—Q4. He develops his pieces on good central squares, but Black has plenty of time for thought.

| | |
|---|---|
| *1.* P—K4 | P—K4 |
| *2.* Kt—KB3 | Kt—QB3 |

R—L

| 3. B—Kt5 | P—QR3 |
| 4. B—R4 | Kt—B3 |
| 5. O—O | B—K2 |
| 6. R—K1 | P—QKt4 |
| 7. B—Kt3 | P—Q3 |
| 8. P—B3 | Kt—QR4 |
| 9. B—B2 | P—B4 |

10. P—Q3 and develops his Queen's Knight and
QB before pushing the QP forward. P—Q3
can also be played earlier, at move five or
six on this variation.

Cognate to the slower Lopez is
*The Four Knights*

| 1. P—K4 | P—K4 |
| 2. Kt—KB3 | Kt—QB3 |
| 3. Kt—B3 | Kt—B3 |

One line of play proceeds symmetrically thus:
4. B—Kt5  B—Kt5 leading to good development, but both
have to be careful of the pin on the King's Knight.

| 5. O—O | O—O |
| 6. P—Q3 | P—Q3 |
| 7. B—Kt5 | B—Kt5 |
| 8. Kt—Q5 | Kt—Q5 |

with great complexity. But 7. ....  Kt—K2 is reasonable for
Black, the doubled BP not being bad.

Very popular has been the Rubinstein Defence.

| 1. P—K4 | P—K4 |
| 2. Kt—KB3 | Kt—QB3 |
| 3. Kt—B3 | Kt—B3 |
| 4. B—Kt5 | Kt—Q5 |

After exchanges, White pushes P—K5.

Alternatively 5. Kt×P   Q—K2 gives Black a good counter-
attack. Of the other, 'symmetrical', variation, here is an amusing example. Someone tries to 'copy' his opponent too slavishly.

| | |
|---|---|
| *1.* P—K4 | P—K4 |
| *2.* Kt—KB3 | Kt—QB3 |
| *3.* Kt—B3 | Kt—B3 |
| *4.* B—Kt5 | B—Kt5 |
| *5.* O—O | O—O |
| *6.* P—Q3 | P—Q3 |
| *7.* B—Kt5 | B—Kt5 |
| *8.* Kt—Q5 | Kt—Q5 |
| *9.* Kt×B | Kt×B |
| *10.* Kt—Q5 | Kt—Q5 |
| *11.* Q—Q2 | Q—Q2 |
| *12.* B×Kt | B×Kt |
| *13.* Kt—K7 ch | K—R1 (Can't copy any longer) |
| *14.* B×P ch | K×B |
| *15.* Q—Kt5 ch | K—R1 |
| *16.* Q—B6 | Mate |

To return to our theme, *3.* B—Kt5 (The Lopez, or Spanish, move) has not always been – and still is not – regarded as the only reasonable Bishop's move, when one is developing the King's pieces.

In the Italian Game – the Giuoco Piano – the 3rd move is B—B4, and this leads to a variety of developments, some fast, some slow – all interesting.

The Pianissimo form is

| | |
|---|---|
| *1.* P—K4 | P—K4 |
| *2.* Kt—KB3 | Kt—QB3 |

(But *2.* B—B4  B—B4 can be played first and nobody in their right senses plays *3.* B×P ch, Jerome's Gambit.)

| | |
|---|---|
| *3.* B—B4 | B—B4 |

(*3.* .... B—K2 is the *Hungarian Defence*, a sort of Philidor.)

| | |
|---|---|
| *4.* P—Q3 | P—Q3 |
| *5.* Kt—B3 | Kt—B3 |
| *6.* O—O | O—O |

In this kind of game it is not necessary to play P—KR3

(Country Move) early, for either side, because B—KKt5 can be met by QKt—K2 and the exchange on f6 or f3 is not unfavourable to the 'exchangee'.

But the 'Slow Game' (which is what Giuoco Piano means) manages to give impetus to some very fast games indeed.

The reader has already seen a fast line when Black's third move was not B—B4, but Kt—B3. (The *Two Knights*.) After 3. . . . . B—B4 White does not gain anything by Kt—Kt5 because of Black's Kt—KR3. If then White's Knight retreats, Black allows White to exchange at h6, and eventually he Castles Queen's side. In the main play (3. . . . . B—B4) 4. P—Q4 can be tried, leading, via Black's P×P and Kt—B3, into the *Max Lange:* but Black can play (after P×P) P—Q3. Also Black can play 4. . . . . B×P; after which 5. Kt×B   Kt×Kt. 6. P—B4 and White has insufficient compensation for his Pawn.

In the Giuoco proper (3. B—B4   B—B4) White can aggress quite quickly with 4. P—B3. If, in answer to this, Black plays such a move as Kt—B3 then 5. P—Q4. If this is taken, then White is left with a very promising centre; but he has to be careful of it.

There are sacrificial lines from the following sequence.

| | |
|---|---|
| 1. P—K4 | P—K4 |
| 2. Kt—KB3 | Kt—QB3 |
| 3. B—B4 | B—B4 |
| 4. P—B3 | Kt—B3 |
| 5. P—Q4 | P×P |
| 6. P×P | B—Kt5 ch |
| (6. . . . . | B—Kt3 is playable because 7. P—K5 met by P—Q4 gives an inferior form of the Max Lange from White's point of view.) |
| 7. Kt—B3 (very safe is B—Q2) | |
| 7. . . . . | Kt×KP |
| 8. O—O | B×Kt |

    *9.* P—Q5               B—B3

  *10.* R—K1 considered good for White. This is
        the *Moller attack.* But there is no need for
        these adventures. *4.* P—B3 can be met by
        P—Q3, after which *5.* P—Q4 P×P.
        *6.* P×P B—Kt3 is safe enough. But even
        better is *4.* . . . . Q—K2. Now White must
        castle if he intends to play P—Q4. Then
        *5.* . . . . P—Q3. *6.* P—Q4 B—Kt3, and
        White is 'biting on granite'.

      Also exciting is the *Evans Gambit* already
      mentioned.

White's 4th is P—QKt4. To decline, with *4.* . . . . B—Kt3 is
safe and sensible, in so authoritative an opinion as that of
Lasker.

If the Gambit is accepted Black needs to walk, as Agag did,
warily, with the risk of being hewn in pieces.

| | |
|---|---|
| *1.* P—K4 | P—K4 |
| *2.* Kt—KB3 | Kt—QB3 |
| *3.* B—B4 | B—B4 |
| *4.* P—QKt4 | B×P (Kt×P is little different) |
| *5.* P—B3 | B—R4 or B4 |

Suppose

| | |
|---|---|
| *5.* . . . . | B—R4 |
| *6.* P—Q4 | |

If now

| | |
|---|---|
| *6.* . . . . | P—Q3 |
| *7.* Q—Kt3 forces | Q—Q2 |

(Not *7.* . . . . Q—K2 because of P—Q5 and the Bishop is
picked up on a fork) after which *8.* P—QR4 with possible
later sacrifice of exchange at a5 is good for White.

Probably, having accepted once, Black is best advised to
accept again. Therefore

| 6. .... | P×P |
| 7. O—O | B—Kt3 |

7. ....    P×P is playable and tenable, but White's development will tax the best Black defenders. A typical sequence is

| 7. .... | P×P |
| 8. Q—Kt3 | Q—B3 |
| 9. P—K5 | Q—Kt3 |
| 10. Kt×P | KKt—K2 |
| 11. B—R3 with a fine game. | |

Black, e.g., cannot usefully play 11. ....    B—Kt3, because of

| 12. QR—Q1 | Kt—R4 |
| 13. Q—Kt4 | |

There is, however, a tenable defence from 11. ....    O—O. From the less compromising

| 7. .... | B—Kt3 |
| 8. P×P | P—Q3 (this position can |
| | be reached from 5. |
| | ....  B—B4) |

Black can hold the various attacks – e.g. 9. B—KKt5   Kt—B3. 10. Q—Kt3   Kt—R4 and 11. B×P ch loses a White piece at least temporarily.

So much for the 'Slow Game'.

Another fast mode of attack is for White to play fairly quickly P—Q4. He can do it on move two. (Centre Game.)

| 1. P—K4 | P—K4 |
| 2. P—Q4 | P×P (here the best) |
| 3. Q×P | Kt—QB3 |
| 4. Q—K3 and Black is not in danger. | |

But White can play, more sacrificially (after

| 1. P—K4 | P—K4 |
| 2. P—Q4 | P×P) |
| 3. P—QB3 This can be 'ignored' with 3. .... | |
| P—Q4 – a good freeing move in many KP | |

openings. But if Black captures the second Pawn, we are in the vortex of the *Danish Gambit*

| | |
|---|---|
| *1.* P—K4 | P—K4 |
| *2.* P—Q4 | P×P |
| *3.* P—QB3 | P×P |
| *4.* B—QB4 | |

Let one line suffice

| | |
|---|---|
| *4.* .... | P×P |
| *5.* B×KtP | P—Q4 (the best) |
| *6.* B×QP | Kt—KB3 |
| *7.* B×P ch | K×B |
| *8.* Q×Q | B—QKt5 ch |
| *9.* Q—Q2 | B×Q ch |
| *10.* Kt×B and both sides have chances. | |

More usual is the delayed advance, P—Q4 on the third move.

| | |
|---|---|
| *1.* P—K4 | P—K4 |
| *2.* Kt—KB3 | Kt—QB3 |
| *3.* P—Q4 | P×P |

Here *4.* P—B3     P×P

*5.* Kt×P is vigorous (*Goring Gambit*)

But *4.* ....     P—Q6 avoids . the dangers of loss of tempo.

*4.* B—B4 gives us the *Scotch Gambit*, which can move into the Max Lange, but need not

*4.* ....     P—Q3 and Black defends with B—K2 etc.

Frequent is *4.* Kt×P (Scotch Game). A familiar sequence is

| | |
|---|---|
| *4.* .... | B—B4 |
| *5.* B—K3 | Q—B3 |

This allows the possibility of the *Blumenfeld*

*6.* Kt—Kt5     B×B

*7.* P×B and Black can check at K4, capture the KP while White checks at c7 — a game slightly in Black's favour. But it isn't necessary for Black to accept the offer. With 7. .... K—Q1 he leaves White disordered.

Therefore normal is

      6. P—QB3             KKt—K2

Now, if 7. B—B4, Black does not Castle because of Kt×Kt forcing the Queen to recapture. But Kt—K4 and a Pawn sacrifice at Q4 gives Black freedom.

If     7. B—QKt5          O—O
       8. O—O              B×Kt
       9. P×B              P—Q4 and 10. P—K5 is
                                     not terrible.

In this type of game P—Q4 is the touchstone of Black's freedom. (Not so in the Lopez or Four Knights.) So we find after another play for Black, when, following

      1. P—K4             P—K4
      2. Kt—KB3         Kt—QB3
      3. P—Q4             P×P
      4. Kt×P

he plays 4. .... Kt—B3
Normal then is 5. Kt×Kt KtP×Kt in order to make possible P—Q4.
So far we have tended to assume that after

      1. P—K4 P—K4      2. Kt—KB3
      2. .... Kt—QB3 is best. This is not certain.

Other possibilities include two well-known openings. One is the *Petroff* (or Russian: Sci. Czarist) Defence

      1. P—K4             P—K4
      2. Kt—KB3         Kt—KB3

This has lost its popularity for non-political reasons. One line of play is:

      3. Kt×P and now, not Kt×P
      4. Q—K2 but 3. .... P—Q3
                 4. Kt—KB3    Kt×P

| | |
|---|---|
| *5.* P—Q4 | P—Q4 with equality, |
| | and not much |
| | scope for either |
| | player. |

In the wilderness with Petroff is *Philidor*, as if in a Franco-Russian *entente*. This opening the reader has seen mishandled by one of Morphy's opponents. Here is the normal.

| | |
|---|---|
| *1.* P—K4 | P—K4 |
| *2.* Kt—KB3 | P—Q3 |
| *3.* P—Q4 | Kt—Q2 |
| *4.* B—B4 | P—QB3 |

The point is that if

| | |
|---|---|
| *4.* .... | B—K2 |
| *5.* O—O | Kt—B3 |
| *6.* B×P ch | K×B |
| *7.* Kt—Kt5 ch | K—Kt1 |
| *8.* Kt—K6 | Q—K1 |
| *9.* Kt×BP | Q—Q1 |
| *10.* Kt×R | and Black, who proceeds to win that |
| | Knight, loses a Pawn more than is necessary. |
| | After *4.* .... P—QB3, White's sacrifice is |
| | more doubtful. (This variation is called |
| | Hanham's Defence.) |

Alternatively, after

| | |
|---|---|
| *2.* .... | P—Q3 |
| *3.* P—Q4 | Kt—KB3 |
| *4.* Kt—B3 | QKt—Q2 |
| *5.* B—B4 | B—K2 allows the sacrifice |
| | already seen, and also allows |
| *6.* Kt—Kt5 | O—O |
| *7.* B×P ch | R×B |
| *8.* Kt—K6, etc. | |

On the whole Hanham's seems to be a better variation.

Black in the Philidor can also relieve tension by *3. ....*
P×P, or do it later. Then he has lost a tempo in getting his
Pawn to Q4, but this may not matter.

By consensus, it seems that Philidor and Petroff are useful;
but that *2. .... Kt—QB3* is preferable.

In consequence, then, of a fear of the Ruy Lopez, a large
number of King's Pawn Games are not mutual. The openings that
make it unilateral are sometimes classed, with some QP defences,
as half-open. The phrase is not important. One problem –
only one of the problems – which is expressed by words like
close and half-open, is the specific difficulty in the development of Black's Queen's Bishop if he does not play P—K4.
One reason for the increase in the proportion of unilateral
King's Pawn openings is the recognition that the development
of Black's QB can be delayed, or can be organized from the
Queen's wing with a fianchetto, or via Q2; in some cases via
Q2 and K1 to the King's side.

One of the oldest of the unilateral KP openings is the *Centre
Counter*. *1.* P—K4 P—Q4.

White gains tempo in the line *2.* P×P Q×P. *3.* Kt—QB3,
because, whether Black replies Q—Q1 or Q—QR4 (the usual)
White has developed a minor piece, as it were, for nothing. But
a lack of pressure is Black's compensation for this.

Typical play is

|  |  |
|---|---|
| *1.* P—K4 | P—Q4 |
| *2.* P×P | Q×P |
| *3.* Kt—QB3 | Q—QR4 |
| *4.* P—Q4 so that Black shall not get in P—K4 (met now by Q—R5) | |
| *4. ....* | Kt—KB3 |

White can now play

|  |  |
|---|---|
| *5.* B—Q2 inducing | P—QB3 |
| If  *5. ....* | Kt—B3 |
| *6.* B—QKt5 | P—K3 (Q—Kt3 is necessary) |
| *7.* Kt—Q5 wins the Queen | |

After 5. ....                        P—QB3

Black can develop his QB, but White's development is easier for some time. There is no great danger to Black.

Many players adopt, nowadays, a different second move for Black. Not 2. .... Q×P but 2. .... Kt—KB3.

White can try to hold the P with 3. P—QB4 but 3. .... P—QB3 followed by

4. P×P    Kt×P

leaves Black with a splendidly free game at the cost of a Pawn. Therefore, after

| 1. P—K4 | P—Q4 |
|---------|------|
| 2. P×P | Kt—KB3 |
| 3. P—Q4 | Kt×P is the usual line. |

Now White gains tempo with 4. P— QB4.

Then 4. ....                        Kt—Kt3 is playable,
                                        allowing

| 5. P—QR4 | P—QR4 |
|----------|-------|
| 6. Kt—KB3 | B—Kt5 |

and Black has solved some problems. Also Black can reply to P—QB4 with Kt—KB3. He has lost tempo but White's development is not yet incisive and Black can so arrange his affairs that White's centre is relatively irrelevant. The absence of White's KP can be greatly in Black's favour.

This situation also obtains in some variations of the *Caro-Kann*.

1. P—K4                        P—QB3

This strange seeming move is quite good, because it projects P—Q4 without the need for the Queen or a Knight to recapture.

1. P—K4                        P—QB3
2. P—Q4                        P—Q4
3. P—K5 is playable. If Black replies 3. ....
        B—B4, then 4. B—Q3    B×B. 5. Q×B gives

White considerable control. Black will later
play P—QB4 in order to undermine the
centre.

Also playable is *4.* P—KKt4 followed, if B—Kt3, by *5.*
P—KR4. The attack is inconclusive, but White develops well.

Most usual play is in two other modes. White can play *3.*
P×P and follow with P—QB4, maintaining pressure on the
centre, which induces P—K3 (Black's Queen's Bishop is closed
in, but is required for the defence of the Queen's side).

Alternative is *3.* Kt—QB3 and Black seems to have nothing
more constructive than *3.* .... P×P.

After *4.* Kt×P P—K4 is not unplayable, but usual is *4.* ....
B—B4.

*5.* Kt—Kt3 B—Kt3 and Black soon reaches a level game.
('Has equalized' is an expression used to indicate that White's
initiative has abated.)

Another treatment, occasionally used by the Author, is

|   |   |   |
|---|---|---|
| 1. P—K4 | P—QB3 |
| 2. P—Q4 | P—Q3 |

a sort of Philidor with delayed P—K4 – very playable.

A defect in the Caro Kann is that Black may have to move his
QBP twice; but this occurs when time is less important than in
a faster type of game.

Let it be added that in recent World Championship games
that great player Botvinnik used Caro-Kann on a large scale.
It is suspected that he learned it from an English umpire.

A quite normal line is the following:

|   |   |
|---|---|
| *1.* P—K4 | P—QB3 |
| *2.* P—Q4 | P—Q4 |
| *3.* Kt—QB3 | P×P |
| *4.* Kt×P | B—B4 |
| *5.* Kt—Kt3 | B—Kt3 |

Possible now is

|   |   |
|---|---|
| *6.* P—KR4 | P—KR4 |
| *7.* B—Q3 | B×B |

Slower, but logical, is 6. Kt—B3 aiming at the control of e5.
Tal, in play against Botvinnik, seemed to prefer 6. Kt—K2
with development on f4, but enjoyed no great success with it.

Another line after *1*. P—K4   P—QB3. *2*. P—Q4   P—Q4.
*3*. Kt—QB3   P×P. *4*. Kt×P is

|         |         |
|---------|---------|
| *4*. ....  | Kt—B3   |
| 5. Kt—Kt3  | P—K4    |
| 6. Kt—B3   | P×P     |

A third:

|          |                                     |
|----------|-------------------------------------|
| *1*. P—K4   | P—QB3                            |
| 2. Kt—QB3   | P—Q4                             |
| 3. Kt—B3    | B—Kt5 (This move is a desirable one for Black in the Caro-Kahn, but it deprives Black as well as White of weapons) |

Perhaps more popular than the Caro is the *French Defence*:
an opening in which Black handles the centre in a way suggestive
of some Q.P. openings, and in which, from the outset, he does
not concern himself with the future of his QB.

|           |         |
|-----------|---------|
| *1*. P—K4    | P—K3   |

2. P—Q4 is almost automatic and Black's reply is

|           |         |
|-----------|---------|
| 2. ....    | P—Q4   |

White has a choice of methods. He can play 3. P—K5, an
old-fashioned move, which received new life this century
through the genius of Nimzovitch.

Or 3. P×P, the Exchange Variation, which was shown by
Alekhine to be good for Black when he won the historic first
game in his match with Capablanca: after which Capablanca
resorted to QP for the rest of the match (implying that he
thought there was no better way, at least for his style, of treat-
ing the French).

Or 3. Kt—QB3, which may be considered the orthodox.

Or *3.* Kt—Q2, with an ambitious plan.

(If White can 'get in'. P—K5   P—QB3. B—Q3. KKt—K2, O—O. P—KB4 and QKt—KB3, he has an excellent control of the centre and play on the King's wing; but this has to be done in the teeth of a counter-attack by Black along the QB file.)

Strategically the French is cognate to the Sicilian and to those QP games in which White blocks the centre aggressively. The counter is by P—QB4. Very unpromising for Black is any play in these systems in which he brings his QKt to B3 before he has moved his QBP.

Here are some typical variants of the Defence.

First, what I may call orthodox.

|  |  |
|---|---|
| *1.* P—K4 | P—K3 |
| *2.* P—Q4 | P—Q4 |
| *3.* Kt—QB3 | Kt—KB3 |
| *4.* B—KKt5 | B—K2 |
| *5.* P—K5 | KKt—Q2 |

(We are now playing a QP with the White KP forward.)

*6.* P—KR4. A move popularized by Alekhine. Black dare not accept the sacrifice, because after *6.* .... B×B 7. P×B Q×P. *8.* Kt—R3, the Queen must return to K2. Elsewhere she can be trapped, and White has gained a lot of tempo for a K side attack.

Of good defences, Black can Castle and stand a strong attack. He can challenge with the risky *6.* .... P—KB3, inviting a sacrificial attack from *7.* B—Q3. But reasonable is *6.* .... P—QR3, with a view to P—QB4. *6.* .... P—QB4 is not unplayable if Black wishes to invite a Knight to d6. In reply to *7.* Kt—Kt5 he may play *7.* .... Kt—B3 and invite an attack which is interesting and dangerous without being fatal.

Against *6.* .... P—QR3. *7.* Q—Kt4 is strong, but it is believed that after *7.* .... K—B1 Black's position is defensible.

In answer to *6.* .... P—QR3, a suggestion of the Author's is *7.* P—QKt4.

Also White can attack with *7.* R—R3, but careful defence

seems to beat off all attacks. However, many players prefer not to encourage the attack in this form; and there are ways of avoiding it.

E.g., after

| | |
|---|---|
| 4. B—KKt5 | B—Kt5 (the McCutcheon is interesting) |
| 5. P—K5 | P—KR3 |
| 6. P×Kt | P×B |
| 7. P×P | R—Kt1 |
| 8. P—KR4 | P×P |
| 9. Q—R5 | Q—B3 |
| 10. Kt—B3 (and Black has a big choice of moves). | |

Another play is the exchange of Pawns by Black

| | |
|---|---|
| 1. P—K4 | P—K3 |
| 2. P—Q4 | P—Q4 |
| 3. Kt—QB3 | Kt—KB3 |
| 4. B—Kt5 | P×P |

which leads to a game in which Black is free from terrors.

Fundamentally different is a policy that can be adopted earlier.

| | |
|---|---|
| 1. P—K4 | P—K3 |
| 2. P—Q4 | P—Q4 |
| 3. Kt—QB3 | B—Kt5 |

This is the old Winawer Defence, revived by Alekhine and much relied upon by Botvinnik.

| | |
|---|---|
| 4. P—K5 | Kt—K2 |

Some prefer 4. .... P—QB4, but this gives White good development with 5. Q—Kt4 inducing K—B1 or a gamble.

After

| | |
|---|---|
| 4. .... | Kt—K2 |
| 5. P—QR3 brings about an exchange analogous to that in the Nimzovitch Defence to the QP. | |

Quite playable is 5. B—Q2 (a move that can be delayed) and after

|       |          |          |
|-------|----------|----------|
| 5.    | ....     | P—QB4    |
| 6.    | Kt—Kt5   | B×B ch   |
| 7.    | Q×B      | O—O      |

8. P—QB3 but White's attack must not be expected to achieve much.

Popular, therefore, is

|       |          |          |
|-------|----------|----------|
| 1.    | P—K4     | P—K3     |
| 2.    | P—Q4     | P—Q4     |
| 3.    | Kt—QB3   | B—Kt5    |
| 4.    | P—K5     | Kt—K2    |
| 5.    | Q—Kt4    | Kt—B4    |
| 6.    | Kt—B3    | P—KR4    |
| 7.    | Q—B4     | P—QB4    |

And now White has a big choice, including 8. P×P, 8. B—Q3. 8. B—Q2, etc. He must so play as to preserve the Pawn at e5, or at least the control of that square.

That theory underlies Nimzovitch's preferential treatment of the French

|       |          |          |
|-------|----------|----------|
| 1.    | P—K4     | P—K3     |
| 2.    | P—Q4     | P—Q4     |
| 3.    | P—K5     |          |

Black attacks, sooner or later with P—QB4, and White does not mind the fall of the Pawn at d4, so long as the KP remains a force.

Capablanca, who thought that White could obtain more open lines in the French than Black, adopted, against Alekhine, the Exchange variation against the Winawer.

The move P×P achieves nothing on move three, though it is playable, but after Black has played his Bishop to a non-central square, White may be gaining tempo.

The first game of the match showed that this belief is not well founded. Here are the first 17 moves of that historic game.

|       |            |            |
|-------|------------|------------|
| 1.    | P—K4       | P—K3       |
| 2.    | P—Q4       | P—Q4       |
| 3.    | Kt—QB3     | B—Kt5      |
| 4.    | P×P        | P×P        |
| 5.    | B—Q3       | Kt—QB3     |

Evidently Alekhine did not wish to risk a weak centre after 5. .... P—QB4. 6 P—QR3 or 6. P×P.

|       |            |            |
|-------|------------|------------|
| 6.    | KKt—K2     | KKt—K2     |
| 7.    | O—O        | B—KB4      |
| 8.    | B×B        | Kt×B       |
| 9.    | Q—Q3       | Q—Q2       |
| 10.   | Kt—Q1      | O—O        |
| 11.   | Kt—K3      | Kt×Kt      |
| 12.   | B×Kt       | KR—K1      |
| 13.   | Kt—B4      | B—Q3!      |
| 14.   | KR—K1      | (Kt×P is better. It is met by B×P ch K×B, Q×Kt P—QB4 Q—R4 ch favourable for Black. Safer seems 14. P—QB3.) |
| 14.   | ....       | Kt—Kt5     |
| 15.   | Q—Kt3      | Q—B4!      |

and White, in difficulties, made the mistake of 16. QR—B1 (KR—B1 is better).

There followed

|       |            |            |
|-------|------------|------------|
| 16.   | ....       | Kt×BP      |
| 16.   | R×Kt       | Q×Kt, winning a Pawn |

and, notwithstanding fine play by White thereafter, the game. Undoubtedly the French Defence is a good defence, but it seems less popular than the *Sicilian*, the evident reason being that in the latter the tension is less in the early stages, and Black's choices are very varied.

|       |            |            |
|-------|------------|------------|
| 1.    | P—K4       | P—QB4      |
| 2.    | Kt—KB3     |            |

Now Black has the choice of 2. .... P—K3, the Paulsen system. 2. .... Kt—QB3 which leaves choice of system open 2. .... P—Q3 which contemplates, *inter alia*, a King's side fianchetto.

The play from 2. .... P—Q3 is instructive.

3. P—Q4. This is White's normal reply to most of Black's second moves.

|   |   |
|---|---|
| 3. .... | P×P Also normal |
| 4. Kt×P | Kt—KB3 |

This is meant to induce, and usually does induce, 4. QKt—B3 which prevents White's playing of P—QB4, the Maroczy system, which is regarded as advantageous to White because of the Pawn control over d5.

(Strangely, a Sicilian position, with P—QB4 played, can occur in the Réti–Zukertort, and the Russian thinkers do not seem to be alarmed by it. However Kt—KB3 is a good move in its own right.)

After 4. QKt—B3 P—KKt3 introduces the 'Dragon' – a sort of King's Indian Defence, and Black has quite a control of the fluid centre, also the chances of an attack against White's Queen's side.

Let us consider this variation first.

|   |   |
|---|---|
| 1. P—K4 | P—QB4 |
| 2. Kt—KB3 | P—Q3 |

The reason for 2. .... P—Q3 is as follows. It is important to prevent White at a later stage from playing P—K5. If Black plays the quite normal 2. .... Kt—QB3, he will also have to play P—Q3, and that extra move will give White a tempo for the Richter attack which prevents the 'Dragon' development, e.g.

|   |   |
|---|---|
| 1. P—K4 | P—QB4 |
| 2. Kt—KB3 | Kt—QB3 |
| 3. P—Q4 | P×P |
| 4. Kt×P | Kt—B3 |
| 5. Kt—QB3 | P—Q3 |

The threat was 6. Kt × Kt followed by 7. P—K5, dislocating the Knight. Actually, after the text 6. Kt × Kt   P × Kt. 7. P—K5 is playable as a sacrifice (7. . . . . P × P. 8. Q × Q ch) but White's superiority in development is insufficient compensation for the Pawn. After 6. . . . .   P—Q3 in this variation. 7. B—KKt5 is good. Now 7. . . . .   P—KKt3 would enable White to exchange 8. B × Kt   P × Kt and Black's Pawn position will require a lot of rectifying, if, indeed rectification is possible. After 7. B–KKt5 P—K3 is required.

Therefore, for Dragon purposes one plays

|  |  |
|---|---|
| 2. . . . . | P—Q3 |
| 3. P—Q4 | P × P |
| 4. Kt × P | Kt—KB3 |
| 5. Kt—QB3 | P—KKt3 |
| 6. B—K2 | B—Kt2 |
| 7. B—K3 | O—O |
| 8. O—O | Kt—B3 |
| 9. P—KB4 | P—QR3 |
| 10. Kt—Kt3 |  |

This move is played sooner or later, because Black can play Kt—KKt5, when the second capture at g4 leaves d4 under-protected. The complications that arise from White's capturing of Black pieces and Black's capturing of White's can be worked out by the reader at his leisure. In any case 10. Kt—Kt3 is necessary to make White's KKtP mobile to g4.

|  |  |
|---|---|
| 10. . . . . | B—K3 |
| 11. P—Kt4 | Kt—QR4 |
| 12. P—B5 | B—B5 |
| 13. B—Q3 | R—B1 |
| 14. P—Kt5 | Kt—R4 |

and White's attack, against careful treatment, will be beaten off. In the modern practice there is a tendency to play B—KKt5 before P—KB4; but the game is indeterminate – as it should be with well-balanced opening play. Against the Dragon the young

American genius Bobby Fischer has popularized B—QB4, a move shown on an earlier page.

| 1. P—K4 | P—QB4 |
|---|---|
| 2. Kt—KB3 | P—Q3 |
| 3. P—Q4 | P×P |
| 4. Kt×P | Kt—KB3 |
| 5. Kt—QB3 | P—KKt3 |
| 6. B—B4 | B—Kt2 |
| 7. O—O | Kt—B3 |
| 8. KKt—K2 (*inter alia*) | O—O |
| 9. B—Kt3 (in order to prevent Kt×P) | |

and White does not mind Black's Kt—QR4 exchanging a good Knight for a not bad Bishop. The advantage of Fischer's B—B4 is that an attempt to strengthen f7 with P—K3 weakens Black at d6.

Another method for White is to play the KB to QKt5, either checking or pinning a Knight. The idea is that the ultimate prospects of the white-squared Bishop are less than that of the Black Queen's Knight.

The other main version of the Sicilian is describable as the Paulsen, or the Scheveningen, according to order.

| 1. P—K4 | P—QB4 |
|---|---|
| 2. Kt—KB3 | P—K3 |
| 3. P—Q4 | P×P |
| 4. Kt×P | |

If 4. .... P—QR3 we have Paulsen's system: if 4 .... Kt—B3 we have the Scheveningen. In practice they work out similarly, because after Black's P—K3 White's P—QB4 is regarded as less desirable than in the other system.

Paulsen's system enables a quick advance of the QKtP. But because one does not wish to rush this the Scheveningen is generally preferred. Also it does keep back P—QB4, for what it is worth.

| 1. P—K4 | P—QB4 |
|---|---|
| 2. Kt—KB3 | P—K3 |

| | |
|---|---|
| 3. P—Q4 | P×P |
| 4. Kt×P | Kt—KB3 |
| 5. Kt—QB3 | P—Q3 |

5. .... B—Kt5 is made dangerous by 6. P—K5 Kt—Q4. (If Kt—K5 White has a sportive attack with 7. Q—Kt4.
Very amusing would be

| | | | |
|---|---|---|---|
| 7. Q—Kt4 | Kt×Kt | 8. P×Kt | B×P ch |
| 9. K—Q1 | K—B1 | 10. B—R3 ch | K—Kt1 |
| 11. R—QKt1 | Kt—B3 | 12. R—Kt3 | B×Kt |
| 13. Q×P ch | K×Q | 14. R—Kt3 ch | K—R3 |
| 15. B—B1 ch | K—R4 | 16. B—K2 ch | K—R5 |
| 17. R—R3 mate.) | But 6..... | Kt—Q4, met by B—Q2. |

renders that line of thought academic; and White stands better, without speculation.

After 5. .... P—Q3 normal is 6. B—K2 (P—KKt3, though it seems to be wasting moves – two openings for the Bishop – is also strategically good).

| | |
|---|---|
| 6. .... | Kt—B3 |
| 7. O—O | B—K2 |
| 8. B—K3 | O–O |
| 9. P—KB4 | P—QR3 |
| 10. K—R1 (to give the B a retreat after 11. Kt—B3 Kt—Kt5 | |
| 10. .... | B—Q2 |

and now White is ready to play 10. P—QR4 or 10. B—B3. If 10. P—KKt4. Black has Kt×Kt B—B3 and Q—B2 which· perceptibly takes the edge off the attack. Black has to arrange for Pawn play while keeping himself prepared to cope with a King's side Pawn rush, calculated to disturb nervous players.

In the last few decades the Sicilian has been analysed exhaustingly rather than exhaustively. What the reader must bear in mind is Black's duty some day to assert himself in the centre.

Moves like P—Q4 and P—K4 (if it can be followed by P—Q4) must be thought about until they are playable.

A completely different treatment of the Sicilian is

|    |         |       |
|----|---------|-------|
| 1. | P—K4    | P—QB4 |
| 2. | P—Kt4 the Wing Gambit | |

After 2. ....                    P×P people have played

3. P—QR3

The Author has preferred to let Black keep the Pawn. 3. B—Kt2, and 3. B—B4 and 3. P—Q4 all lead to good aggressive Chess.

|    |        |       |
|----|--------|-------|
| 1. | P—K4   | P—QB4 |
| 2. | P—QKt4 | P×P   |
| 3. | B—Kt2  | P—Q4  |
| 4. | P×P    | is probably the best and White has a long series of good developing moves ahead of him. |

If   4. ....                    Q×P

5. P—QB4 increases White's 'start'

To move away from the Sicilian, there are other replies to 1. P—K4, e.g. 1. .... P—KKt3. (In effect Kotob–Robatach.) Worth noticing is Alekhine's Defence, already mentioned.

|    |        |       |
|----|--------|-------|
| 1. | P—K4   | Kt—KB3 |
| 2. | P—K5   | Kt—Q4  |
| 3. | P—QB4  | Kt—Kt3 |
| 4. | P—Q4 seems to give White a big initiative: but it is hard to maintain | |
| 4. | ....   | P—Q3   |
| 5. | P—KB4  | P×P    |
| 6. | BP×P   | Kt—B3  |
| 7. | B—K3 (if 7. Kt—KB3 B—Kt5 gains tempo) | |
| 7. | ....   | B—B4   |
| 8. | Kt—KB3 | P—K3   |

| | |
|---|---|
| *9.* Kt—B3 | Kt—Kt5 |
| *10.* R—B1 | P—B4 leads to beautiful complications, which White may prevent with *9.* P—QR3 instead of Kt—B3 |

This one variation (there are many others) shows the opening not to be absurd.

It is not within the scope of an introductory book to investigate many variations. What the reader should be acquiring is a sense of the shapes of game that various openings give. There is a kind of conflict in the mutual King's Pawn which is avoided in the unilateral King's Pawn; and in those the play seems to be deflected from balanced struggle in the centre to the different balance which is the pressing on one wing while one is being pressed on the other.

An attempt to build a solider, if less aggressively designed centre, is made when one adopts the *Queen's Pawn* instead of the King's Pawn opening. As the mutual King's Pawn is a claim to the centre resisted, so is the mutual Queen's Pawn. But the claim is less violent. Thus *Queen's Gambit* is a less aggressive opening than King's Gambit; the pressure on the attacked Pawn is less, and the guarding of that Pawn by other Pawns is easier. Therefore, whereas Black is tempted to accept King's Gambit and fight, he is less tempted to accept the Queen's Gambit; though the acceptance is more popular now that the solid centre has ceased to be a Chess fetish.

| | |
|---|---|
| *1.* P—Q4 | P—Q4 |
| *2.* P—QB4 | P—K3 (shutting in his QB, but there is plenty of play) |
| *3.* Kt—QB3 | Kt—KB3 |

An alternative is

| | |
|---|---|
| *3.* .... | P—QB4 |

the *Tarrasch Defence*.

This gives Black a dynamic game at the cost of an ultimate strategic weakness.

| 3. .... | P—QB4 |
|---|---|
| 4. BP×P (not QP×P | P—Q5!) |
| 4. .... | KP×P |
| (4. .... | BP×P |
| 5. Q×P | Kt—QB3 – the Hennig-Schara leaves White better placed) |

After *4. ....* KP×P White can play Kt—B3 and King's fianchetto. Ultimately, Black will either exchange at d4 or allow an exchange at c5 and a White Knight will blockade at d4. If, instead, Black advances his BP to c4, his Pawn position for the endgame is very weak.

Thus the Tarrasch has a strategic weakness, but Black has freedom.

More usual, however, than the Tarrasch is *3. ....* Kt—KB3 and this is often followed by

*4. B—Kt5.* This is called the Pillsbury development, after an American whose brief meteor course across the Chess skies was a feature of the closing years of the nineteenth century. The older form of the Gambit, preferred by many, is *4. P—K3*, or *4. Kt—B3* (compatible with Pillsbury, but frequently followed by P—K3 instead of B—Kt5). In the slower game, White's QB can wait for the KP to reach K4; or can be fianchettoed.

To *4. B—Kt5* there are playable *4. ....* B—K2 and *4. ....* QKt—Q2 (which the reader has already seen not to entail loss of a Pawn). The advantage of *4. ....* QKt—Q2 is that it reserves the option of a different development than we are now following, namely, the Cambridge Springs.

| 4. .... | QKt—Q2 |
|---|---|
| 5. P—K3 | B—K2 |

To be considered at this point is

| 5. .... | P—B3 |
|---|---|
| 6. Kt—B3 | Q—R4 |

restraining *7. B—Q3* because of *7. ....* P×P, *8. B×P* Kt—K5 with an attack.

That is the Cambridge Springs Defence (so named from a Tournament in 1904 where it was played). White has moves like 7. B—KR4 or B×Kt and Black can put pressure on c3 with the Bishop. But even if White lets a Pawn go lost on the Queen's side, he maintains a compensating development. Another point to be considered at move 5 is that Black can play P—KR3, moving a target Pawn. The main objection is that if and when Black removes his Kt, White's B will be able to move to g3 instead of exchanging. But the move is playable. In the main (orthodox) line,

> after 6. Kt—B3. O—O (and similar reasoning
> applies after 6. .... P—KR3 et seq.)

White has a choice.

He can play 7. B—Q3 or 7. Q—B2, or 7. R—B1. All these are purposive.

7. Q—B2 (with R—Q1 contemplated) is thought to allow 7. .... P—QB4.

That was explored in the Lasker–Capablanca match and found good for Black.

Later experiment has shown that 8. P×QP Kt×P can be followed by 9. Kt×Kt B×B. 10. P—KR4 with a good game. (If 10. .... Q—R4 ch? 11. P- Kt4 P×P. 12 Q×P ch with mate in 3.)

However, a general preference is for 7. R—B1. Before that is discussed, a glance at 7. B—Q3. B—Q3 must be played sooner or later; and the accepted reply to it is P×P. After B×P it looks as if White has lost a move in his transit to c4. But what has Black gained? He is committed to a different type of centre.

Nevertheless, with Kt—Kt3 and Kt—Q4 he has aggressive play.

(Sometimes Black plays P×P without waiting for B—Q3, if he thinks he has nothing better to do.)

The advantage of immediate 7. B—Q3 is that after P×P 8. B×P, KKt—Q4. 9. B×B and the Kt must retake.

If Black has got in P—B3, the Queen can retake; and the threat is then Kt×Kt followed by P—K4.

However, 7. B—Q3 is less popular for strategic reasons than

R—M

7. R—B1. A speculator, playing B—Q3 after R—B1, can play B—Kt1 sacrificially. (This has been done successfully by the Author, but is not recommended.)

7. R—B1. Now if 7. .... P—B4 Black loses a Pawn – though he gains some freedom. The usual answer to 7. R—B1 is 7. .... P—B3, 'overprotecting' d5 and removing a target from c7. That this Pawn may move again in order to attack the centre is not considered a defect in this play. (There are those who prefer 7. .... P—QR3 or 7. .... P—KR3, followed by 8. .... P—QR3, etc., but the BP will move to c6 later.) After 7. .... P—B3 we find usual

8. Q—B2, Rubinstein's move. One idea in this is to build a control of e4. At this point, Black sometimes plays 8. .... R—K1, with the idea of Kt—B1. Alekhine preferred

| | |
|---|---|
| 8. .... | P—KR3 |
| 9. B—R4 | P—QR3 |

The plan is a Queen's side freeing movement:

| | |
|---|---|
| 10. B—Q3 | P×P |
| 11. B×BP | P—QKt4 |
| 12. B—Q3 | P—B4 |

Black's pieces are now free.

In a famous game against Alekhine, Grunfeld played 10. P—QR3 before he moved his Bishop. Black temporized with R—K1. Then on 11. B—Q3 came 11. .... P×P.

| | |
|---|---|
| 12. B×P | P—QKt4 |
| 13. B—R2 | P—B4 |
| 14. R—Q1 | P×P |
| 15. Kt×QP | Q—Kt3 |
| 16. B—Kt1 | B—Kt2 |

and White's threat against h7 seems negligible. There is, however, a tactical point. White may have anticipated here (r3r 1kl, 1b1ktbpp1, pq2pkt1p, 1p6, 3Kt3B, P1Kt1P3, 1PQ2PPP, 1B1RK2R) that he could play 17. QKt×P. If then P×Kt 18. R×Kt! But coming closer to it, he will have seen that 17. QKt×P is met by Q—B3, a winning *Zwischenzug*.

That example is given in order to show that Black can, against a Rubinstein Q.G.D., find a lot of play.

Another counter worth mentioning is *Lasker's Defence*: the following is one form.

| | | |
|---|---|---|
| 1. | P—Q4 | P—Q4 |
| 2. | P—QB4 | P—K3 |
| 3. | Kt—QB3 | Kt—KB3 |
| 4. | B—Kt5 | B—K2 |
| 5. | P—K3 | P—KR3 |
| 6. | B—R4 | O—O |
| 7. | Kt—B3 | QKt – Q2 |
| 8. | B—Q3 | Kt—K5 |
| 9. | B×B | Q×B |

If now White wins a Pawn with Kt×Kt P×Kt. B×P, Q—Kt5 ch recovers it.

The Kt—K5 move, whether now or earlier, seems to involve too many exchanges, and the game can burn out.

In order to maintain a steady, prolonged pressure, many prefer not to play the Pillsbury B—Kt5. The resulting slow form of the Q.G.D. also leaves Black reasonably placed.

| | | |
|---|---|---|
| 1 | P—Q4 | P—Q4 |
| 2. | P—QB4 | P—K3 |
| 3. | Kt—QB3 | Kt—KB3 |
| 4. | P—K3 | Then P—B3 is often played. |

One idea is to try and hold the centre, not loosen it with later P×P. We get an identical position after

| | | |
|---|---|---|
| 3. | .... | P—QB3 |
| 4. | P—K3 | Kt—B3 |

But the interesting point in that sequence is that, at move 4., if White plays Kt—B3, instead of P—K3 Black has the chance of P×P and a defence associated with this author.

Also after 3. .... P—QB3. 4. P—K3 P—KB4 creates the Stonewall, which the reader has already seen. (It is also not bad to play P—KB4 even before White closes in his QB with P—K3.)

That Stonewall theory we also find in the *Dutch Defence*, *1*. P—Q4  P—KB4 an early effort to control R4. In that opening *2*. P—K4 can be played sacrificially.

In the main line the play is for e4,

|  |  |
|---|---|
| *1.* P—Q4 | P—Q4 |
| *2.* P—QB4 | P—K3 |
| *3.* Kt—QB3 | Kt—KB3 |
| *4.* P—K3 | P—QB3 |
| *5.* Kt—B3 | QKt—Q2 |
| *6.* B—Q3 | B—K2 |

Alternative is *6.* ....  P×P leading to the exciting Meran: *7.* B×BP  P—QKt4. *8.* B—Q3  P—QR3. *9.* P—K4  P—B4. *10.* P—K5  P×P. *11.* QKt×P  Kt×P. *12.* Kt×Kt  P×Kt. *13.* B×Pch  B—Q2. *14.* B×Bch.  Kt×B. *15.* Kt—Q3.

This is one of many Meran variations which make the 'Slow Queens' very fast. Recently it has lost popularity.

|  |  |
|---|---|
| *6.* .... | B—K2 (better than Q3) |
| *7.* O—O | O—O (these can be delayed) |

leads to a quieter life.

Now White has two options at least. He can play P—QKt3, B—QKt2, Q—B2 and retain a thrust towards the centre, and Black's Queen side fianchetto is not so good, because on Black's P—QKt3, White with P×P gains tempo. White's alternative is to play his KP forward quickly, gaining a bit of space.

Thus:

|  |  |
|---|---|
| *8.* P—K4 | P×P |
| *9.* Kt×P | Kt×Kt |
| *10.* B×Kt |  |

(Suppose, at this point, that Black is sorry not to have played B—Q3, let him be consoled. If the B were on d6, he still could not play P—K4 because of

|  |  |
|---|---|
| *11.* P×P | Kt×P |
| *12.* Kt×Kt | B×Kt |
| *13.* B×RP ch | K×B |
| *14.* Q—R5 ch, regaining the piece) |  |

Now 10. ....                         Kt—B3
        11. B—B2                      P—B4
        12. B—K3                      P—QKt3 is reasonably
                                      good for Black

Instead

        12. B—Kt5                     P×P
        13. Q—Q3                      P—KKt3 creates a
                                      weakness which seems
                                      unexploitable.

On the whole it seems that White is wise to delay P—K4 and develop his B at QKt2 so as to add a remote control to e5.

So far the orthodox Queen's Pawn. But the players of the early twentieth century were not satisfied to defend the centre. And they were subtle enough to see that a centre can be a hollow façade, and that a centre can be controlled without occupancy. There are several ways of changing the strategic set-up. Some arise in the mutual form of the Queen's Pawn; others develop from a Unilateral Queen's Pawn.

Of the former class, first Albin's Counter Gambit

        1. P—Q4                       P—Q4
        2. P—QB4                      P—K4
        3. P×P                        P—Q5

Playable is 4. P—QR3 but not 4. P—K3 (met by B—Kt5 ch) 5. B—Q2  P×P. Played in strong circles has been 4. KKt—B3 QKt—B3.

        5. QKt—Q2                     B—KKt5
        6. P—KR3 (played: but there may be better
            moves)
        6. ....                       B×Kt
        7. Kt×B                       B—B4
        8. P—QR3                      P—QR4
        9. P—KKt3                     KKt—K2
       10. B—Kt2                      Kt—Kt3
       11. O—O                        QR—Kt1
       12. Q—B2

and now, danger! If *12.* ....     Kt × P

| | |
|---|---|
| *13.* Kt × Kt | Kt × Kt |
| *14.* B × P | R × B |
| *14.* Q−K4 ch | |

Therefore *12.* ....     Q−K2 (to stop P−Kt4) *13.* B−Q2 in favour of White. But *13.* ....     O−O followed by KR−Q1, *inter alia*, give Black plenty of play.

Another process from the mutual QP is the Acceptance of the Gambit. And this can also be done in conjunction with the *Slav Defence*. Noting that the Slav can be converted into ordinary Q.G.D. let us take its aggressive form first.

| | |
|---|---|
| *1.* P−Q4 | P−Q4 |
| *2.* P−QB4 | P−QB3 |
| *3.* Kt−KB3 to prevent a possible P−K4 by Black. | |

Some authorities favour an exchange by White on move three, but the Queen's side attack that may result is defensible.

| | |
|---|---|
| *3.* .... | Kt−B3 |
| *4.* Kt−B3 | B−B4 |
| *5.* B−Kt5 (one line among many) | |
| *5.* .... | P × P (again, one among many) |
| *6.* P−K3 | P−QKt4 |
| *7.* P−QR4 | P−Kt5 |
| *8.* Kt−R2 and there is plenty of play | |

Others play instead of *6.* P−K3 an ambitious process, with Kt−K5, followed by P−KB3 and P−K4. A host of variations were explored in matches between Alekhine and Bogoljubow and Alekhine and Euwe.

To take the Pawn on move two is also possible. White is ill-advised to reply with P−K4, because that gets blocked with immediate P−K4.

| | |
|---|---|
| *1.* P−Q4 | P−Q4 |
| *2.* P−QB4 | P × P |
| *3.* P−K4 | P−K4 and after |
| *4.* P−Q5 Black has the play | |

*3.* Kt—KtB3 is best in order to prevent Black's P—K4.

The normal course of the Gambit Accepted is then for White to play *3.* Kt—KB3 and P—K3, at move *4.* Black will develop with Kt—KB3 and B—B4; and the opening can become very like the Slav.

The theory of the Slav is to liberate the QB, though leaving quite a weakness at b7. But if, with Q—Kt3, e.g. White ever attacks that Pawn Black plays Q—Kt3 or Q—B1.

| | |
|---|---|
| *1.* P—Q4 | P—Q4 |
| *2.* P—QB4 | P—QB3 |
| *3.* Kt—KB3 | Kt—KB3 |
| *4.* P—K3 | B—B4 |
| *5.* Kt—B3 | QKt—Q2 |
| *6.* B—K2 | P—K3 |
| *7.* O—O | B—K2 or Q3 |

and it is not clear how much Black has gained by having his QB at f5. He will probably not be able to prevent an eventual P—K4 prepared by Kt—Q2, P—B3, etc., but while White is doing this P—QB4 can be played by Black. In short, a game with play for both.

But now let us consider those who defer engagement in the centre. First, the *Nimzovitch Defence*.

| | |
|---|---|
| *1.* P—Q4 | Kt—KB3 |
| *2.* P—QB4 | P—K3 |
| *3.* Kt—QB3 | B—Kt5 |

Some players of White regard this as so good for Black that at move *3.* they play some such move as P—KKt3 and do not invite the pin. Others take the view that Black's Bishop is a nuisance to be removed by immediate P—QR3 – a method much used by Botvinnik. White loses tempo this way, but gains the minor exchange, and his Pawns are 'doubled towards the centre'. A third theory is that Black's Bishop is misplaced at White's QKt4. So they ignore it: playing P—K3 (B—KKt5 is far from unplayable) and proceeding to develop KKt and KB and to Castle.

Such a game can proceed as follows.

| | |
|---|---|
| *1.* P—Q4 | Kt—KB3 |
| *2.* P—QB4 | P—K3 |
| (*2.* .... | P—K4. |
| *3.* P×P | Kt—K5 (or Kt5) |

is the highly speculative Budapest.)

| | |
|---|---|
| *3.* Kt—QB3 | B—Kt5 |
| *4.* P—K3 | O—O |
| *5.* Kt—B3 | P—Q4 |
| *6.* B—Q3 | P—B4 |
| *7.* O—O | Kt—B3 |

*8.* Kt—K2 (and if Black exchanges Pawns, White
has the freer game)

Others think that the Bishop move can be exploited by such a move as *4.* Q—Kt3. But *4.* .... P—B4. *5.* P×P Kt—QB3 (or R3) seems quite good for Black.

Nor is *4.* Q—B2, threatening P—K4 very good, because at the worst it induces P—Q4, and Black threatens Kt—K5. By the same token Kt—K5 for Black unprovoked is a loss of tempo. White replies Q—B2.

The variations of the Nimzovitch are too numerous for treatment in a short survey. Two points are worth mentioning: that Black can, in some variations, exchange the Bishop, and having played P—QB4 and Kt—QB3, proceed with P—QKt3. B—R3, Kt—QR4 and QR—B1 to attack the Pawn at c4 (the Sämisch Pawn). While he is doing this, White builds up an attack against the King's side.

The other point is that Black can defer B -- Kt5.

After

| | |
|---|---|
| *1.* P—Q4 | Kt—KB3 |
| *2.* P—QB4 | P—K3 |
| *3.* Kt—QB3 | P—QKt3 is playable, and |
| *4.* P—K4 | B—Kt2 |
| *5.* P—K5 | Kt—K5 |

has points favourable to Black.

But the Queen's Indian, or Nimzo-Indian, is more usually

seen when White's third move is Kt—KB3 instead of Kt—QB3.
Thus

| | |
|---|---|
| 1. P—Q4 | Kt—KB3 |
| 2. P—QB4 | P—K3 |
| 3. Kt—KB3 | P—QKt3 |
| 4. P—KKt3 | B—Kt2 |
| 5. B—Kt2 | B—Kt5 ch |
| 6. Kt—B3 | Kt—K5 |
| 7. Q—B2 | P—KB4 |
| (7. .... | O—O |
| 8. Kt—Kt5 good for White) | |

Black will later play P—Q3 and QKt—Q2.

| | |
|---|---|
| But 1. P—Q4 | Kt—KB3 can herald something very different |
| 2. P—QB4 | P—KKt3 |

The *King's Indian:* not unlike the Dragon form of Sicilian in
its general strategy.

| | |
|---|---|
| 3. Kt—QB3 | B—Kt2 |
| 4. P—K4 (not a 'must') | P—Q3 |
| 5. P—KB4 is playable, but after | |
| 5. ...., | O—O |
| 6. P—K5 | P×P |
| 7. BP×P | Kt—K1 |
| 8. Kt—B3 | B—Kt5 Black is aggres- sive; |

and with P—QB4 sooner or later will render the centre hollow.

Nowadays players treat the King's Indian more respectfully.
Thus

| | |
|---|---|
| 5. Kt—B3 (P—B3 is also very good) | |
| 5. .... | O—O |
| 6. P—KR3, and if now P—B4 we have a Maroczy. | |

Then Black's play is (*inter alia*) to endeavour to attack e4
with P—f5. White's chances include P—g4: also pressure with
B and Q on h6.

Very frequent is the adoption of a White King's fianchetto:

| | |
|---|---|
| *1.* P—Q4 | Kt—KB3 |
| 2. P—QB4 | P—KKt3 |
| 3. P—KKt3 | B—Kt2 |
| 4. B—Kt2 | P—Q4 |
| 5. P×P | Kt×P |
| 6. P—K4 (not essential) | Kt—Kt3 |

or, as we have seen, Kt—Kt5.

Here we are moving into the theory of *Grunfeld's Defence*.

| | |
|---|---|
| *1.* P—Q4 | Kt—KB3 |
| 2. P—QB4 | P—KKt3 |
| 3. Kt—QB3 | P—Q4 |

This could not be played on move *2,* but now there is a lively continuation to it. If

| | |
|---|---|
| 4. P×P | Kt×P |
| 5. P—K4 | Kt×Kt |
| 6. P×Kt | P—QB4 |
| 7. Kt—B3 | P×P |
| 8. P×P | B—Kt2 |

and Black has a target.

A better treatment is to decline the offer.

After

| | |
|---|---|
| *3.* .... | P—Q4, |
| 4. B—B4 | |

followed by P—K3, Kt—B3, and possibly B—K5, has been found, by the Author, very playable on the part of White.

The 'back room' has thoughts in favour of *4.* Q—Kt3 on which much midnight oil has been wasted.

At the time of writing, it may be said that King's Indian (with the variation which is 'the Rubbish') finds more favour than the Grunfeld.

To sum up, it seems that the trend of practice is in favour of the Sicilian against P—K4, the King's Indian against P—Q4.

For the players of both systems, there is a relief from early pressure on pieces, and there is a hope that White will overdo his development. Without derogating from the merits of the non-mutual openings, the author ventures the suggestion that there is a lot of nervousness among the players of Black – a nervousness which is unjustified.

If White is a better colour than Black, then let us all give up Chess!

What is the truth of the matter? First, White has an initiative. In certain well-recognized lines of play, which Black may feel it necessary to adopt (e.g. defences to the Lopez), that initiative lasts a long time. But an initiative must not be confused with an advantage.

There is no opening in which White, without sacrificing unsoundly, can prevent Black achieving full development. When that is achieved, it may well be a better development than White's, because it is a subtler one; in the interstices of a rigid position.

But Black must be patient; and Black has more work to do in the early stages, while White has a few more possibilities in his field of choice. Players, therefore, prefer White through laziness. They prefer not to have to work too hard in the opening stages. But in reality White too, must work. To preserve an initiative as long as possible, without incurring strategic commitments that may prove undesirable, is at least as hard a task as playing a process of development without full initiative. There are a few players, the author included, who actually like Black, precisely because the play for 'equalization' is there to be found, and find its exploitation fascinating. Two propositions, certainly, are true: (1) Nobody ever beat a better player through having White. (2) Nobody ever lost merely through having Black. If it be said that White can so play as to have drawing chances against the best, the answer is: play against the best – and see!

# CHAPTER FIVE

## CHESS COMPOSITIONS: DEVELOPMENTS AND EXPERIMENTS

CHESS is a Science. Not an exact Science, as Mathematics and some of the physical sciences are; rather, an empirical science – in which complete predictability is not always realized, but in which the decisive factors are the objective forces that are available. If one speaks of the 'Art of Chess', one is using that expression, properly, only in the sense that one uses the words 'art of medicine', 'art of engineering', i.e. in the sense of 'skill'. To call a Chess-player an 'artist' in this sense is not, therefore, a denial that he is a scientist.

But to speak of a Chess-player's play as beautiful, or artistic in the aesthetic sense, is to speak as a spectator only – as the spectator who does *not* see the important aspects of the game. To create the 'beautiful' as such is to be controlled by purposes other than the functions of Chess material, and Chess possibilities apprehended as objective forces. A player who was influenced in his choice of move by an aesthetic purpose would be guilty of 'straining after an effect'. In Chess one seeks the 'useful' move – not the beautiful. 'Beautiful', applied to a Chess manœuvre, expresses an appreciation of the thing done – nothing in the doing of it. Diagram 141 shows a position from which Dr Berenblum won in a way that probably surprised the ordinary spectator – perhaps the opponent as well. But from White's point of view the move was effective Chess, not an aesthetic effect. Similarly, many of the moves seen in the illustrative games would be called 'beautiful' by Chess spectators because of the unexpectedness, the pleasing shock of revelation.

Mates from unexpected angles, sacrifices (such as Bronstein's against Wexler) which require great imagination to judge and justify in actual play, will always be called beautiful by the

Black

141

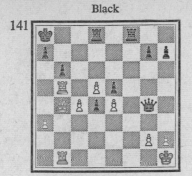

White (Berenblum)

Beautiful because hard to anticipate
1. R×P  Q—K7
2. R—KB6! wins

appreciative player, who says with Brahms, 'Alas, not by me'.
But Bronstein was not 'playing to the gallery' when he sacrificed that Queen. He was scientifically doing the best move on
the board.

But if a composer, seeing a 'clever' movement, decides to
take it, isolate it, give it an economical setting, make a 'study'
out of it, he is doing what a novelist, what many a poet, does
with an experience of life.

In Chess the 'Study' starts very close to Chess life. Many
studies are presentations of realistic positions, with the questions:
How to win? How to draw? Some are purely didactic,
though the selection in the mind of the 'composer' may give
him a slight claim to have created an artistic effect.

Diagram 142 invites the solver to show a way of winning
which is not very difficult to see but is sufficiently so to create
interest and give an aesthetic pleasure.

Diagram 143 pleases by instructing; and there is 'prettiness'
in many a purely didactic study, e.g. (one already seen) Pawns
at c7, b7, a7, facing Pawns at c5, b5, c5, are broken by P—b6. If
RP×P  BP advances: if BP×P, KP advances.

Black

White

White to play and win. Study by Prokop

*1.* B—B7, K—R2; *2.* P—Kt6 ch, K—R1 (not K—R3, because of K—R4, P—Kt4, etc.); *3.* B—Q6, P×B; *4.* P×P, K—Kt1; *5.* P—Q7 wins

Observe how the King cannot stop the Pawn now as it would in answer to *1.* B—Q6

Black

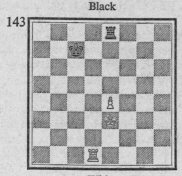

White

Exceptional case

White wins. Study by Frink

*1.* K—B4, R—B1 ch; *2.* K—Kt5, R—K1; *3.* K—B5, R—B1 ch; *4.* K—Kt6, R—K1; *5.* R—Q4 (not possible had Black K stood at c6!) K—B3; *6.* K—B7, R—K4; *7.* K—B6, R—KR4; *8.* P—K5 with a standard win

Similarly, there is prettiness where a game is saved by the sacrifice of a piece at h1, leaving a King blocking its own RP and the other King at f2, in check to a Knight, but never able to be driven from f1/f2, because the Knight cannot lose a move, so as to *zugzwang* the K.

Very many useful technical manœuvres, ingenious promotion themes, ingenious ways of gaining the opposition, of losing a move, etc., are also 'pretty' studies.

But there are composers who aim at THEME and/or FORM – showing movements with an interesting pattern, with echoes, and thematic variations: and culminating in some fine denouements.

These treasures are to be found in the growing literature of Endgame Studies. Great composers include RINCK – a Spaniard, WEENINK, a Dutchman, RÉTI, an Austrian master,

Black

144

White

White to play and win. Study by Kubbel

| | | |
|---|---|---|
| 1. Kt—Kt6 | P—Kt7 | 5. K—Kt6 | P—B6 |
| 2. Kt—Q5 ch | K—Q3 | 6. B—Q3 | K—Kt6 |
| 3. Kt—B3 | K—B4 | 7. K—Kt5 | P—B7 |
| 4. Kt—Kt1 | K—Kt5 | 8. B—B4 Mate |

TROITZKY (perhaps the greatest), a Russian, and following him a wonderful galaxy – Herbstmann, Liburkin, Kubbel, Gorgiev,

Black

145

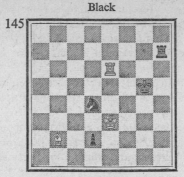

White

White to play and draw. Study by Herbstmann
1. R—K5 ch   K—B3
2. K×P   K×R
3. K—Q3   R—R5
4. K—B4 and the Knight cannot escape
If 2. .... Kt—B6 ch; 3. K—K3, Kt×R; 4. K—K4, R—R4 and the
theme is echoed

Grigorieff, the brothers Platoff, to name only a very few out of scores.

Diagrams 144, 145, 146 are a few gems. They are useful as well as beautiful. Their solution is Chess education. It should be added that many modern composers, in order to achieve clever effects, start from highly improbable positions.

Nevertheless these composers (Kasparian and Korolkov are noteworthy) teach Chess ideas.

The drift away from 'reality' is in the realms of the Chess 'Problem', which is in a different tradition from the Chess 'Study'.

*Problems* are composed for more aesthetic purposes than are most Studies. The solving is an intellectual act, but the purpose is not didactic, and the presented movement expresses a 'form' which gives an aesthetic satisfaction that is different from the thrill of solving a difficulty, or realizing an unexpected possibility.

Black

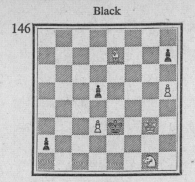

146

White

White to play and win. Study by Kasparian

1. B—B6    P—Q5
2. Kt—K2    P=Q
Now B×P ch only draws
∴3. Kt—B1! This threatens Mate! (by B—Kt5)
3 ....—Q—R4
4. B×P ch    K×B
5. Kt—Kt3 ch wins
    If 3. .... Q×Kt; 4. B—Kt5 ch wins

The old problems used to be 'studies in mating', as if in actual play. But the modern problem takes the form of a position in which the win – the forcing of eventual mate – by one side (White is always chosen) may be ludicrously easy. But the composer says: Mate in 2 or Mate in 3 or Mate in 4, 5, 6, etc. as the case may be. The difficulty is then one of a type unusual in the actual game: to do the mate in less time than it would take in ordinary play. The task is usually a subtle one – hard to see that it is a task – and is solved by a subtlety rather than by spectacular sacrifice.

The key-moves to problems are usually QUIET moves – very rarely checks, rarely captures: just some move that, as it were, redistributes the threats of the pieces. A few examples will suffice. Diagram 147 shows a position in which if Black moves,

Black

· 147

White

Mate in 2. By Nesic

Key: B—B3

        If *1.* .... K—B4; Q × R Mate

As the position stands

        If *1.* .... K—B4; *2.* P—Q4 Mate

The Queen's Mate is a Mutate or Change-Mate

White will be able to mate. But White has to move first – and it appears that whatever move he makes will deprive him of a mate in response to some specific move by Black.

However, if White finds the key, he will discover an alternative mate instead of the one he has abandoned.

The solution of most 'waiters' resets the position, as it were, and gives different mates to compensate for the loss of the old ones – and there are subtleties of relationship between the variations. This is called 'Change-Mate' or 'Mutate' form. There can be 'Added Mates'. But there are problems which do not take this 'Waiting' form. White finds a clever mating process in an unblocked position. These varieties are a special topic of which an introductory volume can only make mention.

Two-move problems require for their solution a small imaginative effort, a projection of a mating possibility, with a slight rearrangement of pieces.

Most good Chess-players solve two-movers at sight. But

Black

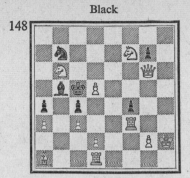

148

White

Mate in 3. Problem by Healey
Bristol Theme (The original 'Bristol')
1. R—R1 (where it remains dead)
1. .... B moves
2. Q—Kt1   B returns to Kt4
3. Q—Kt1 Mate
Note how the Rook has cleared a minimal line for the Queen

there are solvers of two-movers who are not good Chess-players. The effort is a 'special' one.

There are also composers and solvers of longer problems to whom this observation applies.

But three- and four-move problems have more 'Chess' in them.

The next three diagrams show clever play in the very short range that the problem affords. The examples are of three Classical themes.

In the three- and four-move field, 'Themes' are presented, which are Chess movements suggestive of play. In two-move problems (and in some longer ones) the aim is more for geometric pattern. E.g., how many Cross-checks can be met on the mating move? These are good mental exercises. But they can lead away from practical Chess.

Other features valued in problems are the aesthetic value of a model mate (all the White pieces involved and each controlling

Black

149

White

Indian Theme. Problem by A. F. Mackenzie (a great blind composer)
Mate in 4

1. B—R6. P moves
2. R—Q2. P moves (Now Black is in a stalemate position)
3. K—Kt5   K—K6
4. K—B5 Mate (by the piece that moved and was
   temporarily masked)

Black

150

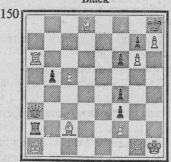

White

Roman Theme (Decoy). Problem by Barry (Amended),
Mate in 3

1. B—R5   Q×B
2. Q×P (At move 1. this would have been met by
   Q×P)

Black now cannot prevent Mate on the back line

one of the King's flight squares). A 'mirror' mate is a mate in which the King's field of eight squares is unoccupied. A 'model mirror' mate embodies a combination of both formal features. A not quite perfect 'model' is seen in one of the variations of the problem which is in Diagram 151.

Black

151

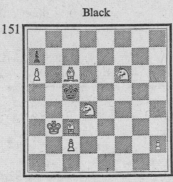

White

Difficult and pretty
Mate in 4, by Dr Planck
1. B—B3
if 1. .... K—Kt3; 2. Kt—K6 K×P
3. Kt—Q7, K—Kt4
4. Kt—B7 Mate
if 1. K—Q3; 2. B—Kt4 ch
K—K4; 3. Kt—Q7 ch K moves. 4. B Mates

In this way geometrical pattern becomes the essence – and not 'Chess difficulty', though that is always an added merit.

In order to create good formal effects, and with the purpose of making ingenious puzzles, composers have set problems in which there is co-operation in the creation of the mate (Help-Mate). Very intriguing and difficult are Self-Mates (or Sui-Mates). Here White is called on so to play that he compels Black in all variations to administer the mate. Often this is achieved with a ridiculously small Black force and in quite a surprising way.

These are 'not Chess', but they can call for great Chess ability in the solving of them. The name of Shinkman (a fine player), is of a great pioneer in that field.

The logically next move is to composition on the Chessboard, but with the assumption of different rules from those of the ordinary game.

'Why,' asked the late T. R. Dawson (in effect), 'should the evolution of Chess be stopped by the fortuitous European discovery of the printing press?'

That argument (not conclusive) justifies Fairy Chess, with its extra pieces, with its 'special rule' problems (Maximummers: e.g. in which every Black move must be over a maximum of squares). Those topics take us beyond the scope of an introductory volume and they take us, also, into a world of puzzles, rather than of Chess. Here we find Cylindrical Chess, Three-Dimensional Chess, etc., all very difficult.

But one type of puzzle is well worth mentioning – Retrograde Analysis. One has a problem, e.g. in which a difference is made to the defence by the apparent ability of Black to Castle. Prove by working out 'what must have happened' that Black has forfeited his right to Castle.

Retrograde Analysis can go very far back. But a very simple instance occurs where the solution of a problem is P×P e.p. This depends on the demonstration that Black's last move had to be a double move by a Pawn: there could have been no other. But, strictly speaking, this is a puzzle using the rules of Chess rather than a problem in Chess (see note at end of Chapter).

Specially amusing 'games' include 'Alice Chess' in which two boards are used – every piece, moving on one board, being directed to its objective square on the other.

Near to real Chess is *Kriegspiel*, a game for Chess detectives. White plays on one board: Black on another. They are concealed from each other. Between them is a third board, concealed from both players, and controlled by the Umpire.

On the Umpire's board the moves of both players are made, but each opponent only knows his own moves, and has to infer, from his questioning of the Umpire, what his opponent has done.

The Umpire announces checks and their direction; he also announces the very first occasion on which a Pawn capture can be made (e.g. Black has moved and White is in check on the long diagonal; or White has moved and Black has a Pawn capture).

For the rest the players ask, 'Have I any?' (Pawn captures). The answer is 'no' or 'try'. If the try is successful that move must be made. A shrewd player will try the unlikely before the likely, unless he wishes to capture.

Some 'schools' of Kriegspiel only allow one Pawn capture try per move, others allow any number.

The player also asks the Umpire: 'Can I move there?' indicating, say, B—R8. If the reply is 'Yes', he must make the move. If not, and in any event, he has gained information.

Opportunities for deception are infinite. One discovers, by elimination, that a Pawn can capture; so one does the capture with a Kt or Q, etc. The game can be so well played that, towards the end, one player's board will be almost exactly like the Umpire's. Ideally, he will have put his opponent's pieces – the right pieces – on the proper squares. To this ideal the good inferrer, with Chess imagination, will approximate.

---

### NOTE ON THE CHESS RULES IN PROBLEMS

Here is something amusing by the late C. S. Kipping: rk2K3, KtPR5, 4O, 4Q3. (Mate in 2.) The solution 1—Q—Kt4 leads to nice sub-promotions, and to a 'model-mirror' mate. But the position is an impossible one. (What was Black's last move?) Question: Is it a valid problem?

### SOLUTION TO STUDY ON PAGE 16

*1.* Q—QR1 ch  K—R2. *2.* Q—Kt1 ch  K—R1. *3.* Q—Kt2 ch  K—R2. *4.* Q—B2 ch  K—R1. *5.* Q—B3 ch  K—R2. *6.* Q—Q3 ch  K—R1. 7. Q—R3 ch. (It took 7 checks to get there.) 7. .... B—R2. *8.* Q—B3 ch  K—Kt1. *9.* Q—B8 (threatening to win the Q: and note how helpless she is). *9.* .... K—B2. *10.* B—B5 and the Queen is DOMINATED and won.

# NOTE ON THE CHESS CLOCK

IN order to make games of Chess terminable within lifetimes, rules were made compelling the players to make, each, so many moves per hour – or other unit period. E.g., 20 per hour, 40 in 2 hours, or 40 in 2½ hours, etc.

To measure the time used an ingenious method was devised.

Two clocks are geared together. When White is thinking, preparatorily to moving, his clock is going; not his opponent's. When he moves he presses a knob: his clock stops, and his opponent's commences to go. So each player only registers on his own clock the time consumed during his delays in moving. At the end of e.g. 4 hours – each clock will register what has been consumed by each. Fifty moves may have been made, one player has used 2½ hours, the other 1½. Very usual is it that, towards the end of 4 hours, each player has not yet completed his quotient, and has to move fast. He is in *Zeitnot* (Time need). If the 'flag' falls before he has completed his required number of moves he loses 'on the clock'.

This is sometimes considered unsatisfactory, but the justice of the rule is clear. You must play well, within the time allowed. The time need is one of the difficulties. Good players, according to Capablanca, should play well at 20 per hour.

But Parkinson's Law operates. Given more time, one consumes more time. Some very fine players are perfectionists and do, at points of the game, think hard and deeply, and use more time than they have. Reshevsky, one of the fastest players in the world, is famous for his capacity to concentrate beyond his clock. Few players can use time like that. They gaze at the same line, without adding to their awareness. Very often they are wasting time on regrets.

---

In order to make the 'timing' system work, players in tournaments, etc. must record their moves. That makes notation important. At adjournments a move is 'sealed' by the last player because, obviously, if it were made on the open board, the opponent would have gratuitous time in which to think about it. In the sealed move there must be no ambiguity. An ambiguous recording (or the recording of an impossible move) forfeits the game.